D1248492

Daffodil Hill

Daffodil Hill

Uprooting My Life, Buying a Farm, and Learning to Bloom

JAKE KEISER

THE DIAL PRESS

NEW YORK

Daffodil Hill is a work of nonfiction. The order of some events has been adapted to the story but all are authentic. Some of the names of the persons discussed have been changed to disguise their identities. Any resulting resemblance to persons living or dead is entirely coincidental and unintentional.

Copyright © 2022 by Jake Keiser

All rights reserved.

Published in the United States by The Dial Press, an imprint of Random House, a division of Penguin Random House LLC, New York.

THE DIAL PRESS is a registered trademark and the colophon is a trademark of Penguin Random House LLC.

Library of Congress Cataloging-in-Publication Data
Names: Keiser, Jake, author.
Title: Daffodil Hill: uprooting my life, buying a farm, and learning to bloom / by Jake Keiser.
Description: First edition. | New York: The Dial Press, [2021]
Identifiers: LCCN 2021025830 (print) | LCCN 2021025831 (ebook) | ISBN 9781984854810 (hardcover) | ISBN 9781984854834 (ebook)
Subjects: LCSH: Keiser, Jake. | Daffodil Hill Farm (Oxford, Miss.) | Women farmers—Mississippi—Oxford—Biography. | Divorced women—United States—Biography. | Farm life—Mississippi—Oxford. | Life change events. | Self-realization in women. | Oxford (Miss.)—Biography.
Classification: LCC S521.5.M7 K45 2021 (print) | LCC S521.5.M7 (ebook) | DDC 338.109762/83—dc23/eng/20211028
LC record available at https://lccn.loc.gov/2021025830
LC ebook record available at https://lccn.loc.gov/2021025831

Printed in the United States of America on acid-free paper

randomhousebooks.com

2 4 6 8 9 7 5 3 1

First Edition

Book design by Caroline Cunningham
Frontispiece: Dover Pictura: Flowers/Daffodil

For my family, thank you for your love and support,

and for giving me the space to evolve.

In memory of Kahuna, Maybelle, Rupert, and Gemma Jane.

Thank you for loving me and helping me heal.

"And the day came when the risk to remain tight in a bud was more painful than the risk it took to blossom."

—ANAïS NIN

Daffodil Hill

Dirty Secret

I planned each outfit the way celebrity stylists plan for the Oscars. Boats and yachts meant cover-ups and hats. Polo, depending on the side of the field, meant upscale picnic or Kentucky Derby chic. Girls' nights out meant, well, Prada, Dior, Gucci, or some other fashionable designer. Tampa Bay was rich with see-and-be-seen events, and I lived two blocks away from everything: bars, restaurants, dress shops, a high-end movie theater, and a farmers' market.

It was a warm, sticky October Saturday, and I was returning home with my typical farmers' market haul of fresh cut flowers, vegetables, handmade porcini pasta, and free-range eggs. The cruelty-free movement spoke to me, but I couldn't help wishing that the splotched, irregularly sized eggshells had the same pristine uniformity as the kind in the grocery store.

As I entered my apartment, a strong odor of fish smacked me in the face. I drew a breath through my mouth and greeted my little designer dog, Kahuna. Kahuna was an eight-year-old, seven-pound black Yorkie-poo who'd been with me since he was a puppy, ever since my divorce. I gave him a kiss while searching for air spray, scanning the shelves, the countertop, the dinette. The scent was intense. The Spanish-style detailing and soaring ceilings made the place feel like home, but I couldn't change the fact that my apartment was sandwiched between two undesirables: to the left, a lady with a knack for stinking up the building with her cooking; and to the right, a single man with a parade of partners almost nightly. Air spray, earplugs, and a noise-canceling app had become necessary quality-of-life items.

My heartbeat quickened from anxiety as I rushed from room to room. I hated to be late to anything, but I also didn't want to smell like my neighbor's fish dinner. Finally, I spotted the can and walked around spraying while wiggling out of my romper. Glancing at my phone to check the time, I dashed to my closet. There wasn't a second to lose. I had brunch with the girls. "Ten minutes until you're late," I sang to myself, trying not to work up a sweat in the Florida humidity. The very idea of not being on time made my lungs feel like they were filled with cement. These days, everything triggered my anxiety. But instead of crumbling under the weight, I forced myself to take a deep breath, and when I threw open my wardrobe doors, the pressure lifted. My clothes hung neatly in a row. I took a mental inventory, pairing each potential outfit with complementing accessories, from over-the-top baubles to delicate heirloom pieces. In the Tampa social scene, fashion was as much a sport as it was a science. Keeping up appearances required not only an expert knowledge of the playing field, but also a well-developed understanding of weather patterns.

I pushed past the understated Burberry and brightly colored Versace, and then my eyes landed on the perfect mix of form and function. "We have a winner!" I said to Kahuna, shimmying into an easy black maxi dress made even more perfect by a pair of hidden pockets. With a simple base, I layered on the silver statement jewelry I had purchased in Mexico, black Prada slippers, and Chanel sunglasses. After fluffing my long, chocolate brown hair, I twirled in front of the mirror, appraising the comfortable yet effortlessly sophisticated look. With a parting smile, I scooped up Kahuna and grabbed my key chain, heavy with keys.

Racing from one temperature-controlled environment to another, I moved from the lobby, to the car, to the restaurant. I arrived with five minutes to spare, the first of the group to the table, a critical bit of social maneuvering. As every socialite and Mafioso knows, having the best seat is vitally important. With a prime position, I not only had the best view of the scenery, but also a strategic advantage should an ex or a frenemy walk through the door. I'd see them before they'd see me.

After settling in and ordering a Bloody Mary, I pulled out my phone. In the three minutes since I'd last checked, I'd racked up thirteen missed texts. All from *her*. Laura. The reality TV "starlet."

I took repeated deep breaths. *In through the nose, out through the mouth.* This was de rigueur. This was my *job*. I was a publicist, and she needed publicity. But did that mean I had to sacrifice my nights, weekends, and every available moment? Her never-ending calls, texts, and emails were starting to give me gray hair. I was going to have to increase my Botox dosage just to keep the worry lines at bay. She paid well, sure, but was it worth it when most of the money went toward covering the very spa treatments she drove me to need?

After shooting off a couple of messages, I attempted to ignore the magnetic pull of the flashing notification. It was a sunny, mild day, and I vowed I would *relax*. Defying the vibration, I turned my chair to the side, making sure to stay under the giant umbrella. I loved the sun but preferred to keep my fake tan out of its reach. Freckles were not my friend. On point, the server

brought Kahuna a fresh bowl of chilled water along with my
Bloody Mary. I made a mental note to increase his tip.

Relax, it isn't that difficult, I told myself, sipping on the humid,
autumn air and trying to enjoy the peaceful view of the park
across the street, with its expansive banyan trees and tall slender
palms. I watched the breeze make the leaves sway in a graceful hula and tuned out the noise of midmorning traffic. Instead, I listened to the sounds of people running and biking,
the awkward-looking tourists on the Segway tour, the rolling
bar with its boisterous pedaling occupants. The city was bustling
with activity. The sidewalks were busy. The birds were busy. Even
the sparkling bay water was busy. Sailboats were out in full force
and dolphin fins broke the crystalline surface off in the distance.
The tables around me filled quickly, and I listened to the music
of several conversations in various foreign languages. The atmo-
sphere felt sophisticated, worldly. I loved it.

Well into my second Bloody Mary, I heard the telltale click of
heels. I didn't have to look up to know it was the girls.

"Jake! Why can't you ever just *wait?*! You're so rude!" Kelly
said, exasperated, dropping her huge leather purse next to her
chair. A petite, blond spitfire, Kelly was a French-trained hairstylist with a penchant for extremely high heels and a knack for
making any outfit look fabulous—even if it made her late every
day of her life.

"Why can't you ever be on time?" I responded tartly, sipping
my cocktail.

Kelly thought the world should wait for her; I thought the
world should run according to plan. Clearly, we disagreed on
what made someone rude.

Hugs passed from one set of toned arms to another, and
phones were pulled out and placed next to plates.

"As you all know," Kelly began, calling the brunch to order, "we've been trying to find some new places away from the usual Tampa crowd." She paused, waiting for everyone to lean in. Surrounded by a circlet of gold and bronze heads, she continued. "So, last night, Jake, Angi, and I pregamed at a *hotel bar*."

"Oh, that's right!" Nicole jumped in. "How was it?" She tossed her long, red locks, the tips appearing to catch fire in the bright sunlight.

"Well, the food was amazing," I replied. "They grow their own salad greens on the roof."

"I'll bet it was nice not seeing the usual suspects," Adria joined in. Kelly nodded and went on, "We bonded with some hot businessmen. God, I love a well-dressed man."

I laughed. "Not to mention one of them picked up our entire tab."

The girls nodded with approval.

"I want to go with you next time," Nicole said.

"Well"—I paused to collect my thoughts—"I don't think we're going back."

After a rustle of rejoinders, Kelly held up her hand.

"We loved it," she agreed. "But when we ordered our last drinks, the bartender asked if we were . . ."

"Hookers," I filled in. "We thought she was joking, so we laughed and told her, 'Of course not!' Then she looked at us, dead straight, and said: 'But *IF* you were . . . I could totally hook you up.'"

The girls broke into hysterics, and my pulse returned to its resting rate. But as Kelly ordered a drink, my phone started vibrating again. I peeked at the screen. Laura. I let it go to voicemail. She needed to learn to respect boundaries, and I needed to learn how to make them. My phone buzzed again. One new voicemail. I dug my nails into my palms and drank down another Bloody Mary.

Turns out, anxiety doesn't mix well with vodka. By the time we paid the bill, my stomach felt like a lead balloon, and my breathing was shallow and quick. My palms were branded with eight half-moons, and I could feel myself about to flip from well-adjusted type A personality into bitchy and intolerant, or as my friends were kind enough to call it—"business mode." After a closing round of hugs and air kisses, the valet brought my car. There was only one cure for my anxiety. Retail therapy.

I didn't plan to spend fourteen thousand in a couple hours, but that's exactly what happened. Perched on an overstuffed chair, I sat while the salespeople presented one item after another, offering to tailor things for the perfect fit. I felt like a princess and refused to deny myself anything. Which is how I ended up with a fabulous red Fendi handbag and another pair of Chanel sunglasses. (Sunglasses are a wardrobe of their own in Florida.) Clutching my shopping bags, an intense euphoria flowed through me. I couldn't wait to get home to re-admire my purchases before changing, once again, for the evening's black-tie event.

One charity ball and an Epsom salt foot soak later, I was more than ready for bed. As I rubbed my tortured feet, I looked out the window and noticed a chubby raccoon rifling through a trash can. He methodically pilfered through his banquet, and when he finally waddled away, I felt a twinge of regret. Even with Kahuna curled up next to me, in a building and city full of people, I was all alone.

I turned my attention to the late-night news loop. It featured a couple in their midforties. The husband had lost his job and the wife was concerned she might lose hers next. They were worried about making ends meet financially. The economy was precarious and this had been an ongoing theme for several years.

The reporter interviewed the couple from their sizable back-yard. I noticed there were lots of toys visible, but no garden. "How are we supposed to feed our kids without decent employment?" the wife lamented. Stories like these struck me to the core. Being self-employed and single, I was always concerned for my financial fate. The thought of being unable to feed myself was more than I could bear. I couldn't take watching the news any-more. It served up even more panic onto what already felt like a full plate. I quickly turned the TV off.

Now in full anxiety mode, I rolled onto my side and pulled out my laptop. A pang of shame ran through me as I opened a new browser. As the web address autofilled with familiarity, I realized I might have a problem. An addiction to which I was turning way too often these days. I was sure I could stop if I wanted to—but for now, it was my only release. My peace. My go-to es-cape from my grueling professional life. With a few practiced clicks, I logged in and was welcomed back to my account on MyPetChicken.com.

For well over a year, I'd been browsing chicks, hoarding them in my virtual shopping cart. Even though I never had any inten-tion of pressing the checkout button, seeing them all lined up gave me a sense of tranquility. But it also made me feel like a freak. Back when I lived with my ex-boyfriend Chad, I took pre-cautions. I used headphones and erased my search histories. But one afternoon, in need of a quick fix, I forgot to turn off the sound and couldn't click out quickly enough. Chad turned to me, eyes wide with concern. "Are you looking at chickens again?!" I was mortified. Devastated. It felt worse than if he'd caught me looking at porn.

As my face turned a ghostly white, Chad laughed, shaking his head. Eleven years my junior, he couldn't understand my longing for connection, for children, for nature. I tried to get him on board, dragging him to farmers' markets like they were Saks. But how could I explain?

I'd never held an adult chicken, and I didn't have a single friend who had a chicken. There was just something about the endless variety of colors, shapes, sizes, patterns, and fluffiness. Chickens seemed like the ultimate accessory. Even the sounds they made gave me a feeling of peace and took me away from my ever-present anxiety. I could fantasize about a different life, one where I felt free, happy, and maybe even creative again.

And yet, as soon as I stepped away from my virtual farm, whenever I had to face my life head-on, I was deeply unhappy. I tried to discuss things with Chad, but as much as I loved him, he had no idea how to help and I couldn't bridge the widening gap between us. Serious conversations just weren't his thing. I was too tired to confront the issues, and worse yet, I couldn't even really define what the issues *were*. So I started to sleep more, slipping gracefully into a quiet depression. I became antisocial under the weight of hidden emotions I hadn't dealt with; and I became resentful. Chad started to feel more like a human puppy than a life partner, and over time, I started to feel more like his mother than his lover. I should have broken up with him sooner, but I loved him immensely. I didn't want to hurt him, and I didn't want to have to deal with the shitstorm inside me. So I left things as they were—for over a year. All the while, I felt myself disappearing, acting solely on autopilot. I thought to myself, repeatedly, *There has GOT to be more to life than merely existing.*

But it was more complicated than even questioning my existence. My ego factored in as well. I feared that as soon as we broke up, he'd jump into yet another relationship and I'd be left alone, validated in my suspicion of his codependency, and feeling worse than I already did, if that was even possible. Which is exactly what ended up happening. After I finally summoned the courage to end things, within weeks of our breakup, he got together with a girl who'd recently joined our circle of friends.

I was devastated and my ego pricked. Was I so easily replaceable? Had I been merely a placeholder? Had Chad ever loved *me*, or had he just needed *somebody*? The truth punched me in the gut. Chad was a relationship monkey, going from woman to woman as if they were branches on a tree.

He had met me when he was separated from his wife, and he often spoke about exes going back to second grade. How had I not seen the pattern sooner? One thing I was sure of: It's not a compliment to be chosen by a codependent person.

And worse, I'd wasted precious time frittering away what the medical community deemed to be the last of my fertile years. My anxiety and depression grew even more severe, and my life felt small and increasingly unimportant. I suffered from panic attacks, shortness of breath, and a growing helplessness. *This is what drowning must feel like,* I told myself. Clothes became my anchor to the world. I put on one outfit after another and threw myself into work. This was still the South, after all. People locked up their emotions right along with their fine silver.

My sole therapy came in the form of MyPetChicken.com. Of course, I didn't tell anyone.

God only knew how Kelly and the girls would react. It was a secret so deep I refused to share it with most people in my life. Only my family was aware of my growing desire to *one day* retire to a little farm of my own. But it was a pipe dream, that was all.

Lying in front of my laptop, I browsed through the regal Silver Laced Cochins, the sweet puffy Brahmas, the fluffy black Silkies, the quintessential Barred Rocks, and the stars of egg laying, Leghorns. Between the brightly spotted yellow Mille Fleur D'Uccles and the adorably squat Bantam Cochins, I spotted an olive-colored egg I hadn't seen before. Who knew that chickens could lay olive-colored eggs?

"Oh, I must have you!" I sighed, adding it to my shopping cart, which had approximately two hundred dollars' worth of fluffed and feathered damage. It was a relatively inexpensive habit, because I never got further than hovering over the checkout button. I didn't intend to actually *buy* the chicks. I was simply a virtual collector.

After updating my shopping cart, I opened a folder called "tax documents," and with a double click, the most important spreadsheet on my computer unfurled across my screen. It was my dream farm, complete with columns of chickens, goats, sheep, vegetables, and anything I thought would make my fake farm prettier or more enjoyable. I added my new acquisition to the list, all the while fantasizing about tranquil breezes, screened doors, and sweet animal sounds. I would make baked goods, I decided, and collect vintage tablecloths and tea sets.

Basking in the glow of my fantasy, I powered down for the night, crawled under the blankets, and turned off my bedside lamp. And then my phone lit up. Laura. Livid, I answered.

"It's three A.M.!" I shouted at the screen. "You better be dying or in jail."

A high-pitched screech filled the darkness. She was beside herself. Her limo for an event was *white*, not *black*, and she *deserved* black. "Real celebrities have black limos," she slurred through muffled sobs.

Shocked into silence, I blinked several times. Laura was, at best, a D-list celebrity.

Where did she get off? I wasn't the limo fairy. I wasn't a miracle worker. I was just a regular woman, trying to unwind after a long week by going on the internet to look at baby chicks. Was a quiet bit of daydreaming in the wee hours of the morning too much to ask?

"Don't call me again for shit like this," I snapped. "I'm not your assistant, or your babysitter."

I threw the phone across the bed, pissed—at her, at myself. Weariness clawed at my soul. Most of the time I could ignore the fact I was chasing money, but clients like her made me hyper-aware of the fact that I was selling my time and ultimately my health for the highest price tag. As I lay there, yet again, considering my profession, my thoughts took a nosedive into a pool of anger and anxiety.

Bullshit was thick in the media world, and lately, fame was a pursuit unto its own. My most demanding clients didn't have a talent, a skill, or a message, they just wanted exposure. They wanted their homes displayed in local brag mags. They wanted to make a "best-of" list. They wanted to be adored or admired by strangers to appease their bottomless self-esteem issues . . . and I was there for them, egging them on, for a price. Of course, I had some great clients, but many were like wax figures in a museum, void of authenticity and poised for optimum public perception. Genuine connections had been replaced with inauthentic inter-actions. I suppose this was the inevitable result of any PR profes-sional. As all publicists know, our very occupation stems from Edward Bernays, the "father of public relations." He coined the term "public relations" after the Nazis took over the original word, *propaganda*. Now, I was acutely aware how accurate (and frighteningly brilliant) he was. It could be argued Bernays and his marketing mind-control concepts (it's no coincidence that his uncle was Sigmund Freud) have completely formed the mod-ern world in the way of business, education, and, of course, poli-tics. My whole world revolved around propaganda, disseminating it for public consumption and broadcasting my own. As Bernays suggested, education is often simply socially acceptable propaganda. I'd lost count of how many times I'd used the phrase to close a client. "It's my job to *educate* the public about your . . . cause, product, idea, etc."

Deep into the night my mind went further down the rabbit hole of my chosen profession. Often public relations exists not to free or truly inform us of truth, but to elicit behaviors to benefit particular people or groups. In other words, to enslave us into conformity (ex: keeping up with the Joneses). It's certainly not here to promote individuality . . . that wouldn't benefit the entities who hire publicists. Companies and groups can't exist for long unless there's public demand. Bernays was a big proponent of "interest groups." We see these people on the news daily. Interest groups assist in legitimizing ideas. And the use of "influencers" isn't a new thing. Bernays was the first to use socialites to make products or movements take flight. He created "causes" to elevate ideas . . . like successfully getting women to smoke cigarettes. This is what my profession was all about and it was starting to leave a bad taste in my mouth.

Bernays has a great many quotes, most of which concerned me.

"Whatever of social importance is done today, whether in politics, finance, manufacture, agriculture, charity, education, or other fields, must be done with the help of propaganda."

Reading the many writings and quotes of Bernays had been starting an awakening in me. As my beliefs began shifting, my professional self was crumbling at its very foundation. I found myself questioning everything.

The entire goal of PR is to shape public perception for better or worse. To make us turn away from our own ideas and experiences . . . turn away from original thought. It can serve to make those who don't conform to feel somehow lesser and not a part of the included. The modern way of life was breaking me from the inside.

Everywhere I turned I could see the deception. The more I looked into things, the more I wanted to find my own way. To hear my own soul speak and lead me in whatever direction felt good.

With my mind in overdrive, I was exhausted. I had been perpetually unhappy in my career and in my life. To be honest, I couldn't remember the last time I was happy for more than a few minutes, and I wasn't even sure if those fleeting moments of excitement were even real happiness. What did "happy" even mean to me? I needed to get off the hamster wheel in my head. So I popped a sleep aid and passed out.

Hours later, I heard the telltale buzz of an incoming call. I smashed my face into my pillow and felt around for the offending noise. If it was Laura, I was going to throw my phone through the window.

"Hello." I tried to sound as alert as possible.

"Did I wake you up?" my stepmother jumped in. "I found a farm for you!"

Leap of Faith

My heart was racing in fear and possibilities as I ended the call. Pushing myself out of bed, I stared out at the manicured trees and the vintage brick parking lot. The landscaping, despite its best efforts, couldn't hide the giant concrete highway ramp. Florida was my home, but in almost twenty years of being a resident, I'd rarely opened my windows for longer than a few minutes. The breeze always smelled of road, rubber, and sulfur from sprinklers or chemical treatments, and the chemicals in the lawn sprays gave Kahuna seizures.

In my head, I replayed the conversation with my stepmom, trying to digest everything I'd just heard. She'd called to tell me she'd found a house with five acres of land in Mississippi. Did I want it? The homeowners were about to accept an offer but said they would be willing to give me a couple days to get to Mississippi and look at their property. In a bit of shock, operating on autopilot, I opened my calendar and moved a couple things around . . . Kahuna pawed at my leg, snapping me out of my foggy dream state. Was I really going to consider this? It was ludicrous. Just the *idea* of moving to Mississippi scared me.

Moving to the Bible Belt as a divorced, non-Christian woman could quite possibly seal my fate as a childless single woman forever. All I'd need to complete the picture was a few cats.

Also, I was a city girl. I liked designer shoes and boutique businesses. I'd never had farm animals, let alone a garden. And yet . . . All I wanted was to cuddle chicks, pick flowers, and breathe deeply.

"Jake, you have to chill out," I admonished myself. "You're not actually moving to Mississippi." Hearing those words out loud brought a sense of relief. I made my choice. If I ever decided to buy a farm, I'd do it somewhere else, *in retirement,* far, far down the road.

For now, there was no harm in looking . . .

The next day, I left for Mississippi with Kahuna perched securely on his little pillow in the passenger seat of my car. "What the hell are we doing?" I asked. "Do you think I'm crazy?" He stared at me with his little baby doll face. The longer I drove up I-75, the more I was convinced that yes, I was, indeed, completely crazy. But as the hours melted away, and the landscape changed from Florida's flat, never-ending highways into a beautiful, hilly countryside readying itself for a long winter sleep, my head seemed to clear. The winding roads passed by expansive fields outlined with hardwood forests. The cotton plants were high, and the landscape was dotted with farm equipment, both well kept and junky but incredibly charming. The grass was still green, but the trees were alight with the colors of fall. It felt as if I was driving through an oil painting.

Only when I looked down at my phone did I realize just how deep into nowhere I'd gone.

The cell signal was gone. I vigorously rubbed the screen with

the cuff of my shirt, hoping that the effort would bring the signal to life, but it was useless. I tossed my phone into my bag
and turned my attention back to the endless eternity of my
surroundings—presently, a herd of brown-and-white pinto
horses intermingling with cows.

After twelve hours on the road, I joined my stepmother at the
property. At first glance I noticed there was a house situated on a
hill, another house across the street, and one more, barely visible,
off to the side. The long driveway was lined with pecan trees and
assorted fruit trees that were overrun by kudzu and thorny brush,
threatening to choke them out. "What a poignant metaphor," I
mumbled. Tampa was crawling with social vampires who scaled
the ranks and sucked the life and authenticity from everything. I
knew the feeling of suffocation all too well.

When we pulled up at the foot of the house, I thanked my
lucky stars. I knew I would never, *ever* live here. The home was an
awful-brown, one-story relic of the 1960s. Part brick, part wood
plank, it had a large but unattractive concrete porch with two old
rocking chairs and a porch swing—the only redeeming qualities.
The landscaping was sparse and there were holes in the lawn
from their dog. This was definitely not the charming old farm-
house that I'd imagined.

A rustle of leaves drew my attention to a large double-trunked
oak in front of the house.

There was a mark on the side where a sizable branch had fallen
off years ago; it looked like a large eye, crying. I followed the
trunk up into the tree's canopy, which hung over the porch, casting a cooling shade on the side of the house. There were several
bunches of mistletoe throughout the top of the tree. According
to Celtic mythology, mistletoe in oak trees was supposed to be
lucky. *Well,* I thought, *I could certainly use some luck.*

A light breeze danced through a wooden and metal wind

chime, and a gust of fresh air brushed against my cheeks. It smelled like fall. I inhaled deeply—something I hadn't done in earnest for a long time, even in yoga class. All I wanted to do was sit on the porch swing and embrace the moment, but my reverie was interrupted by the homeowners: a sweet country couple with two sons. They invited us inside, smiling with kind, round faces. Even the people here had a totally different energy and manner than the people in Tampa.

After forcing the front door open over an old, moth-eaten carpet, I took a quick glance around.

The windows were hidden by thick, dark brown wooden blinds. The popcorn ceilings were low and stained. The walls were wood paneled, painted in mustard yellow, red, and light brown. The house was uncomfortably dark.

I hated it.

The tour that followed supported my initial assessment: The house felt exactly like I did, ill-fitted with no character or life. Eager to get out, I asked to see the back porch, and soon we exited through a late 1960s–style back door. An overhang extended from the house, low and full of nails, all pointing down. It reminded me of spiked torture coffins in old horror movies.

Aiming my eyes to the horizon, I hurried to the grass and inhaled all the fresh air my body could hold. The owner began walking us around the property, toward a brownish-gray-colored wooden car shed. We passed a small orchard of five fruit trees, which appeared to be very old and barely alive, overrun by vines. On one side of the property was a small gully, and on the other, a nice-size pond. "It was stocked a few years back with bass and brim," the owner explained, following my gaze. I nodded in quiet acknowledgment, watching the ripples play across the water. They reflected the soft afternoon sun and sparkled with millions of tiny lights. Dragonflies were busily going about their business, sweeping over the water and the surrounding overgrown reeds. The pond seemed to beckon to me, as if the water knew something I didn't. My mind flashed back to childhood when I used to catch tadpoles with my parents in our goldfish pond. It was the only good memory I had of when my parents were together. Looking over this much larger body of water, I visualized myself meditating here and instantly felt a sense of relief.

Technically, the property checked off all the boxes. It had a hilltop home with a real wood-burning fireplace, established fruit and nut trees, a tranquil pond, and even an outbuilding that could be turned into a barn. I hated the *look* of the house with every particle of my being, and yet . . . I didn't want to leave.

Visions filled my head—winters drinking hot chocolate by the roaring fire, springs sitting on the porch swing lost in the view of the sparkling pond. This place was a vortex of peace I hadn't known since I was a little girl, when I lived in Guam and the Philippines, as a stepchild of a navy officer. This property had all the same haunting beauty I'd experienced in those jungles. There are just certain places in nature whose presence won't be denied. They have a way of grabbing the soul, commanding attention, and setting your mind free into the present moment, as if it were a universe of its own. It felt like one of those rare moments in life when you look at someone or something you love and the world goes silent, only the two of you exist. For me, this was one of those places.

My stepmom's voice interrupted my peaceful thoughts. "There's another offer on the table; you have to decide if you want it now." My mind raced. I had to make a decision to entirely change my life or not, and I had to make it immediately. I was scared. Scared of saying yes and scared of saying no.

What exactly was I waiting for? A man? The family I'd tried to have and repeatedly failed to create? I felt pathetic and tired.

Change seemed to be all around me while I stayed the same. My life was too small for who I wanted to be, and, in my thirties, I still didn't even know who that was. The thought of spending another night in my city condo hunting for air spray after yet another fish dinner made me sick. I couldn't do it anymore. I couldn't wait for someone else to come along and save me. I needed to make the change myself. My brain called me crazy, but I swear I could hear my soul speak for the first time in years, and it whispered *say yes.*

Ignoring the fear screaming inside me to retreat, I decided to take a leap of faith.

I'd buy the house.

I might not fit in Mississippi, but I knew I belonged to this land.

Upon my return to Florida, before I even started packing my belongings, I logged onto MyPetChicken.com. My mouse hovered over the button I never thought I'd press. I could hear my heart beating rapidly as I clicked Buy. My chicks would be shipped on December seventh. I could hardly wait. To celebrate, I rewarded myself with my first pair of farm boots—black and brown Hunters that seemed like the perfect mix of city and country. Proud of myself for making such a sensible purchase, I decided to continue crafting a practical shopping list. My first step was the internet. Surely there was a YouTube video, or a blog, that could prepare a single city girl for the farm lifestyle. I searched, and searched, and searched . . . but . . . nothing. I found only women who blogged about farm life with their families and women who blogged about redesigning their second homes in the country. I couldn't find a single city girl who was doing what I was about to do alone. If I needed any confirmation that I was totally off the wall, this seemed to be it: The internet, which had *everything*, was empty.

Sheepish and self-conscious, I decided to keep my move a secret. Only immediate family and my closest friends would know about this drastic life decision. I'd tell Kelly and Nicole, Adria and Angi, and then I'd make the move quietly—just me and help from my younger sister Jenifer. I wouldn't post any pictures on social media. If this thing didn't work out, I could easily pull the plug and move back to Florida without anyone being the wiser. The last thing I needed was for people to judge me, or worse, fire me because they thought I was losing my mind. Which, maybe I was.

I said silent goodbyes to the bars, restaurants, dress shops, movie theaters, and farmers' markets. I packed up without fanfare. Then I sat on the floor of my closet, surrounded by boxes.

Wiping a smudge off a pair of Gucci peep toe pumps, I felt a familiar pang of anxiety. I picked up the shoes, hugged them to my chest as the fear washed over me, and cried.

Into the Unknown

Within weeks, my official move date arrived. Jenifer had flown in from Mississippi and with the help of a couple hired, grumpy men loaded the U-Haul with clothes, shoes, home goods, and mystery boxes that I still hadn't unpacked from my breakup with Chad. With one final look, I waved away the last sixteen years of my life and clambered into the big truck. Jenifer hopped into my BMW SUV, Kahuna by her side. For the next fifteen hours, she would drive behind me as I lumbered along. I had no idea driving the big truck would add three more hours to the trip.

As the time passed, I shifted my weight back and forth, hoping to ward off a growing ache in my backside. I was used to managing pain. For years, I'd numbed myself, multitasking my feelings away, ticking through any free time I did have watching reality TV while playing solitaire on my phone and simultaneously flipping through fashion magazines. Distractions had been the name of the game. But now, finally, I was ready to be present. I just wished the present came with a softer seat cushion.

Shortly after midnight, we entered Mississippi. As we drove deeper into the state, the streetlights ended. The starry sky, occasional house lights, and our headlights were the only things illuminating our way. After seeing a fourth shooting star I called Jenifer, still keeping pace behind me. "Are you seeing these meteors, too?" It seemed nature was putting on a light show that urged us onward. We spoke briefly, trying to break up the monotony of the slow drive. The radio selection was limited to mostly Christian stations and country music, so I settled on some classic Christmas music. It was only early November, but I was in a festive mood for the first time in years.

When we made it to the town of Oxford, Jenifer and I stopped to hug each other goodbye and go our separate ways. She handed me Kahuna, and with one final squeeze, I was on my own. I would circle back to drop off the truck and pick up my car later.

It was 3:30 A.M. when I pulled the U-Haul up my new driveway. There were no lights on in the house or on the porch. I sat parked in the giant truck holding my little city dog, trying to muster the courage to step out into the cold, pitch-black darkness. I counted to ten and pushed open the door. Hugging Kahuna under my arm and using my phone as a flashlight, I jumped out.

A large meteor rocketed by. It was the last of five I'd seen that evening and by far the biggest and brightest. I remembered that in numerology, five is a number of change.

Before I took a step, I heard the bloodcurdling howl of a coyote close by, and then more began to chime in. "Nope," I said to Kahuna, leaping back into the truck and slamming the door. Coyotes were surrounding the property in the cover of darkness. Their howls and yips sounded like the wailing of women and children. I clutched my trembling little dog to my chest and tried not to cry. My new life would have to wait a bit longer.

After spending what was left of the night in the truck, I unfolded onto the driveway with cramps in places I didn't know existed. I massaged my butt, which felt like one giant bruise, and shook out my feet. And then, I released a sigh I didn't realize I'd been holding for the last twenty years.

Everything looked different covered in the morning Mississippi dew. Even the sunlight felt brighter and cleaner than the city sun, I thought, as I watched it filter through the large oak tree and hit the porch floor in a dappled pattern. I squinted against the brightness. The hill, the trees, the pond. Everything that I saw was *mine*. I had my very own canvas on which to create and play and *be*. I felt something shift deep inside me. It felt similar to anxiety—but not. For the first time in a long while, I felt . . . anticipation.

I fished around in my purse and pulled out the key. *The* key. The one and only key. There was no mailbox key, building key, pool key, or gym key. There was just one little piece of metal that would open the front and back doors. Life was already simpler.

After letting myself into the dank, dark hallway, I faced a challenge I hadn't considered: How did one get electricity around here? I fumbled around with my phone, struggling to find two bars, and prepared to do battle. Dealing with utilities was always a time-consuming task, trying to get service online, fighting to speak with someone on the phone, and then enduring lengthy holds, animated prompts, and payments. Expecting the worst, I dialed the number for the Northeast Mississippi Electric Power Company. One ring, two rings, and then . . . a real human being's voice.

"Hello?" I said, startled. "Is this, um, the electric company?"

"It sure is, honey," said a thickly accented woman on the other end. "How can I help you?"

Collecting myself, I replied, "I'm sorry, I was expecting an automated system."

She laughed. "Where is it that you're calling from?' she asked, indicating that this was business as usual in a small southern town.

I explained that I'd just moved from Tampa, and, as I rifled through my wallet for my debit card, I asked what form of payment they needed in terms of a deposit. Her response stopped me in my tracks.

"Oh, honey, we'll get your electric on right away. You just come on into our office when you're available and you can pay then, no rush. Don't you worry about it."

I thanked her profusely and got off the phone, smiling. I could get used to life in the country. The sun was shining and there was that ever-present breeze gently stroking the old chimes on the porch. I made my way through the dark house throwing open windows and doors along the way. Sunshine splashed through the hallway, pouring onto the crumbly old carpet and dated linoleum floors. I removed the age-stained curtains and let the light and fresh air into the house. That's when I noticed the ladybugs.

There were thousands of ladybugs flying around the inside and outside of the house.

They were everywhere. It was as if the house itself were inside a giant swarm. It felt magical. As I watched them flying around the room, I let out an awe-filled "Wow." Kahuna barked, not quite sure what to think of them.

My wonderment stopped short, though, when I suddenly remembered that I also didn't have my water service turned on. With stale breath and unbrushed teeth, I didn't even bother to try the faucet; I texted my stepmom and asked who to call to have my water turned on. She replied, "You have a well."

"What the hell?" I said to my empty kitchen. The idea of having a well instead of city water horrified me. Did a well connect to a treatment plant? Visions of hand pumping water into buckets for my horse as a kid in the Philippines filled my head. It wasn't an easy task. I didn't recall seeing a pump on the property. Where would I even find it?

I slipped on my Hunter boots, Kahuna dashing around my feet, eager to explore his new surroundings. When I opened the door, his courage disappeared, and he waited for me to scoop him up. Riding around in my handbag or traveling in the basket of a beach bicycle were among his favorite activities; could he adjust to farm living? Instinctually, I lifted him with one hand and pulled out my key to lock up with the other. Then I looked to my right. I looked to my left. I was in the middle of nowhere. The key returned to my pocket, unused.

A quick stroll across the lawn proved that there was, indeed, a well; but it was electric. No hand pumping required. I had been so citified it hadn't even dawned on me to try the faucets first. I had just figured that since I hadn't set up an account, there would of course be no water. In that moment, I realized I needed to try to go about my new life a little differently. I bent over and helped myself to water fresh out of the ground. It was chilled and had a crisp, bright taste. I had rarely drunk the Florida tap water because it smelled of rotting eggs and chemicals. But this . . . I could get used to this. It was the freshest water I'd tasted in years. And I wouldn't miss having a water bill each month, either.

Feeling better already, I practically skipped back to the house, Kahuna bounding ahead, yapping at squirrels. And then, seemingly out of nowhere, Kahuna's ears pricked up, and he dashed to the back of the house.

I ran over to see what had him so agitated and found a crawl space near the porch. Deep in the darkness, muffled by spiderwebs and dust, I heard a meow. I shushed Kahuna, and then heard it again—*meow*. Less than thrilled about the prospect of crawling under the porch, I tried to muster my most trustworthy voice, calling out "kitty, kitty, kitty," as sweetly as possible. After a long stretch of silence, I heard a loud purr deep inside the damp darkness, just out of view. I went to grab my phone and what was left of a turkey sandwich I'd eaten earlier—the only food I had in the house.

Using my phone as a flashlight, I could see a white-and-tabby kitten walking back and forth, bumping along the foundation of the house on its tiptoes. Its big yellow eyes glowed. Its little velvet nose and lips were pink, and it was purring loudly. "You must be starving, little one," I cooed. I pulled some turkey from the leftover sandwich I had and sucked off the condiments. Then I ripped off a small piece and threw it toward the kitten, startling it. Its fear turned to excitement, though, when it realized the mysterious flying object was food, and the kitten ate voraciously. That was all it needed to grow brave enough to cautiously approach me.

I'd always been a little afraid of cats, but I held out another piece of meat hoping it wouldn't bite, or scratch, or worse. If this kitten could muster the courage, so could I. After several minutes of sniffing and staring, it finally ate from my hand. After that, I was able to draw it out into the sunlight. It was a little girl. She was surprisingly clean for living under a dusty old house. Her eyes glowed like golden marbles, and she purred like a tiny motor. I touched her little pink nose and held back a sneeze. Between my cat allergies and the safety of my future baby chicks, this was the last thing I wanted. In fact, I had specifically stated on my dream-farm spreadsheet that I was *not* getting another dog, much less a cat.

But as I watched the kitty dance and wind herself around the deck stairs, I understood that my head was in direct opposition to my heart. With a heavy sigh, I realized that much like the property itself, this kitten had chosen me. She belonged here. "Well, crap. I guess you're my first farm animal," I said to her.

She responded with a string of meows.

"I think I'll name you Gialla. It's Italian for yellow," I explained to her. "I'll call you Gia for short."

Gia took Kahuna's lead and followed me into the house. I didn't have the heart to shoo her away. And the old carpet was in such a worn-down state, I figured she couldn't do any significant damage. For the rest of the day, she came and went as she pleased, wallowing on the old tattered carpet and offering her belly to me while I bustled about trying to clean and unpack. It took longer to do everything with her constant need for attention, but I was surprisingly smitten by my new, unexpected addition. "Live it up while you can," I told her. "When this house has new flooring, you'll be an outside kitty again."

After the eventful morning, I found my teapot and put some water on the stove; but my tea break was interrupted by a loud roar. I looked out the window to see a petite woman wearing large sunglasses coming up my driveway on a four-wheeler, a pie miraculously balanced on her left hand. An incredulous smile spread across my face. The woman parked at the top of my driveway and jumped off the ATV, along with a big Labrador, who bounded for the pond.

As soon as I opened the door she began talking.

"I'm Tricia," she said, brushing her long blond hair out of her eyes with her free hand.

Before I could get a word in, she handed me the pie and pushed into the house to look around.

"I have a lot of work to do," I said apologetically, embarrassed by the condition of things.

I looked down at the pie, not really believing this was actually happening. "Thank you for the pie," I said. "It looks wonderful!"

"It's egg custard. I didn't have time to bake so it's store-bought from the Piggly Wiggly, but it's real good," she informed me in a thick southern country accent. "Do you mind if black dog swims in your pond?" To clarify, I responded, "Are you referring to your chocolate lab?" She said, "Yes. Her name is 'Black Dog.' We called our yellow lab 'Yellow Dog.' And the dog before that was 'White Stinky Dog.'" I laughed to myself. I had spent countless hours coming up with elaborate names for the farm animals I didn't even have, and she just called 'em like she saw 'em.

We chatted for a few minutes about my plans for the property. I expressed my desire for farm animals and asked if she thought the other neighbors would mind. She replied, "Guuurl, naw! We love animals. I'm forever rescuing unwanted animals that people drop off out here. Well, I'll let you get back to it. Don't hesitate to let us know if you need anything!" She pulled her oversized sunglasses back over her eyes, turned, and sauntered back to her ATV. She was so open and out there with her personality, I couldn't help but like her.

She started the engine, and Black Dog, realizing she was being left behind, ambled out of the pond, tongue hanging from the side of her mouth, her big butt swaying heavily back and forth from swim exhaustion. I waved goodbye as Tricia hollered, "Gurrrl, welcome to the neighborhood!"

I'd just put a fork in the pie and had shoveled the first bite in my mouth when I heard yet another loud motor coming toward the house. I had a fleeting thought of how odd it was to notice sounds, since in the city I rarely even heard the sirens that seemed to blare daily. Now, every vehicle passing by was a stark contrast to the country quiet. "*Oh my god*, this is good pie!" I exclaimed aloud as my eyes rolled back from the edible ecstasy. Kahuna stared me down, willing me to give him a bite. Ignoring him, I swallowed the whole bite of creamy goodness and peeked out the kitchen window. A tractor was pulling up my driveway. A freaking *tractor*.

Sitting in the driver's seat was a man who appeared to be dressed in his Sunday best: a freshly pressed button-down tucked into slacks with boots. He took off his hat when he spoke, revealing a full head of gray hair, brushed back, and introduced himself as "Farmer John." He informed me that he and his family owned most of the land surrounding mine, and then he plowed right into the heart of the matter: "My wife is out of town and I don't cook. She said it wouldn't be neighborly of me if I didn't take you to dinner on your first day here."

So Farmer John came back at five P.M. and took me to "the" Cracker Barrel, as he called it.

Surrounded by sweatshirts, plaid, and cowboy boots, it was clear I wasn't in Tampa anymore. There were no tourists or snowbirds—only truckers and country folk from wall to wall.

Farmer John opened the conversation with a question I would soon come to expect from everyone in Mississippi: "What church do you go to?" Throughout my life, there always seemed to be a primary question I was asked: What do you want to be when you grow up? What college do you want to go to? What sorority are you in? What's your major? What do you do for a living? Do you have kids? And here in Mississippi, in the heart of the Bible Belt, a new primary question would emerge: What church do you go to? These were questions people asked in order to categorize someone new.

I looked at him blankly; it had been years since anyone had asked me that question. I'd lost my faith the Christmas I lost my first baby. Since then my relationship with God wasn't exactly on good terms. And the last thing I wanted was to purposely put myself in a place full of happy families flaunting what I didn't have. I could tell him the complicated version of the truth, but instead I told him the short version: "I don't have a church here." It wasn't a lie, I reasoned with myself.

"Then you'll have to come to mine," he said. "I'm the deacon. It's for all types of folks." I had no intention of accepting his invitation but I appreciated it for what it was worth.

Farmer John offered his help for anything I would need. He seemed amused by my utter lack of country knowledge and asked what I intended to farm on my small acreage. "Any productive animal that's also pretty. And I'm going to have a fabulous garden," I said.

"I see," he said, seemingly appraising me. "You're an *unusual* girl." His southern way of speaking emphasized the word *unusual*. I tried not to be offended. He clearly had something on his mind, and his tone turned serious. "It doesn't matter the age, race, religion, or if you have money or nothing, we have a tight-knit community that comes together in times of need. When and if tragedy strikes, we are your family." It was the last thing I expected to hear—this serious, earnest sentiment from a person I barely knew—and yet that sense of community resonated with me deeply.

When I returned home, I collapsed on my bare mattress. Even with Kahuna by my side, I felt all alone. For the first time, I felt the weight of what I'd done. I hadn't told most of my friends or any of my clients about this plan; for all they knew, I was out of town for work. While most people were getting married, having babies, or climbing the corporate ladder, I was embarking on a wildly different and secret journey.

In need of some kind of connection, I pulled out my laptop and searched for my bible: my spreadsheets that neatly outlined all the chickens I would buy, and all the eggs they were going to lay. I scrolled through a collage of images I'd copied and pasted from the internet—an animal and vegetable menagerie that broke down the various species and gave details on each of them. My farm philosophy was simple: form and function. Everything had to be visually appealing as well as productive. I envisioned something along the lines of Disney meets Martha Stewart. The animals would have pink collars and they would never ever get dirty or sick. I would have a magnificent green thumb regardless of weather patterns and soil quality. I felt exceedingly confident about my spreadsheet plans and remained blissfully unaware of the fact that the only person in the world who would think to operate a farm via Microsoft Excel is a person who had absolutely no clue about nature or farm life.

Exhausted, I popped in my headphones to listen to music. And then, slowly, a realization sank in. I no longer had to wear headphones. I no longer had to talk quietly, or even be sensitive to the paper-thin walls of city living. Here, I was entirely free. Here, even my private shames could be celebrated. Here, I could blare Jessica Simpson as loudly as I wanted without fear of judgment. This was my kingdom, and I could be as naked as I wanted, literally and figuratively.

That first night in the house, I had restless sleep and strange dreams. One dream was especially vivid. I was walking down a country road when a lone coyote walked out of the overgrown weeds on the side of the road. My heart stopped. The coyote looked battle-scarred and weary. It didn't seem to notice me. When it crossed to the center of the road, it paused and looked directly at me. I held my breath, too fearful to move. As we stared at each other, the old coyote started transforming into an orange-and-black-striped tiger, healthy and free of its old wounds. It continued to hold my gaze, secure and confident in its power. I swallowed nervously. I knew I couldn't run, so I watched as it closed its eyes in a slow blink, then turned its massive head and calmly walked to the other side of the road. I woke up, sweaty and heart racing, just as its tail disappeared quietly into the weeds.

Into the Wild

On my second morning living at the farm, I needed to shake off the silence, so I decided to explore my neighborhood. Back in Florida, I exercised by walking the waterfront parks as dolphins played by the seawall. I'd always loved it, as a way of easing my busy brain—getting lost in my environment with the help of music from my Walkman when I was younger, then my iPod, and eventually my cell phone. I was used to the flat Florida landscape, so the hill country of north Mississippi was going to present more of a physical challenge. I was still achy from the long U-Haul drive, but I was ready to stretch my muscles and explore my cute country road.

Kissing Kahuna goodbye, I made my way down the driveway and turned onto the road. The air was cold as hell to my thin Florida blood and I didn't have gloves, but that was just the motivation to get me moving and warmed up. The small hills proved to be no joke compared to the flat terrain of Florida, and it was harder to adjust my stride than I'd expected. I took deep breath after deep breath, filling my lungs with the cold, amazingly fresh air. There wasn't a trace of exhaust or rubber or chemicals to be found.

Not one car drove by. There was no traffic noise. As I continued walking, the road passed through a ravine, where thick woods lined both sides. Walking into the ravine gave me an uneasy feeling, like I was Little Red Riding Hood about to encounter the Big Bad Wolf. Freaking myself out with that image, I increased my speed until I broke out into a full uphill run.

When I made it through to the next clearing, there was an expansive fenced-in pasture full of cows. Startled by the sudden appearance of an odd human, the cows froze and stared at me. Heaving from my run, I stopped to catch my breath, doubled over, hands on my knees. I couldn't even run a short distance without feeling like my lungs would burst. *This is just embarrassing*, I thought.

I looked up as a couple brave cows took cautious steps forward. They were far enough away that it didn't concern me. Then a few more started following the leaders. Then the whole damn herd started coming toward me. As the cows got closer, I could see how massive they were—much, *much* larger than me. *Uh-oh.* There was nothing between us but a flimsy barbed-wire fence. Still heaving and breathless, I decided to play it cool and continue walking as if there weren't fifty-plus giant beasts seemingly intent on invading my personal bubble.

I could sense them gaining on me. Then, in the periphery of my vision, I saw the leader emerge past my right shoulder. I tried to avoid making eye contact, but I couldn't help it—I looked straight at him, and he stared right back at me. Miraculously, he made no effort to destroy the fence and attack me. This interspecies interaction felt incredibly bizarre. For some reason, I was compelled to squeak out an awkward "Hi." Aware I sounded like an idiot, I looked over my shoulder and saw the entire herd following along, matching the pace I'd set.

This is when I lost my composure.

Panicked by being with these big-eyed beasts in such close proximity, my feet started to speed walk of their own volition. My arms pumped so high I felt like a windmill. The head cow sped up and matched my pace perfectly, and the whole herd followed. *Oh god, oh god, oh god.* Then my feet, ignoring my still-searing lungs, broke out into an all-out run.

Full disclosure, I'm not a runner. I don't understand people who run. For me, the problem is a boob thing. There are no boob contraptions in the world that hold them down enough where I don't feel the need to cup them with both hands for support while I'm running. So, in a full-out, boob-holding sprint, I looked over my shoulder to see over fifty cows running with me, easily keeping up. Several bucked and farted in pure delight, but all I felt was intense, irrational fear. When I finally made it to the end of the fence line the cows stopped, lined up, and watched as I put distance between us. My heart was pounding loudly in my ears.

Before I could feel relieved, I heard ferocious barking coming from a property along the road. A large, ratty-looking dog was running full speed, straight for me. I slowed to a walk and crossed to the other side of the road, hoping to show the dog I wasn't a threat. It suddenly stopped, right at its property line, and continued barking at me but made no attempt to approach. I presumed there had to be an invisible fence. Once I passed its home, it lay down and watched me. I had already seen several shaggy, unkempt farm dogs—nothing like my tiny Kahuna. I couldn't understand why anyone would let their dogs get so ratty. I felt sorry for the dog and annoyed with the owner, but I had a more pressing issue: *How the hell was I going to get back home?*

There were no cars to rescue me, so I had no choice but to retrace my steps. My heart rate slowed and the herd, which I could still see, gradually lost interest and dispersed. Finally, when I was too cold to wait any longer, I decided to put on my big girl panties and brave the walk past the pasture again. It was my only option.

As I made my way back past the dog, it commenced its vicious barking but, again, made no attempt to leave its property. *Whew, one threat down.* This time, as I approached the pasture, every single cow was waiting for me. Alerted to my return by the tattling dog, they greeted me at the fence line. Since they didn't attempt to eat my face and trample me the last time around, I relaxed a bit. *Shake it off,* I told myself. With me on one side of the fence and the herd on the other, as before, the cows perfectly matched my pace. Slightly amused, and feeling much more relaxed, I sped up. They sped up. I slowed down. They slowed down. I jogged. They "jogged." I stopped and faced the fence. They stopped and every one of them turned toward me.

I looked at their giant, expectant faces and their big soulful eyes. They weren't so scary. They were absolutely adorable. "You have no intention of hurting me, do you?" They just stared eagerly, so I continued, "You're so cute, every one of you needs a spankin!" This was my thing: For some bizarre reason, I always threatened "spankins" to anything I thought was cute. I also had this uncontrollable baby voice that I used on animals. Several cows started chewing their cud, still watching me in a superchill stance. These guys were just gentle giants. It was like I'd had a scary alien encounter, but the aliens turned out to be really cute, even kind of cool. I realized that my little country road, despite the mean dog, was the best gym I could ask for. There was no musty smell, no waiting for machines, and I didn't even mind being ogled by the members, who all chewed with their mouths open.

Leaving the cow pasture behind, I continued my walk and came back to the creepy ravine lined by dense woods. My knees and hands hurt from the cold, so I couldn't run through this time. It felt like I was sneaking through a haunted house, looking left and right and walking as quietly as I could. I was halfway through the ravine when a giant, antlered buck emerged from the forest. He stood just fifteen feet in front of me. I gasped. He was majestic. And yet, his sheer size and the fact that he didn't seem the least bit intimidated scared the shit out of me. *What the heck do I do now?* Videos I'd seen of humans being pummeled and punched by deer ran through my mind. The buck stomped and let out a snort, his breath visible in the chilly air. I almost peed my pants.

I clasped my hands together as if in prayer and said out loud, "I don't know what that means! *Please* be cool, I just want to go home!" This was too much nature for one day. At least in Florida there were usually clear boundaries between humans and wildlife. The buck gave me a hard stare, looking down its nose at me, then leapt high in the air and disappeared back into the woods. Adrenaline kicked in yet again and I hauled butt home, holding my boobs and running like I was competing for Olympic gold. I probably burned more calories than I ever had at my city gym.

After the wilds of the countryside, I needed to get back to the human world so I could stock my fridge. I threw on my fancy farm boots and a black pashmina and jumped in the car.

My property was one of the smaller plots of land in the area. The little country road was home to mostly cattle, expansive fields, and large trees. This part of northern Mississippi had beautiful rolling hills, etched with vast hardwood forests, crop fields, and generous water elements such as ponds, small lakes, and streams. Nearby Oxford was small-town posh, but just a few

miles from town, the land quickly became rural. Despite having
gone to college at Ole Miss and living on and off in Oxford as a
child, I had never really ventured outside the town limits. The
rural area was home to people of different races and socioeco-
nomic statuses. Many properties were working farms, handed
down through generations; others belonged to wealthy people
who enjoyed dabbling in farm life, such as a former pro football
player, originally from D.C., who now had cattle milling around
the huge workout facility he'd built in his pasture. Still other
people were just seeking less expensive places to live. Everyone
had one thing in common, though: They tended to be intensely
private.

As I headed toward the little town of Water Valley, formerly
known as "the watermelon capital of the world," I got my first
taste of a "country traffic jam," which I quickly learned was far
better than a city traffic jam. The slow-moving tractor in front of
me gave me time to notice all the wasted cotton bolls along the
road, which must have blown away during harvest and now lined
the road like southern snow. A mile later, I had to stop as a small
group of deer crossed the road. I didn't mind the wait; in Tampa
it could easily take twenty minutes to drive a mile due to traffic
congestion and accidents. I quietly observed the little family of
deer as they slowly ambled by. Ahead, hardwood trees were over-
hanging the road, creating a cathedral of rich autumn colors. I
felt like I was driving through a bowl of Fruity Pebbles.

Water Valley turned out to be almost charming, if somewhat
run-down. It had the layout of an old southern railroad town,
with a long avenue running along an old railroad, and homes that
looked like they had once been grand but time had taken its toll.
The street was lined with vintage brick buildings in varying states
of decay; fortunately, several appeared to be transforming into
new life. I admired the character in the architecture. Even the

side roads had magnificent old Victorian-style houses and delightful 1920s bungalows oozing with charm. The town seemed to be positioning itself for a rebirth. Businesses were trying to multitask in interesting ways—a quaint coffee shop, for example, proudly offered that one could also get a bronzy summer glow in their tanning bed.

Driving down the main street, I found an adorable old-fashioned-looking grocery store. The interior had exposed brick walls, and they offered handwoven Amish picnic baskets for customers to fill with all kinds of specialty items. Toward the back of the store, a small freezer caught my eye. It was loaded with local ice cream, homemade desserts, and home-cooked meals. My stomach growled. I filled my picnic basket with a slice of homemade French silk pie, freshly made chicken salad with basil and parmesan, local vegetables, raw honey, and, finally, what I'd soon learn was the most delicious local milk packaged in a glass bottle. I hadn't had fresh milk from a glass jar since I was a kid living in the Philippines. One of my favorite childhood memories was putting our used glass milk and juice bottles outside our house each evening and each morning, like magic, finding them replaced with bottles full of fresh milk, mango, and guyabano juices. Similar to the Philippines, I would find unique grocery items in Mississippi but the selection was drastically limited.

Farther down Main Street, I found a Piggly Wiggly grocery store. I'd seen these grocery stores as a kid, but didn't know they were still around. Upon entering, every employee greeted me with a big smile. "Good mornin, miss!" I heard repeatedly. Their cheery attention made me feel like a celebrity. It felt like, at any moment, these people were going to break out into a Broadway musical number, twirling around me as we moved through the aisles. I had never experienced this in any city market or grocery store, ever. Did these people actually *like* their jobs?

On my way to check out, I passed a small dining area near the center of the store, next to the greeting cards. There was a table full of old men of different races, most dressed in overalls or well-worn clothes, eating together. They appeared to be having a heated debate.

"*Nawww*, you don't know what you're *talkin* about," one man said, shaking his head and swatting his hand in the air dismissively. He looked utterly disgusted. "That's not the best *eatin* variety!"

Half the men nodded in agreement. Another farmer chimed in to argue his own point: "Yeah, but they're bigguns!"

There was another chorus of "*Uh-huhs*" and head nods.

I couldn't help but smile. Here, people didn't get heated up about politics. But watermelons were worth fighting over.

While I was confident that as soon as I found my farm legs, it would be smooth sailing, I wasn't so sure that I wouldn't suddenly realize I'd made a huge mistake leaving my city life. I had no idea country living was so solitary, and the quietness threw me for a loop. But I was used to challenges. I'd started and ended my own businesses; I'd left an abusive marriage; I'd suffered miscarriages, sexual molestation, and sexual violence. I'd been a navy brat and lived in cultures where people didn't look or sound anything like me. If I could survive all that as well as living in the Philippines and Guam, where death loomed by way of wild monkeys, venomous wildlife, and other bodily threats, couldn't I tackle rural Mississippi as an adult, even though I was alone? Certainly, I could deal with subpar grocery availability and not having a French-trained hairstylist nearby. Besides, I had the vast knowledge of the world at my fingertips, via the internet.

Although my natural confidence had helped me get through

some trying situations over the years, in middle-of-nowhere Mississippi, it was proof that I was the typical city person worthy of country folks' deepest suspicions. To country people I not only had zero credibility, I was also just plain "unusual," as Farmer John called me.

My uncle had warned me about this. On one of our first visits since my arrival, he cautioned me, saying, "I'm proud of you for doing this, but you know your business is going to suffer there." I asked him why he thought this, and his response was, "Women won't let you do business with their husbands." *What?* While I'd always respected his business acumen, the sentiment was ludicrous. Who would think *I'm* a threat? By southern beauty standards, I was easily average. I laughed at my uncle and told him I was flattered, but my business would be just fine. People would hire me because I was the best for the job. I was far more concerned that *I* wouldn't want to work on their small-budget projects.

From the towering height of my Gucci heels, I looked down on the country community, secure in my superior book knowhow and city smarts. My complete lack of basic farm and animal information didn't factor in. But confidence is no replacement for experience. Fueled by my arrogance, I pushed aside even the real, tangible danger of Mother Nature—until Tricia texted a picture of a bobcat she shot coming off my property. I forwarded the message to Kelly.

She responded: "OMG, they shot a tiger on your property!??"

I replied, "Yes, Kel. Tigers run rampant around the jungles of Mississippi."

Sigh.

Her comment made me think of the dream I'd had about the tiger. With this reminder that predators were all around me, the darkness and deafening silence of night began to feel oppressive.

In the evenings, I sat on my porch in the dead silence of winter with only the occasional sound of my wind chimes and the rustling of god-only-knows-what off in the woods. My mind filled the dark spaces with demons, rabid animals, and Peeping Toms. As much as I wanted to enjoy being outside under the brilliant night sky wrapped in heavy blankets, I couldn't get past my imagination and the silence of the winter air. When I did attempt to stargaze, the sound of coyotes and the occasional unknown animal noise made me scurry back inside. In Tampa, I could barely see the stars, but at least I had never been worried about bobcats trying to stalk and eat my little dog.

While my first days were full of the excitement of a new life and getting my house in order, I felt terribly lonely and out of place. As I continued to unpack my belongings, the feeling of isolation settled over me, and the stillness started to overwhelm my senses. I'd heard of the phrase *silence is deafening;* now, the silence thundered in my ears.

The quiet that surrounded me was intense and unsettling. Not having noisy neighbors was one of the things I wanted, but without the distraction of sound, my brain went into overdrive. My mind became a damp cemetery of trauma where I struggled to find solid ground. All the things I'd thought I'd overcome through years of soldiering on were now, like zombies, pushing their way to the surface. I refused to look at them, but that didn't stop them from surrounding me.

I was only a kid when I learned that not every adult is trustworthy. I had been molested as a girl, from ages seven to nine. I wanted to tell my parents, but the predator had threatened the lives of everyone I loved. Out of fear, I kept my mouth shut. Molestation creates complicated emotions and circumstances. At that point, my parents were happily settled into new marriages. Even if his threats weren't real, speaking my dirty truth would lob a bomb into all our lives. I loved seeing my parents happy, so I couldn't let that happen. Instead, I did the only thing I could think of—I voiced my hatred for him to any adult who would listen. It was a cry for help that not only went unheard, I was reprimanded for speaking badly of him.

I kept my secret until my late twenties, when I was planning my wedding. I refused to allow this man to come. I knew banning him would mean I'd have to tell my truth, but I couldn't bear to have him there. Upon hearing about my decision, my older stepsister called and gently demanded to know why he wasn't invited. I will never forget the quiver in her voice. We hadn't been very close as children but she deserved to know. Summoning every ounce of courage, I told her why. On the other end of the phone, I could hear her break down. "He did it to me, too," she sobbed. I was shocked. All at once, we were tied together in a sisterly bond much stronger than a contract or blood. We were forged in trauma. Scared to death of what would happen to our family, we had both kept our awful secret. People don't give enough credit to children. Parents aren't the only ones who take on a protective role in a family. Sometimes, kids quietly carry heavy burdens all on their own. I often wondered what two little girls could have done if only we'd known each other's truth? But we didn't know, and when a predator threatened our lives and the lives of everyone we loved, we lived within our fear and shame and kept our little mouths tightly shut.

I needed something to focus on and I couldn't wait to start populating my property with fur and feather babies. To combat the silence that kept plowing up my past and while I awaited the arrival of my baby chicks, I ordered the best satellite TV and internet available in rural Mississippi. Even the best tier was too slow to download movies and videos, though, and I was left desperate for familiar sounds and human voices. In my uncertainty, I told myself that if I failed, I could always run home to Tampa and civilization. But somehow, I already knew I didn't fit in there, either, anymore. The very act of the move itself had already changed me. Now, I felt I was existing between two worlds: city and country, lies and truth.

I had to learn to restructure my days. My old routine wasn't going to work in my new life, with a few exceptions. One morning, as I made breakfast and pondered what my new daily rhythm would look and feel like, I heard my phone ding.

It was a text from Farmer John: "I'm going to come by later and pick you up on my mule to show you the property lines."

What?

I understood that land is country currency and fence lines were to be respected, so it was important for me to learn my property lines, but I was immediately uncomfortable about riding on the back of an animal with a man I barely knew. I had grown up riding dressage horses and had even been on a donkey in Greece, but never a mule, and never with a stranger. I started typing a response several times, but I had no idea what to say. I didn't want to offend him. Then my phone rang. It was Farmer John.

He started speaking as soon as I answered: "Jake! Do you think I'm trying to pick you up on the back of an *animal*?" Still uncomfortable, I simply said: "Um, yes." Farmer John started chuckling. "*NAW!* A *mule* is an ATV, an ALL TERRAIN VEHICLE!" he informed me in his thick southern drawl. Relieved and feeling silly, I laughed nervously. He continued, "We need to get you country educated real quick!"

Where'd You Get Those Peepers?

One month in, it was clear that my perfect farm plan was perfectly ridiculous. Some of the animals I wanted simply weren't available in my area, or even in the United States. And many of my garden selections couldn't survive or produce in the hills of north Mississippi. After weeks of struggling to get by on my own, I received a text from my new farm friends, Brice and Danielle Noonan.

The Noonans were in their early thirties and, like me, originally city people from Florida. Brice was a biology professor at Ole Miss and a friend of my dad, who also taught biology at the university. Tall and bald, Brice's mustacheless beard wrapped neatly around his face, giving him the appearance of an Amish hipster. His wife, Danielle, reminded me of comedian Amy Schumer: foulmouthed, real, and fabulously hilarious. Having made the city-to-country transition themselves, they knew much of what awaited me, and they thoroughly enjoyed their ringside seat to the misadventures of my new farm life.

Like many country people, the Noonans weren't into small talk. Their text that day got straight to the point, asking if I wanted their geese for my pond. They'd raised Toulouse geese and didn't want them anymore. Just reading the text made me anxious. Toulouse geese? What even were those? They sounded French, which I was totally into, but geese weren't on my farm plan, so I knew nothing about them. I ignored all the questions in my head and boldly responded that I'd be willing to take ONE. The Noonans replied, "You'll take all three. We'll drop by Sunday afternoon."

Great. Now I had two days to learn all I could about geese. *What the hell do geese even eat? Where would I put them? What if they hated me? What if they weren't pretty?* I spent the next three hours at the computer reading about the breed, their preferences and requirements. Just weeks into this new life, I was about to come face-to-face with my first real farm animals and, like Gia the cat, they weren't a part of my original plan.

As I frantically researched geese, I received a call from the post office. The pleasant lady on the phone told me there was a package waiting for me. "And . . ." she said, "it's peeping!" *Oh, thank God,* I thought. *They're alive!* It was my order from MyPetChicken.com. I still couldn't wrap my head around the fact that live baby chicks could fly via U.S. mail. Apparently, birds absorb the egg yolks into their abdomen just prior to hatching. They can live off the yolk without additional food or water for up to three days, allowing them to travel. Even so, it was unnerving to think of how rough the journey must have been for my soon-to-be babies.

The entire twenty-five-minute drive to the post office, I trembled as if I'd had too much caffeine. I had been daydreaming about these chicks for so long, had spent so many furtive hours looking at them on the internet, and now I couldn't get to them fast enough. My emotions vacillated wildly from euphoria to fear. Then the questions began. *What if they were sick? What if they were hurt? What if I couldn't keep them alive or I failed them in some way?* My excitement was quickly weighted down by fear. The prospect of having new animals seemed to be opening old wounds. So many times, I had wondered what I could have done better to save my failed pregnancies. I had rethought everything I had eaten, I had chastised myself for every negative thought I'd had. And now, the question of whether I was a bad mother was bleeding over into my quest to care for my new animals. I decided I wasn't going to let this line of thinking destroy my excitement and quickly brushed off the darkening thoughts.

After I parked, I practically bolted out of the car, smiling like an idiot. You'd think I was about to meet Coco Chanel herself, and not just the baby chicken I'd decided to name after her.

"I'm here to pick up the peeping package you called about!" I announced a bit too loudly as I entered the post office. My heart was pounding so hard, I was afraid others could hear it. Strangely, this felt like the moment just before walking down the aisle to get married over a decade earlier—excited and scared, with an odd, plastered grin and no clue of what I was getting myself into. The postal worker returned with the sweetest-sounding package I'd ever received. I had been instructed to open the package in front of witnesses, so I carefully handled the small, hole-filled cardboard crate like it held priceless jewelry or the world's finest candies. There, inside, was my dream come true, my very first chickens.

I heard several exclamations of "Awwww" around me. I had an audience, and I felt like a proud parent. I couldn't wipe the huge toothy smile from my face; it was as if I'd hatched the chicks myself. They were tiny multicolored balls of peeping fluff. To my great relief, they looked perfectly mobile and healthy, if a little confused. Loudly protesting the rush of cold air, they all huddled tightly together. Except for the chubby yellow chick—she was ready to conquer the world, actively trying to escape her cardboard prison. My heart was bursting, but I was still too nervous to touch them. Breathing a sigh of relief that they were alive, I gently closed the lid.

I drove slowly all the way home, trying my best to comfort the little ones and not jostle the box. I resisted the persistent urge to open the lid and check on them, their occasional peeps giving me some comfort. Less than an hour into it and I was already scared about failing as a chicken mom.

Once I got home, I did my best to follow the online instructions. Again, I opened the lid, and now I lightly petted each one with my index finger. A rush of sweet emotion and happy tears washed over me. Kahuna's curiosity was sending him into a whiny panic. He'd never met a chicken before. Standing on his hind legs, he tried desperately to see inside the box. I cupped the first chick and held her up for inspection. Her yellow down was baby soft and she had the cutest delicate orange legs and feet. I brushed her against my cheek and she nestled into my hair. "I think I'll name you . . . Babette," I told her, as if I didn't already have all their names and placeholder photos on my spreadsheet already. Next, I inspected Fiona, Mae Mae, Coco Chanel, and finally, Prada.

After I confirmed that they didn't have any of the common issues newborn chicks can have, such as curled toes, splayed legs, or crossed beaks (thank goodness!), it was time to step into the mother hen role. "Please don't let me accidentally drown these babies!" I murmured to Kahuna. I took each chick and dipped the tip of their beak into their water. One by one, they tilted their heads back to swallow their first sip of liquid. They were thirsty from their long journey and, to my delight, they quickly learned to drink.

Next, it was time to teach them to eat. I set their food dish into their heated enclosure and sat back to see what they would do. None of them went for it, even though I'd bought them expensive organic chick crumbles, like a cereal for baby chickens. They were too interested in exploring their new digs and pecking at each other to care about eating. I knew they needed sustenance so, placing the tip of my finger directly into their food, I started poking in and out, simulating a hen pecking at the ground. This got their attention. They rushed to my finger and stared, and then the bravest one mimicked me with her beak. That first taste was all it took for the baby to start eating voraciously. Then the others joined in, excitedly scratching around. I sat back and watched until the babies had had their fill and started passing out from a combination of food comas and travel exhaustion. I was satisfied, with myself, and with what was obviously my natural farming ability. I wondered what my Tampa friends would think if they saw me now.

While the babies slept, I sat hugging my knees to my chest and marveled at their little bodies. I couldn't wait to learn their personalities and preferences. I could already tell that Mae Mae and Babette liked to stay away from the heat lamp. The other three piled together under the warm glow, snuggling into one another's down. They were so cute and peaceful. I fought the temptation to disturb them and constantly checked to see if they were still breathing. I watched as Babette fussed herself awake, then stretched a tiny leg out, followed by her adorable little T. Rex arm, which looked nothing like a wing yet. There was something so humanlike in the sleepy way she stretched. I knew they all needed rest, so I kept my hands to myself and observed everything I could about their behavior. This was the best programming ever. Farm people refer to it as "Chicken TV," and now I knew exactly what they were talking about—I was instantly hooked.

There's a popular phenomenon in the farm world called "chicken math." This refers to the magical way new chickens seem to show up in your life. You plan for five chickens and suddenly you have ten—not unlike nice handbags, or shoes. You have a black one but now you need a yellow one. It's about variety. *Somehow*, delightfully, they multiply.

I had been a chicken keeper for only a day when I received a call from an organic vegetable and pig farmer, a young man named Farmer Bradley. Farmer Bradley knew little about chickens, but despite his lack of poultry knowledge, he wanted to buy my first adult bird for me as a welcome gift. That way, he reasoned, I wouldn't have to wait months for my baby girls to start producing. With the winter solstice approaching, if I had adult chickens, I could have my first eggs in a few weeks. In the Northern Hemisphere, the winter solstice triggers the girls to start laying eggs in preparation for spring (chickens often don't lay year-round unless they are given artificial light, which forces the process). Never mind that I didn't have a coop or even a crate to transport an adult chicken in. But the next day happened to be the popular Ripley flea market, otherwise known as "First Monday," and so ready or not, Farmer Bradley and I were off to get me a chicken.

Farmer Bradley was younger than I was by several years, but our conversation flowed easily during the hour-long drive. Thinking of all the chickens and baby animals that awaited me, I could barely contain my excitement. We pulled in just after eight A.M.

and there were already people everywhere. It was a crisp, beautiful morning, and I was ready to *shop*.

The market reminded me a bit of a carnival or fair—it was dusty, and the air was thick with the aroma of food being prepared. The Ripley First Monday Trade Days originally opened in 1893. Today, there are over six hundred vendors, and the market is one of the largest and oldest in the country. I couldn't resist this shopping experience. My mother had often taken me to markets when we lived overseas. She was an incredible treasure hunter. She had a knack for finding anything from beautiful handmade textiles to antique weapons. Once, while on a road trip in the Philippines, she pulled over to buy a handwoven rattan hat from a woman working a field with her caribou. My mother bought the hat right off the woman's head. Many of the things she owned had a story like that. As I began walking the market, a comforting sense of nostalgia settled in. I hoped to find feathered treasures of my own.

We passed a taco booth and I felt my stomach growl. *It's too early for tacos*, I tried to convince myself. Food would have to wait. Once my mission was complete, I could relax and eat. For now, I had to get my new feather babies.

The number one rule of any market is to get there early. Unless you contact a vendor to hold something for you, the good stuff sells quickly. We walked past booths ranging from high-quality cast-iron cookware and antiques to cheap junk like socks and stinky candles. My head felt like it was on a swivel. The sheer number of available animals was staggering. I could see everything from rabbits to peacocks to pigs to lizards. Some vendors kept their animals in great conditions, but others . . . didn't. Seeing this, I snapped into rescue mode, talking about how I'd buy *all* the animals that were living in such shitty conditions. But Farmer Bradley cautioned against it, recommending I stick to rewarding only those vendors who cared for their animals. "Those assholes who keep their animals in deplorable conditions will only keep doing it. They *count* on people like you to save what they have." He had a good point, and I made a mental note to report each horrid vendor to the people who ran the market. (Soon after, the market hired someone who walked the grounds making sure the animals had everything they needed.) In the meantime, we stuck only to the conscientious vendors and continued perusing the feathered and fluffed wares. I was itching to open my wallet. Then I saw *her*.

In front of us was a beautiful lavender-colored pullet, a young female chicken. It was love at first sight. I was instantly taken with her feathered feet and feminine coloring. She was the stuff of my Disney farm dreams—feminine and fabulous. I couldn't believe my luck! She would have the honor of being my very first "real" chicken and would, I knew, be my number one prized girl. Farmer Bradley handed over the $6.00 asking price for her.

As beautiful as she was, having never held an adult chicken, I was too afraid to touch her, so the vendor unceremoniously plopped her into the ten-dollar transport crate I'd purchased earlier. Lifting the crate to eye level, I inspected my new love. She was hunched down, frightened. I told her she would be home soon. "From now on you'll be my Francesca!" I whispered. I felt like a little kid, and this was my Chicken Christmas.

We continued our quest and added four more young hens to the carrier. Clueless about what to look for, I based my decisions purely on appearance. This buying experience was nothing like the clean, informative website I was used to browsing, and I was flying blind. But with money to burn and the excitement of a shopping spree—it was the same kind of euphoria I'd once gotten from Dior and Chanel—I bought two red hens, a black-and-gold laced hen, and a chubby yellow hen.

As we left the market, an old farmer in well-worn overalls waved at us. He was sitting on his tailgate overlooking the crowd like it was a spectator sport. He commented on my prized lavender girl, saying, "That's a fine blue cockerel you have there, young lady." Instantly offended that he would mistake my gorgeous girl for a boy, I spat out, "Thanks, but it's a girl!" and hurried past him in a huff. *Silly old man.* Obviously, he was clueless about chickens.

On the way home, Farmer Bradley decided to take a detour. We stopped at his small parcel of rented farmland where he kept his free-range pigs and late fall crops. I had never seen such a variety of food growing from the ground. I recognized the vegetables, but only partially; I was used to seeing them neatly washed and packaged for public consumption. At all the farmers' markets I'd been to, the vegetables were always pristinely displayed. Bradley pointed out the various types of organic kale he was growing, then he started plucking leaves off different plants. He took a bite and offered me a leaf.

"Eat this," he commanded.

"Um. No thanks. You just pulled that from the dirt, something could have peed on it," I retorted, flatly.

"Don't be silly, have a sense of adventure."

"I think secretly moving to Mississippi qualifies as enough of an adventure. Besides, I just bought kale at the grocery store."

But he insisted, shoving the kale at my face, and finally I acquiesced.

I'd never been a huge fan of kale, but this was a completely new taste experience. It was, without a doubt, the best kale I'd ever had.

"OMG, why does it taste so different? It's the pee, isn't it?" I said inspecting what was left of the leaf, only partly joking. This tasted *nothing* like the stuff I bought at the grocery store.

"Ha. Not funny. It's because it's straight from the ground and hasn't lost any of its nutrients and flavor. At some point, I'll convince you that local, fresh food is always better."

Sunday afternoon, when the Noonans were coming with the geese, rolled around slowly. I did my best to keep busy with the baby chicks and spent the morning watching the flea market chickens shuffle around their small coop from the safe distance of my living room window. Farmer Bradley had given me his old coop, a five-by-four-foot wood-framed box that was elevated a few feet off the ground by wooden legs. The entire frame was wrapped in wire and it had a cute tin roof. There were two nest boxes and a perch inside. It was small, but worked well for a temporary house until I could build the permanent coop—again, of course, with the help of Farmer Bradley. I was quickly learning that without the wisdom of the farmers and neighbors around me, I would be totally lost in this new world.

When the Noonans drove up, they got right down to business. Before they even pulled the large crate from the car, I could hear the geese honking. They were surprisingly loud and sounded extremely distressed. Already I was afraid, and I hadn't even laid eyes on them. I smiled at the Noonans and nervously twirled my hair. *What are these people getting me into?* I thought.

"Where do you want them?" Brice asked as he and Danielle balanced the crate's weight between them. I kept my distance, my arms hugging my midsection for comfort. Sensing my trepidation, he continued, "Why don't we put them by the pond? They've never had a real pond before; we can see what they'll do." I nodded and followed the couple with the pissed-off French geese to my pond. I couldn't see through the crate, so I still had no idea what they looked like, but they sounded *big*.

The Noonans set the crate down at the water's edge and undid the latch. One by one, the heavy-bodied, slate-gray geese with bright orange bills slowly made their way out into the fresh air. Their necks stretched out, heads held low to the ground in defensive stances. All three were hissing wildly. I remembered a quote I'd once seen someone post on social media: "It is said geese are the descendants of dragons. They have teeth on their bills, and while they have lost the ability to breathe fire, they hiss to remind themselves they once could." This made perfect sense to me now. These geese moved and sounded just like the dragons I'd seen in Hollywood movies. I suppose that if chickens originated from T. Rex, maybe geese could have some equally frightening ancestry?

I watched as the birds hesitatingly waded into the water, carefully inspecting their liquid surroundings and bitching at us the entire time. Then, as if it suddenly dawned on them that they were free and we meant them no harm, they plunged into the pond. We watched as they transformed from mean, hissing creatures into graceful water dancers. They flew around the water, dipped, glided, and made haunting calls that filled the air. The bright sun reflecting off the water made it look as if they were paddling through molten gold. They had their own space, they were totally free. Goose bumps ran up my arms.

I glanced over at Brice and Danielle. We were all misty-eyed and aware that we were watching something beautifully transformative. None of us spoke. These creatures, who had never even seen water before, instinctively knew this pond was their home. Just one hour prior, they had been landlocked animals. Then, after enduring a traumatic event, they were delivered into the life they were born to live. I couldn't help but hope the same would happen to me.

You Can't Leave Your Past Behind

It had been a couple years since my last miscarriage and yet the memory and grief still hit me like tsunami waves, seemingly out of nowhere. I couldn't understand why the emotions were so strong, but the effects were paralyzing, sometimes for moments, sometimes for much longer. But eventually, I was able to pull myself out of the tailspin. I had become a master of ignoring . . . or what I like to call "refocusing."

Now with my farm animals rapidly accumulating . . . I started to question myself. If I couldn't keep my own children alive, what made me think I could care for other lives? I was biologically programmed to bring life into the world and yet had failed at the simplest of tasks.

I was twenty-nine years old when I lost my first baby. Then I lost my marriage, and finally, I lost my faith. I was devastated, but at the same time, the pain almost didn't feel real, as if it were too much to bear. It felt like something that would inevitably vanish, because I was young, and I had time, and I fully expected I'd have a family of my own one day. Dealing with the pain felt optional, in a way, because *surely* I would find a way to fix this.

The day of my first miscarriage, the technician at the doctor's office, looking at the baby on the monitor, wouldn't make eye contact with me. Not ready to concede defeat, I sat up and craned my neck to view the screen. When the technician turned the monitor away from me without comment, the verdict was obvious. Afterward, the doctor said, "Women have been doing this for thousands of years. Miscarriages are like a heavy period."

That was on Christmas Eve. My body held on to my dead baby for another week. I don't know if I was grateful for the extra time, or if it made it worse. I spent long hours sitting at our patio table in St. Petersburg staring blankly into the air. I had no idea what to do with all the pain. All the self-loathing. I questioned everything I had eaten, every action I had taken. Did I not love my baby enough? I still had morning sickness, but now with nothing to show for its torture. Amid the holidays, the irony of the timing didn't escape me. The upcoming year was supposed to be the year in which I became a mother. The new year, my new beginning, was the exact opposite of everything I wanted.

That New Year's Eve, the actual process of miscarrying brought with it an overwhelming sense of physical schizophrenia. The waves of pain were so intense that I didn't know if I had to vomit, urinate, or shit. Excruciating pain shot through my back and legs. It was the first time I truly felt the closeness of death. I was afraid and alone, with a husband who didn't seem to care at all, when even just a hug would have meant the world to me. There was an increasing heaviness in my uterus, which I tried desperately to fight. I held it inside, refusing to yield to the pressure. But ultimately, my body didn't care what my heart wanted.

When the pressure became too great, I made my way to the toilet. Even before I could sit down, my muscles contracted and my body seized. A rush of blood and fluid exploded. The pushing was involuntary, and I knew what was happening. I couldn't bear to look in the bowl of the toilet; I was too afraid of what I'd see. Horrified and in pain, I screamed for my husband downstairs. In all his sensitivity, he had decided to go ahead with hosting a New Year's Eve party for his friends. It was surreal, hearing a party full of laughter downstairs while I suffered my worst heartache and physical pain only feet above it. When he finally came in, I begged him to find our baby. I just wanted to see any emotion in his face, any sign that he cared at all. But there was nothing. Just his drunken stupor and annoyance.

I made it back to our bedroom just in time for another contraction. I was exhausted, sick to my stomach, and bleeding profusely. My husband came into the room and said he couldn't find anything. He had flushed the toilet. I knew he hadn't even tried.

He lay down beside me and passed out, drunk and snoring loudly. As our bedroom filled with the stench of his alcohol breath I looked over at this man I no longer wanted to know. When I calmly said, "I'm leaving you," he didn't break from his drunken snoring. For the longest time, I didn't know people like this actually existed. I had always found reasons and excuses for his angry, insensitive behavior; mostly I blamed myself. To me, if someone was mad at me, I always assumed it was my fault. I had never known abuse in a committed relationship before, and I couldn't figure out how I'd gotten myself entangled in this mess. I thought about the times he yelled at me for not having dinner ready when he came home from work, never mind the fact that I worked full-time over an hour away. Or when I finally confided in him about being molested as a child—he blamed *me*. It was an instant reminder of what it had felt like as a kid, when, one time I had gathered all the courage I had and tried to express what was happening to an adult I was close to—who immediately informed me that the molester was a good person. I discovered that often adults prize decorum over ugly truth. My husband's reaction triggered me deeper into shame and caused me to keep my mouth shut about the abuse for many more years. I presumed everyone felt as he did—that I was damaged and lucky anyone would want me at all. I thought about when he threatened my life for touching his TV remote. Looking back, I'd lost count of how many times he'd threatened me. My life was one of walking on eggshells and bottling up my emotions, never knowing what would set him off. I had lived in fear for so long, but the loss of my baby had created a vacuum and bestowed the kind of strength that only anger and despair can. It was an emotional earthquake that shook me awake from the nightmare marriage I was in. There was no fear of him left, there was nothing but anger and hatred—for him, and for the God who had forsaken me.

It took four more hours of contractions and blood loss that soaked every pad and towel I had laid under me until, finally, my body had nothing left to give. One year ended and another began. I don't remember much of the months that followed except that I couldn't bear to see pregnant women or babies. Most of all, I couldn't stand it when people told me I could always have another baby. I wanted *that* one.

Fear and Ruin

After several weeks of keeping the market chickens in the temporary coop, Farmer Bradley arrived to "help" me build the permanent coop. He was remarkably strong and clearly no stranger to this kind of work. As I watched him roughly but expertly handle the materials, I realized I wasn't so keen on wrecking my manicure, so I just sat back and tried to follow his lead whenever possible. Sometimes I was helpful, and other times I was clearly just in the way. Despite my assistance, it only took a few short hours before my new chicken coop was finished. I added fresh straw and was giddy with the idea of finally moving the adult chickens to their permanent home. But because I was still afraid of them, I called Jenifer to see if she would assist me. Up until now, I'd somehow, miraculously, managed to care for the chickens without ever touching any of them.

"Not gonna lie," I told my sister. "I'm not crazy about catching and holding these things." She nodded in nervous agreement. With visions of flapping wings and pecked-out eyes swirling in our heads, the two of us psyched ourselves up to make our first physical contact with the birds. After a few minutes of hesitation, we decided to rip the Band-Aid off and just go for it. Of course, the girls didn't want to cooperate. When we opened the door, they went to the back of the coop and bunched together squawking. This meant that, to reach them, we had to stick our upper torsos *inside* the small coop through a wire opening a little over a foot wide.

In a whirlwind of feathers, screeches, and face slaps from frantic wings, we captured the chickens one by one and carried them to their new digs. It was traumatic for both the shrieking chickens and the squealing women. But Jenifer and I came out of it relatively unscathed, if not completely disheveled and exhausted from adrenaline, with a few feathers in our hair. I hoped the move would mark a new beginning in my relationship with these girls. Now that they were in a much larger coop, I could sit with them and get properly acquainted . . . from a comfortable distance.

Later that night, I finally got around to unpacking my boxes of books. Since I was a child I had always been a voracious reader. At least, I had been until I got together with Chad. His codependency was so strong it made him uncomfortable when I tried to read before bedtime. He needed my full attention, always. I hadn't gotten through the first chapter of the thick historical fiction novel I bought when we first moved in together and by the time we broke up a few *years* later, I was no further along.

On the farm, I was looking forward to again filling my nightstand with a stack of books. As I sorted through my boxes, I found a copy of the memoir *Eat, Pray, Love* by Elizabeth Gilbert. I felt my heart sink a bit. This woman had a movie-worthy life and what had I ever done besides shop and go from distraction to distraction? At least she had the courage to attempt something different. I wasn't even sure I'd make it on the farm for a year.

Unlike most people I knew, I rarely remembered exact lines from books I'd read. Usually, I could recall how a book made me *feel,* but rarely any of the specific words. This book had been different, though. One line had haunted me for years, and it came to mind the second I laid my hand on the cover.

"Ruin is a gift." *What?* When I'd read those words years ago, I couldn't fathom what she meant or how anyone could even *think* such a thing. But worse, I found I just couldn't get that line out of my head. Whenever I thought of those words, I immediately felt a quickening of anxiety in my chest. They seemed to be written specifically for me and yet, I had no desire to look deeper into myself, to find out *why* they tormented me. As I unpacked, merely holding *Eat, Pray, Love* made me feel uneasy. I shook my head and quickly shoved the book to the bottom of my bookshelf.

City Life Meets Country Life

My animals quickly multiplied. By the end of my first December, I was chasing around chicks, Toulouse geese, and five adult chickens who continued to scare the shit out of me. As it turned out, the flea market chickens were untamed roughnecks with serious street cred. Somehow, they all knew they were the boss of me. The one exception was the oldest, Serafina, who had a sweet disposition and the oddest habit of suddenly taking a nap in the middle of anything she was doing: drinking water, eating, or just walking around. Her eyes would close and her head would bob down for a few minutes, and then she would wake up, look around, and resume her normal activities as if nothing had happened. Since I had no idea what normal adult chicken behavior looked like, I wasn't sure whether this was weird or not, and I just continued to sit back and observe it.

After a particularly harried week of running around tending to the various birds, I noticed my beautiful Hunter boots were now ripped at the ankles and my dainty socks were getting holes in the toes and heels. My wardrobe was painfully inadequate, especially as the frost crept in. In Florida, I had always despised winter clothes. Every bulky item had taken up the space of at least two summer dresses, so I bought very few things for winter. Now, I still didn't even own a proper winter sweater. My idea of winterwear consisted mostly of scarves and cute boots. My "winter coats" were much more fashion than function, and my go-to yoga pants and tights certainly weren't made to provide real warmth. Plus, they looked like crap tucked into my now-ripped boots. My scarves quickly started to show wear and tear, and I found myself wasting valuable time picking straw and God knows what else out of their fringe.

With few options, and not wanting to spend much money on clothes that would just be used for farm chores, I decided to visit a secondhand store in town. There, I found a never-used, tags-still-on pair of hunting overalls in camo green. They were made for little boys, and were a little short on me, but otherwise they fit perfectly. They were padded for extra warmth, but not too bulky and (bonus!) they made my boobs look *great*. And they were only *nine dollars*!

I texted a picture to Kelly and told her about the price. Amused, she decided it was time to visit and see just what I'd gotten myself into. She drove from her new home in Atlanta the very next day. When I ran out of the house to greet her, she took one look at me and my budding farm and said, "I give this six months before you're back in Tampa."

"Well, my mom said she gives me two YEARS. So I guess we'll see who's right!" I replied.

Kelly spent the next week sitting on my porch swing, swaddled in blankets, cuddled up with Kahuna and glasses of wine. It was an odd feeling, having this person from my old life suddenly in my new one. I felt nostalgia for city socializing, and a little self-conscious about giving someone a glimpse into my odd, solitary world.

Kelly was terrified of the adult chickens and wary of my baby chicks, who were growing like adorable fluffy weeds. Even while refilling glass after glass of wine, she never took her eyes off the animals. She was particularly leery of the geese, who roamed the property like a band of noisy, bossy thugs. Kelly's Scorpio sensibilities meant her trust was hard-earned—ironically, she had this in common with the geese. I didn't blame her, though; the birds were beautiful jerks who were only lately starting to tolerate *my* existence. Between wine runs, Kelly helped me hang photos and art, and my little house finally began to feel more like a home. It was comforting having a familiar friend with me, even if she was constantly screaming for help when one of the animals got too close to her. At one point, while sitting by my fireplace she commented, "I'm sitting in front of a fire, knitting, next to some chickens that are in the house . . . this is some country-ass shit." I laughed and nodded.

On her last night, we took our spots on the porch to talk. Throughout the week, I had found her extreme fear of my feather babies curious and wanted to discuss it. I understood that my own fear was due to my inexperience and the fact that it was obvious my adult animals weren't tamed. But I wasn't scared of the chicks and the geese, who, I had come to learn, simply wanted their boundaries respected.

"You seem to have a genuine fear of the animals?" I gently prodded.

She paused for a moment and adjusted the giant messy bun on top of her head, considering her answer.

"That's because they really scare me," she replied as she sipped her wine and pulled the blanket up to her chin.

"I mean, I understand you're not familiar with them but you seem to really believe they *want* to hurt you. Why?"

She shrugged. "My dad has a scar on his face from trying to catch a chicken when he was a kid. I think I'm afraid of them because of what happened to him."

I nodded in understanding and we sat quietly rocking for a while until Kelly changed the subject.

"I can't believe you actually moved to a farm. I remember when you were depressed before your breakup with Chad, I thought you would get better naturally. I thought it was just because of the miscarriage and that all you needed was time, but then you started sleeping all day and never left the bed . . ."

"I remember," I said quietly. Being reminded of my depression made me uncomfortable, but she continued, "I'd sit on your bed and beg you to go outside, or anywhere, with me. I was lonely and missed my best friend and felt angry that you wouldn't just snap out of it. You refused to even talk about anything."

"My feelings were so complex I guess I felt paralyzed." I tried to explain something I still didn't really understand myself. "And I believe your exact words to me were, 'You need to get the fuck out of bed!'" I said, grinning.

Kelly laughed and went on, "Then you started spending all your time on your computer looking at farm stuff. I thought you were just hyperfocusing on a fantasy to feel better. When you kept talking about it, I couldn't believe it. I told you it was silly."

Her use of the word *silly* still stung. I knew this would be a shared sentiment with nearly everyone who knew me back in the city. In that moment, I solidified my intention to keep my move quiet as Kelly continued, "The point of this is, I wanted to tell you that I was being selfish; I didn't want you to leave me and I'm sorry for that. But that being said, I love you very much and still, I give this six months."

The next morning Kelly was loading her car and called me over. "Your red hen has passed out several times since I've been out here. Is that normal?" I watched Serafina scratching around with the rest of the flock. Before long, she stopped and slowly slumped to the ground. A minute later, she popped up as if nothing had happened, shook it off, and continued foraging. For the first time I began to think that *maybe* this wasn't normal chicken behavior.

As I said goodbye to Kelly, I swore her to secrecy: Under no circumstances would she tell anyone in Tampa of my whereabouts. Most of my friends, as well as my clients, still had no idea and I would keep it that way. So much of my work was done over the phone or email, and as long as I remained accessible, they could think I was anywhere: on work trips, or even sitting in my office in Florida. Social media still named Tampa as my city and I was careful not to accidentally post anything farm-related on my personal page or add pictures of myself on my farm page. My new life still didn't feel real; it didn't even feel like it was really fully *mine*, in a way. It all felt precarious, like a facade hiding a deep shame. My soul still felt exhausted and disconnected. The last thing I wanted was the spotlight of judgment aimed at me. I feared the fallout would cost me my business and friends. For now, I was comfortable staying in hiding, safe from prying eyes and the opinions of others.

Country Busy

Quickly, I was learning that "country busy" was entirely different from "city busy." I spoke to my mom and stepdad back in Florida more now than I had in the sixteen years when I lived only an hour away from their Orlando-adjacent home. Time at the farm passed slowly and calmly, and I was more willing to keep them informed of all I had going on. (To be honest, I had never been too keen on filling them in on my city nightlife escapades.) In many ways, I was starting to feel like a kid again, excited to share all that I was learning. The deep regret I expected to have over the move still hadn't set in, and yet I lived in constant fear that it would.

My life in Tampa had been ruled entirely by the passage of time; clocks and technology mattered immensely. As soon as I woke up in the morning, the first thing I did was grab my phone, and I was mindful of exactly what minute it was all day long. There were scheduled meetings and deadlines almost every hour. In my new life, though, time was becoming the least of my concerns. Gradually, I was falling into nature's rhythms. Each day, I woke up, without an alarm, to the sun pouring through my window. The first emotion I felt in the morning was no longer anger over an abrupt alarm, or frustration while rushing around preparing for the demands of the day. Instead, I eased out of bed, made my way outside to feed the animals, and filled my lungs with fresh, life-giving country air. That act alone felt like a gym workout and morning meditation wrapped in one.

I had always been heavily motivated by the idea of freedom, which is why I started my own marketing and PR business in the first place. I've always known that I wanted to work for myself. But it took me a long time to realize that what I had in Tampa wasn't freedom at all. Running my own business meant that I didn't just have one boss, I had many. And rather than ending a day at five o'clock or walking out on a Friday afternoon into freedom, my business demanded nights, weekends, and holidays. On the farm, though, I often wasn't even sure what day it was. Holidays snuck up on me. I still ran my business, but now I tried to condense my active participation in human interaction (e.g., conference calls) to one day a week. There were some immediate benefits to this. The biggest was that I no longer spent my Sundays in mental and emotional anguish in anticipation of the upcoming week.

As a publicist and marketing professional, I had a very responsive personality and an intense need to please. When someone needed something, I jumped. It's a major holiday but you want stories for your newsletter, in the middle of the night? Done. You procrastinated and failed at your own job but need me to fix it for you over the weekend when I had special plans? Sure! You accidentally sent out a letter to major donors two days ago but now, on Sunday morning, you just remembered your website needs several new pages addressing the issue? I'm on it. Being responsive was a huge part of what made me good at what I did. It was the only readily available tool I had to combat my overwhelming anxiety but it also earned me major props professionally. At one point, a particularly hardcore journalist told me: "What I appreciate about you is that you are always available. You're prepared and when you don't have an answer, you find it. You make my job easier."

At the time, I'd felt this was great praise. I'd always had a healthy respect for journalists, and in many ways, I viewed them more as my clients than the people who were actually paying my bills. But looking back, I was starting to see that it was that desperate need to please that compounded my anxiety. Constantly trying to get ahead of the needs of others meant neglecting myself; it meant rarely taking a simple break. And, I was starting to realize, it had been slowly killing my spirit.

The clock had been my brutal master, but slowly, it was releasing its death grip on me. On the farm, I found moments of freedom in the smallest details. Now, I was starting to truly live by the whims of my body: I ate when I was hungry, slept when I was tired. Sometimes my stomach wanted lunch at ten A.M., so I would have it. Some days I went to bed at six A.M., other times at six P.M. There were major changes I'd been expecting when I moved to the country, but it was the small adjustments like this that took me by surprise. Still, nothing rocked me more than the most difficult parts of my past suddenly rising up from where I'd long ago buried them.

When I first moved to the farm, several things about the property had been hard for me to swallow. One of the kids' rooms was painted bright green and yellow, in John Deere tractor colors with a matching faceplate on the wall. The children's decor triggered my sensitivities, but I quickly tamped down these feelings with differently colored paint—an easy fix.

There was also a heavy wooden treehouse cemented into the ground that the previous owner had built for his sons. Each time

I glanced at it, my mood sank. At first, I considered making it into a cool chicken coop or goat playground but, truly, I just wanted it *gone*. Right in the heart of my property, visible from the house, it was a constant reminder of a life I didn't have. Fortunately, the former owners contacted me shortly after, asking if they could have it. I readily agreed; I never wanted to look at it again.

One day, shortly after the winter solstice, I was on the porch swing with Kahuna, getting mooned by my little flock of adult chickens. Their adorable fluffy butts were high in the air as they foraged the sparse winter ground for tidbits of food. Had I not still been terrified of them, I would have delivered "spankins" to each little feathered bum. I watched as Serafina woke up from one of her minute-long naps. She looked around, seeming nervous, and then, abandoning the flock, she took off toward the barn, running like a toddler with a loaded diaper.

Oh my god! Could she possibly be about to lay an egg?! I put Kahuna back inside the house and, like a thief in the night, stealthily made my way to the barn, creeping slowly around the corner to get a view of the coop. There was Serafina, inspecting the nesting boxes one at a time. She would jump in, scratch around, jump out, and go to the next box. None of them seemed up to her exacting standards. Crouching like a baseball catcher, my legs were getting tired, and I wished she would hurry the hell up. *How long does this process take?* I wondered. Serafina then apparently decided the coop itself wasn't good enough and walked back outside. *You'd think she was about to lay a golden egg, the way she's acting.* I rolled my eyes. She made her way closer to me, and I held my breath, frozen in place.

There was a cardboard box just outside the barn door, leftover from my move. I'd unpacked it the day before and had forgotten to break it down. Serafina suddenly noticed it, hopped up on the ledge of the box, and, after aerial inspection, jumped inside. *Seriously?* I thought. *An ugly freaking moving box?* I'd provided perfectly lovely, luxurious nest boxes, full of soft fluff to cushion an egg. I heard her scratching around on the cardboard bottom and then . . . silence. Ten leg-numbing minutes passed and still nothing, not a scratch or a peep. I was dying of curiosity. Then suddenly Serafina popped out of the box, jumped down, and started belting out her egg song. Chickens tend to cluck loudly to announce they've laid an egg. "*Bok bok bah GAWK!*" She was like a town crier, yelling repeatedly with a very serious expression, turning in all directions to achieve optimum range. It was the first time I'd heard an egg song in person. Serafina wanted the whole world to know what she had done.

And just like that, she took off running back to her flock. Inside the box was a beautiful, large brown egg. The protective bloom was still drying. I'd learned from the internet that, while laying an egg, the bird's body adds a clear protective coating over the shell. This coating seals the pores of the egg shell so bacteria can't get into it. It also helps prevent moisture loss, which keeps the egg fresh longer. I recalled buying my first farm-fresh eggs from a farmers' market in Florida. When I opened the carton and inspected the eggs, several of them weren't clean at all. Then I researched it; it turns out you don't wash farm-fresh eggs until you're ready to eat them, otherwise the protective bloom is removed. I lifted the egg out of the box and inspected it like it was a rare jewel. I wasn't expecting it to be so warm.

I ran back to the house, cupping my little treasure, and proceeded to stare at the egg for far too long, delighted and amazed, wishing there was someone else around to share the moment with. I took picture after picture of my first egg, positioning it in different ways, and yet nothing could capture its perfection or the way it stirred my spirit. My mind was simply blown. I'd always known that food doesn't originate from a store, but I didn't really *know* it until that moment. *One tiny step closer to self-reliance,* I thought.

A knock at the door startled me out of my photo shoot. It was Farmer John. "I don't know if you like bacon and sausage, but I make it and thought I'd bring some to you," he said.

"Bacon and sausage are two of my favorite things! I can't wait to try them, thank you so much!" I said, beaming at the unexpected gift. Farmer John, not being one for long conversations or awkward silences, quickly said his goodbyes and left. "First local kale, then Serafina's egg, now local bacon and sausage!?" I said to Kahuna. "Looks like someone is trying to tell me I need to make breakfast!"

Serafina's egg had the most brilliant orange yolk that stood tall in the pan. The egg white was thick and solid, unlike most store-bought eggs that have a thinner consistency and light yellow, watery yolks. Factory eggs tend to have a bland flavor but this egg . . . the orange yolk was rich and the white was as decadent as a fine, delicate cheese. I thought of how lucky my hens were to freely roam the property, basking in sunlight, breathing fresh air, and hunting for their own food. Just the thought made me smile and the results of their healthy lifestyle were obvious. It was, hands down, the best breakfast I'd ever made.

The Noonans came over a few days later and I told them all about my first real egg experience. They smiled proudly at me. Getting your first egg was a huge milestone for any chicken keeper. We all seemed to have the same euphoric wonder that our animals could provide this beautiful food, food most people could only find in grocery stores.

"I didn't know what to expect, I was afraid it was going to have dirt or poop all over it," I said, laughing.

Danielle chimed in, "Yeah, crap and dirt on eggs used to disturb me, too. Just wait, eventually when you collect dirty eggs you'll just flick it off. Now I don't even make the effort to flick it off, I just crack them in the pan."

I laughed nervously, hoping she was joking. Danielle, sensing my recoil, backtracked.

"*Nooo,* I'm totally kidding. I wouldn't do that," she said. But then, sheepishly, she confessed: "Actually, I'm not kidding at all, I totally do that."

My nose wrinkled and I pursed my lips at the visual. We all broke out in laughter. I was starting to like the Noonans more and more, but still I made a mental note not to eat eggs at Danielle's house.

On the farm, I'd started going to bed earlier and earlier. It was easy to fall sound asleep well before I ever would have in the city. Darkness descended early in winter, and there were no city lights, sounds, or muffled neighbor conversations to keep me awake.

Occasionally, there were lonely moments when I wondered what I was missing out on in Tampa. Winter in Florida meant an abundance of social activities: polo, outdoor music events, galas, food and wine festivals, and one of my favorite celebrations, Gasparilla—a citywide event similar to Mardi Gras, but pirate themed. From social media, I saw everything my friends were doing. The social scene went on as if I'd never existed, and this stung a bit. Envy reared its head often, but I continued to remind myself that leaving had been my choice. And I began to question all the fun I used to have. *What had been my purpose, back in Tampa?* There had to be more depth to life than just socializing and endless workdays. In the sobering silence of my new surroundings, I could see that those old distractions of social media or games on my phone weren't going to help anything; the emptiness of my old life was what had driven me here in the first place.

As time passed, I started to become quieter in my solitude. Before I'd left Florida, I'd taken up knitting in an effort to cut dependency on my phone. I started with making a baby blanket when my friend Adria got pregnant with her second son. The baby's birth came and went, though, and I couldn't bring myself to stop knitting it. The texture of the fine yarn gave me comfort; it was connecting me back to a fleeting past, to something that should have been my future. In a way, every row felt like I was weaving my own children back into my life. With each knit, I considered the memories I'd never have and let my mind ponder things like what my kids' faces would look like. Would their hair be dark or light, curly or straight? Knitting the blanket became a labor of love, a meditation on my lost future, a tribute I knew I'd never finish, because I never wanted to.

I kept up the knitting on the farm. I also read a lot, from historical fiction to how-to books about farming. Often, I would spend entire days cooking feasts for myself: roasts or soups, fresh bread and veggies, all of it happily eaten alone by the warm glow of the fire. Since I had no one else to cook for, I started making warm meals of oatmeal, various grains, herbs, vegetables, and proteins for the animals, too. They gorged themselves before cuddling up next to one another for the night. Serafina particularly liked my oatmeal concoctions and developed a tendency to wipe her messy face on my clothes. I became her personal napkin.

I pored over cookbooks, the kind that didn't call for overly processed and convenient ingredients. I took more control over what I put in and on my body. I started reading labels on packaged foods and beauty products and learned how to simplify. It was a crash course in a whole new way of living; my brain was a sponge and I was hungry to learn everything. Each time I found a way to simplify, I felt a little freer, a little more in control. Even with a few new friends in my life, my phone barely rang, but the silence no longer bothered me. Despite not having much of a social life, and only occasional interactions with my city friends, I was physically and mentally exhausted at the end of each day and slept like the dead—just like Serafina, who, it turned out, was legitimately *narcoleptic,* by the way; it was a real thing that could affect chickens. *Of course* I would buy a chicken with narcolepsy.

Early one frigid evening in January, I was enjoying the warmth of my roaring fireplace, snuggled next to Kahuna, holding a mug of hot spiced cider. Gia was lounging on the back of the couch, belly up, purring. She had quickly gained weight and seemed to love her new life. Periodically, she would stretch her white paw over to gently touch the side of my face. I'd never had anyone or anything in my life randomly touch my face like that. Maybe she sensed that I needed support, maybe this was just something cats did. It seemed odd, but it warmed my heart, and it reminded me that I wasn't totally alone: There were living creatures all around who depended on me and some who even showed me love and affection in return.

Mother Nature Is an Asshole

As the temperatures in January began to dip below freezing, my house was like a sieve, ushering in the outside air from every crack and crevice. I was completely unprepared for my first winter and the brute force of Mother Nature. The cheap, single-paned windows of my house certainly didn't help. I had no idea that cold could physically *hurt.*

Spending just a few minutes outside made my nose lose all feeling, turn red, and start to run profusely. The animals seemed fine so long as they had fresh water, so I stayed inside as much as I could, struggling to keep the fire alive. Of course, the proverbial understanding of Murphy's Law dictates that the colder the day, the harder it is to start a fire and keep it going. Often I sat near the fire looking like a human teepee of blankets, shoving my hands under my laptop for warmth. Each night, I took a long hot bath to soothe my cold bones.

One bitter morning, as I forced myself out of bed to brush my teeth, no water came from the faucet. I couldn't understand what was happening. I kept turning the faucet on and off, on and off. Not a drop.

I needed water. The animals needed water. I texted Tricia and asked if they had water, still not fully grasping what the whole having-a-well thing meant. Maybe I had used it all up? I truly wondered if the groundwater had run out. Tricia responded, "We do, but I'll send Jeff right over!"

While I waited for Tricia's husband, Jeff, to come rescue me, I decided to do what any tough farm girl would do: get water from my frozen pond. The geese and chickens drank from the pond and puddles, anyway, so until I could get fresh water again, I figured it could work. I felt energized by my own ingenuity. "I got this!" I said to Kahuna, who alternately seemed to love and hate the chilly air. Throwing on my little boy's overalls and new down coat, I took two five-gallon buckets and broke up the pond ice with an old rusty hammer. The ice-filled buckets were heavier than expected, and I could only lug one at a time up the hill to my house. After two trudging trips, I heated up the water that remained in the teakettle from the day before and poured it on the ice. That worked well enough for one bucket, but I still had the second to melt, and my animals needed to drink. Waiting it out wasn't an option.

Staring at the fireplace, an idea popped in my head. I hauled out an old cast-iron pot I'd found under the house, placed it into the fireplace, and started a fire. Next, I went outside and collected fist-sized stones from around the property. By this point, the pot was too hot to touch, so I added the rocks to the hot pot with a pair of long grill tongs. I waited for the stones to heat, and then picked them up with the tongs and placed them in the bucket of ice. The entire process took a long time and made a mess, but it worked. "God, I'm so good at this!" I said to Kahuna.

Jeff arrived after all the animals had been watered. He took one look at the well and asked if I had a light source on it so it wouldn't freeze during the winter. *Huh?* I cocked my head at him. He continued, "Did you leave your faucets running last night and your cabinets open?" Again: *Huh?*

I was clueless. He might as well have been speaking Greek. It turned out my well was frozen. He informed me that my pipes might have burst, too, and then gave me a rundown of basic winter well management. One, always keep a light bulb on the well during winter months. Two, always keep the faucets dripping at night. Three, always keep cabinets under sinks open and wrap any exterior pipes or spigots in bubble wrap, cloth, duct tape, anything I had on hand to insulate them. He instructed me to have an extension cord and use a blow-dryer to unfreeze the well mechanism if it happened again.

Jeff was kind enough to not make me feel stupid, but as he was leaving he said, "Don't hesitate to contact Tricia if you need anything. And if you don't know what something is . . . call me before you touch *anything*." He knew I was in over my head.

With the well working again, it took time for the water to flow freely through the house. Even then, though, the pressure was abnormally low. I couldn't figure out what was going on. Then a text came in from Tricia: "Girl, you have water running down your driveway!"

Outside, sure enough, there was a full stream of water running down the hill. In the garage, the pipes had burst and water was spewing like a geyser. When the plumber arrived, he fixed the main pipes, then asked if he could check the pipes under the house. "Knock yourself out," I said.

I could hear him cussing up a storm through my floorboards. Then he started counting out loud "One! Two! Three!"—sounding incredulous. For some reason, I imagined he was counting all the spiders under my house. When he got to "SEVENTEEN!" I yelled at the floor, "I CAN HEAR YOU, YOU KNOW? WHY ARE YOU COUNTING? YOU'RE FREAKING ME OUT!"

I watched from the window as he crawled out. He was soaking wet. I met him on the porch with a towel and asked why he was counting. "Ma'am, you have *twenty-four* leaks under the house."

Wonderful. I wasn't thrilled with the unexpected expense, but my brain was fixated on a more pressing issue. "Okay, but did you see spiders?" The blank look on his face told me that wasn't a question a real country person would ask.

My, What Big Teeth You Have

....

For several nights that winter, I'd been observing a very large possum eating the cat food I left on the back porch for Gia. Amused, I posted a picture of the animal on my farm Facebook page. My "Gucci to Goats" farm page was my online safe haven. I was incognito and could be my true farm self, away from the judging eyes of my city friends and acquaintances. Moreover, I had found an amazingly supportive community. The post prompted a few farm people to comment, cautioning me that possums will kill chickens.

But in the name of my "being one with nature" philosophy, I welcomed the hungry creature. If it was well-fed, I reasoned, it would have no need to go after my animals. When it growled at me one night, I called my dad, a biologist, and asked if the possum posed any danger to my chickens. His response was, "No. Possums don't eat chickens. *But* animals don't read the textbooks, so anything can happen if given the opportunity." Nonetheless, I stopped leaving Gia's food out at night. I hadn't seen the cranky possum for days, and so I figured that maybe my problem was solved. A small thought crossed my mind that maybe I wasn't *quite* ready for a life filled with *all* of nature's unpredictability, but I brushed it aside.

One night, it was nine o'clock, pitch-dark, and the animals had been in bed for hours, except Serafina, who had for some reason refused to go into the coop for the second night in a row. I was sitting on the couch, about to get ready for bed, when I heard a bloodcurdling screech coming from my back porch, just a few feet from where I was sitting. I knew by the sound that it was Serafina. Panicked, wearing nothing but my airy nightgown, I raced into the cold night.

Out in the darkness, I could see the large possum. From the pale glow of the outside lamp, I watched it chase down my squealing Serafina and rip off her rear end, tail feathers and all. I'd never seen brutality like this in real life. Serafina screamed and ran as fast as she could toward the coop, which was closed up for the night. The possum would corner her easily.

I took off at a full, barefooted run across the cold, hard ground. I was frightened, but I was going to kick the shit out of the possum. Arms flailing to make myself look bigger, I ran toward it, screaming wildly. For some reason, the possum missed the turn Serafina made and went around the other side of the barn, which gave me the opportunity to catch up to my injured girl.

It was completely dark on that side of the barn and although I could hear Serafina's labored breathing, I couldn't see her. Listening intently in order to find her, I could hear the possum returning. His mucus-laden breathing gave him away. He was coming back to finish what he'd started. As my eyes focused in the darkness, I could make out the silhouette of a rake leaning against the barn. I'd been in a constant state of distraction on the farm, going from project to project, and had left farm tools all over the place. This was one time I was grateful for my lack of organization.

I grabbed the rake just in time for the possum's approach and swung it at him like a golf club. I hit my target hard and heard myself squeal as the rake made impact. The possum was heavier than I expected. The fan of the rake scooped it up and sent it flying with a surprised growl. It upset me to fight an animal, even a wild one that was dead set on hurting my baby. Shaking and scared, I waited for the snarling piece of shit to come back as I searched for my hen. I again listened for Serafina's injured whining in the pitch black of the night, but she was silent. I was still skittish about picking up the chickens, but the life-or-death situation gave me the courage, and the adrenaline, that I needed. Reaching down, I searched the ground for her with my bare hands.

I could hear the snotty-sounding possum, again, ambling back in our direction. It was as determined to finish the job as I was to stop it. Then, my hands found Serafina's soft feathered body. I grabbed her, hoisted her in my arms, and—praying not to step on anything with my bare feet—sprinted past the possum to the house, holding my injured hen like a football.

I looked back over my shoulder to see the huge possum running behind me. I made it inside and slammed the door, leaving the filthy beast to rifle around on my back porch. I *hated* him. The thought crossed my mind to go back outside and beat him with the broom or stab him with a kitchen knife, but then I noticed the blood running down my arm. Serafina was still alive, but in shock, bleeding, and totally quiet. At this point, she was probably as scared of me as she was of the predator.

Much of her buttocks was missing and her tail was completely gone. There was a lot of blood and matted feathers. I had no idea how to help her, or even *if* help was possible. She was going to die, and I had no clue what to do. Putting an animal out of its misery wasn't anything I'd thought to prepare for. So, instead of doing the merciful thing, I locked Serafina in the garage for her own safety and said my goodbyes, feeling like the worst of human garbage. I went to bed and sobbed for what felt like hours before finally falling asleep.

The next morning, I avoided going into the garage and as I went to let the rest of the chickens out of the coop, I noticed the back porch had been ransacked. The possum had knocked down and shattered my flowerpots. Gia's food bowl was broken. I had no idea animals could have a temper or be so destructive. Clearly, this was war.

Before I could deal with the possum I mustered all the courage I could. I dreaded going into the garage to find my girl, who I was sure would be dead. But when I opened the door, all I saw was a broken egg in the middle of the floor. I looked around for Serafina's lifeless body, but when I finally saw her, crouched behind some boxes, she was very much alive. She was alert and greeted me with a sweet *churr churr churr* sound. "My sweet girl!" I exclaimed, as tears sprung to my eyes. I made a makeshift hospital suite for her out of Kahuna's crate and gave her food and water. She ate and drank right away, which gave me hope. Serafina stayed in the garage for two weeks, and I dutifully watched over her as her wounds healed and new feathers started growing in.

But I still had a predator with a taste for blood who needed to be dealt with. I was completely out of my comfort zone now. My father brought over a live trap to catch the possum. He gave me advice on how to bait it with cat food, and before he left, he added, "Call me when you catch it and I'll relocate it . . . *but* . . . if you catch a skunk, *call somebody else!*"

The first night, Gia got caught in the trap; she had licked the can of cat food clean. Fortunately, she wasn't hurt, but the thought that a raccoon or bobcat could have found her trapped before I did gave me chills. The second night I put Gia in the house, and this time, I caught the possum. Its body filled the now damaged trap. For a possum, it seemed huge, much larger than my seven-pound lapdog, and it was battered-looking, with bloody sores in its mouth. It growled and fully opened its mouth, displaying very sharp teeth.

The geese, nosy as usual, approached to see what I was doing. When they saw the possum, they instantly went into full dragon mode, putting themselves between me and the predator. Wings and necks fully extended, they surrounded the cage. In perfect unison, they marched closer to the possum, completely unafraid.

It was a powerful, magnificent display. The geese bobbed and weaved like the snakes on Medusa's head. They hissed in pure fury. It felt like a beautiful full-circle moment: I had to defend Serafina from the possum, but now the geese were defending *me*, and our home. All of us on the farm were united, in a strange way, against this predator. The possum opened its large mouth wide again, displaying its teeth and bloody sores throughout. I felt like Little Red Riding Hood staring down the Big Bad Wolf. "You will never hurt my babies again," I said as I threw a blanket over the cage and hoisted it into the back of my car. When I delivered it to my dad he commented, "That's a very large male. He's old and deserves to live out his life." Seeing the predator again gave me chills and reminded me of our fight. The possum would be living the rest of his life in a forest far away, thanks to my softhearted father. That was good enough for me. I never wanted to see it again.

Three weeks after the attack, Serafina laid an egg again. This time it was whole and beautiful.

After the possum attack, my father gave me his vintage gun he'd had since childhood. It was a beautifully kept bolt-action shotgun that held three shells. It was large and heavy and, frankly, I was terrified of it.

I had been posting updates on Serafina's recovery when one guy in particular, in his midtwenties and familiar with rural life, reached out. "You know how to shoot a gun to protect yourself and your animals, right?" This wasn't the first time I'd been asked this question. Everyone seemed concerned about my safety and cited everything from home invasions to wild dogs and hogs. I told him about my father's shotgun and explained that I was unnerved by it. The guy, who had been in the military, offered to come spend a couple hours showing me how to use it and hesitantly, I accepted.

The young man took his teaching seriously, and when he arrived a couple days later, he came equipped with protective glasses, earplugs, and targets. Still, none of it made me feel comfortable handling the large gun. At the end of our lesson, even though I still felt intimidated, I wanted to document the new skill I'd acquired. Right as I pulled the trigger, he took a photo of me. It turned out to be a pretty badass picture, I have to admit; I look calm and confident and you can even see the orange flame exiting the barrel. What the picture doesn't show is the outrageously loud squeal I let out. Every time I pulled the trigger that day I squealed. It was humiliating, but I was slowly learning.

Still, I could never get used to the large gun. It wouldn't be until my brother, Mark, gifted me with his childhood .22-caliber rifle that I would become comfortable with a gun. As I held it and felt its light weight and much smaller size I was only mildly afraid to take it for a test drive. The magazine was much easier to

load. I inspected the small, brassy bullets closely. They didn't appear to be as deadly but that meant I'd have to learn to have true
aim. With a little practice, the fear and thoughts of a violent tool
dissipated and was replaced with a feeling of empowerment and
self-protection. Predators, guns, learning to shoot . . . none of this
violence and vigilance had been a part of my plan. With my past
as a sexual victim and now my extreme awareness of being alone
and a very easy target to predators both animal and human, this
one small skill gave me a measure of protection I had never
known before.

The Senators

After weeks of cold, rain, and frost, by late February there was a hint of spring in the air. I was excited about the new season and the whole new range of animal behaviors I'd get to observe. Gradually, I was beginning to unlearn the book knowledge and presumptions I'd accumulated over the years. My fear of missing out on the social scene was dissipating, too. On Friday nights, I no longer automatically wondered what was happening back in Tampa. At first, cultivating true presence took a bit of work. I had to break some long-standing habits. Throughout my entire adult life, I'd had a monkey mind of worry. But the quieter my world became, the more I took the time to observe my surroundings and focus on what I wanted my farm life to become. The sense of presence and peace became easier. Like anything, it required practice and persistence, but eventually it felt like my most natural state. Now, the bulk of my "social" life revolved around my animals and a handful of new human friends, and I was starting to feel okay with that.

To celebrate the arrival of spring, the Noonans were hosting a small dinner at their house. After what felt like a long, solitary winter spent hibernating by my fireplace, I was excited for a chance to hang out with people. They lived about a twenty-minute drive from me, on a gorgeous property with an abundance of daffodils and other spring flowers. There was an adorable red barn on the property, which gave me barn envy, another common feeling I experienced in the country. As I pulled up the drive I noticed a multicolored herd of goats milling about in a small fenced paddock. Most of the goats were pregnant and looking as if they were about to pop. And, oddly enough, intermingling with the goats were giant tortoises, who—I looked closer—were . . . having sex.

I'd never seen or thought about turtle sex before. I stopped and got out of my car to verify that was really what was happening. Maybe it was some form of turtle play? I looked closer. Nope. It was sex. Did you know that giant tortoise sex is painfully slow? For me, it's not unlike watching golf. It takes place on the grass, there's not much to see, and then there's a grunt during each stroke. Even the grunts happen in slow motion. The female appeared expressionless and unimpressed . . . like me, watching golf.

Before I even walked in the Noonans' door, I could smell something sweet and heavenly wafting from inside their house. I followed the scent of warm bubbly goodness into the kitchen, and Danielle waved me to the stove, where she was overseeing a vat of fresh caramel sauce, known as *cajeta*. I'd never been hugely into sweets, but seeing and smelling the creamy caramel made my mouth water. "It's almost done," Danielle said. My stomach growled.

After enjoying a fabulous home-cooked meal, we started talking about the benefits of farm-fresh food. I snottily informed everyone that I didn't like goat milk. I was talking out of my ass; I'd never even had goat milk. But I'd heard other people back in the city eschew it, and I insistently parroted their criticism: that it smelled bad and tasted funky. In rebuttal, Danielle offered me a bowl of ice cream with fresh goat milk caramel sauce drizzled on top. I hesitated, and then lifted a spoonful to my mouth.

The whole family watched, waiting, as I let the decadent goodness melt on my tongue. I closed my eyes and nodded my head. It was *easily* the best caramel I'd ever tasted.

Danielle interrupted my reverie. "You know the ranch dressing on the salad you ate *two* helpings of? It was made with goat milk." She let that sink in before she continued. "And you know that lasagna you loved so much? Goat milk ricotta." Her eyebrows rose as she waited for me to rethink my goat milk prejudice. I smiled—I was busted, but on the other hand, a whole new world had just opened to my taste buds.

We were all gathered outside on the front lawn when several large tom turkeys decided to join our conversation. Toms are fully grown male turkeys over two years old. These guys looked intimidating, with their big bald heads and long snoods (the retractable dangling skin that hangs from the top of their beak), but every time someone laughed, the turkeys responded with a round of loud gobbles. It was hilarious. We would laugh, they would gobble, then we'd laugh harder, which would just start another round of gobbles. It surprised me how foreign the sound of my own laughter was to me. And then, suddenly I realized that I couldn't remember the last time I'd laughed like that . . . *really* laughed, uncontrollably, with all my body and heart. God, it felt good. The Noonans referred to their turkeys as "the senators," because they always needed to have the last word. I was so enamored by these funny birds that right then and there I decided I needed a few of my own, and I made a mental note to add these to my spreadsheet immediately.

When I left the Noonans, my head was swimming with new possibilities. As soon as I got home, I bought my first goat milk cookbook and began to research turkeys. After browsing a number of online sources, I decided I much preferred the "Royal Palm" breed. They tended to be smaller in stature, and their beautiful white-and-black color pattern reminded me of Chanel branding. This was the perfect sophisticated turkey breed. Within days, I found a breeder and drove the hour and a half to pick up my four new babies. I asked the breeder why some of their coloring was so light compared to the pictures I'd seen on the internet. The (very) young man responded, "I don't know. Maybe those are the girls."

As it turns out, they were not girls, and they were *not* Royal Palms. I'd made an accidental, rookie purchase. This is how Rupert the turkey entered my life. Over time, the tiny poult would grow into a huge tom and prove to be my champion, as well as the most feared and beloved animal on the farm.

The turkey poults quickly outgrew their little coop. They needed to roam free, but I was concerned they would escape into the woods and never come back. When I finally got the courage to free them, they excitedly raced around the backyard, wildly flapping their wings, leaping high in the air and flying short distances. I was thoroughly entertained by their antics and even happier that they didn't appear to have any inclination to leave the safety of my property.

Occasionally, gangly young Rupert would puff up and strut, following me around. He became my shadow and I started to call him the "sheriff" of the farm. I hadn't guessed how lovable these turkeys would be. I adored them more and more each day.

The poults quickly figured out my daily regimen and knew when it was feeding time. Day after day, when they heard me refilling the water buckets, they'd come running. For several days in a row, they ran to me at top speed only to clothesline themselves on the water hose, falling like bowling pins. I laughed at first, then I wondered if there was something wrong with them. Evidently, young turkeys simply aren't the sharpest crayons in the box. In fact, they are total ditzes. It would take time before they grew into their intelligence. In the meantime, they were the hilariously awkward, spastic goobers of my farm.

The Noonans' young son Caden volunteered to help me with farmwork one morning. I was grateful for the help, even if it was from a nine-year-old. He was used to farm chores and wasted no time getting started.

We talked farm stuff while he helped me clean the chicken coop. It was hard work, loading shovel after shovel of heavy muck into the wheelbarrow. Once we had a full load I dropped the shovel and started to pull the wheelbarrow toward the compost pile.

"This wheelbarrow isn't nearly full enough," Caden said.

"Looks pretty full to me, Caden."

"No, we can fit a lot more into it." He proceeded to hop on top of the feces-laden bedding. He rolled back and forth with his body, packing down the mess. When he was satisfied he jumped down and said, "See?!"

"Yep. I see that you have poop all over you now. Your mother is never going to let you help me again when you come home all stinky."

"It's okay. She's used to it," he said, shrugging. I couldn't help but smile, even as a little pain stung my heart. If I ever had another chance at having a child, I hoped they would be as selfless and kind as Caden.

There was one chicken Caden was enamored by in particular and he talked often about how she reminded him of a chicken he'd "had." "Caden," I said, "you keep referring to one of your chickens in the past tense. Did something happen to her?"

"Yeah." As he continued shoveling crap, he said, "We ate her."

The only response I could come up with was, "Oh."

Spending time with Caden was bittersweet. I loved being with him, but it also made my heart ache, thinking about what I'd lost and what was missing in my life. Kids have this way of being wonderfully authentic. There's no pretense with them, no walls. Their true self is easily accessible. When I was growing up, I had always just presumed I'd be a mother by the time I was in my thirties. Now, I was less than a year away from turning forty and there was no man in sight. Not to mention the fact that small-town USA wasn't the prolific pool of dating that city life had been. Motherhood had always seemed like a guaranteed right, like the only path toward true womanhood. But what if that didn't happen for me? This question was a can of worms I couldn't bear to open. There was no way I was ready to concede defeat. There was no way life would be so cruel. I shook my head and pushed the thoughts away.

What's Got Your Goat?

One morning in early March, the Noonans called to say their goats had given birth. One little doeling had the blue eyes the Noonans knew I coveted for my dream goat. (Of course, I already had a name picked out for her: Valentina.) They asked if I wanted to visit the new arrivals? *Hell yes I did!*

The baby goats were the size of teenage kittens. Unlike kittens, however, they were born with their eyes already open. They had long, wobbly legs and were endlessly entertaining with their spastic movements and awkward, stumbling attempts at running and jumping. After only a few hours of life, several of the kids were already bold enough to leave their moms. We watched as they tried to jump on the backs of the tortoises. It didn't take long before one of the bigger bucklings (a baby male goat) was crowned king of his tortoise mountain. I wondered how the tortoises felt about being blatantly used as toys. Soon, the kids were all played out and returned to their moms for a snack and milk coma. As sleep descended, they became impossibly sweet and looked so soft. Danielle handed me my little blue-eyed princess, my future Valentina, and my heart melted. Her coloring was a beautiful light brown, with darker brown boots. I snapped picture after picture of her and then took turns cuddling the other kids, not wanting to play favorites too much.

As we started discussing when Valentina would be ready to come home with me, the Noonans casually mentioned a young goat named Maybelline (Maybelle, for short) who just had twin kids. The problem was, they couldn't get Maybelle to stop nursing from her own mother, who'd just had two new twins of her own. They were Maybelle's younger siblings, in a sense, and they needed the milk Maybelle was stealing. Danielle asked if I'd be willing to take Maybelle and her twins until the babies were weaned. Then they would bring Valentina to me when she was ready, and pick up Maybelle's kids. This would mean that, eventually, I'd have a young adult doe (female goat) and a doeling (baby female goat). I really wanted baby goats to bond with, but I hesitantly agreed—worried, as always, about what the Noonans were getting me into.

"Great! We'll bring them over in a couple days," Danielle said.

"But wait," I said. That was a really quick turnaround. "I don't have fencing or anyplace to put three goats!"

"You'll figure something out," Danielle said. "No one is ready for animals when they get them. That's what motivates you to get working."

She was right. Getting animals before you were ready seemed to be status quo in the farm world. It was a similar feeling I'd get with clients when I wanted their project so badly I'd commit to things I had no experience doing. That's always when real motivation kicked in—when I had very little time to pull something off, and it lit a fire under my butt. When I explained the situation to Farmer John, he suggested that another neighbor, Farmer Alfred, could help me put up a pen around the barn area. Three days later, I had a pen, and Maybelle arrived with her kids in tow.

How fitting that I was the accidental recipient of a goat named after a makeup company. When Danielle told me Maybelle's mother's name was Cover Girl, I knew it was a destined match.

Maybelle proved to be high maintenance. She had the attitude of an alpha animal and little time for me. Neither did her kids. For several weeks, they avoided me and my good intentions, and eventually, the Noonans came to replace the kids with Valentina. I was stoked to finally have my beautiful Valentina, but it somehow hadn't dawned on me that Maybelle's babies would be going away.

After Brice jumped out of his truck, he hauled a stack of wood out from the bed.

"What's all that?" I asked, gesturing to the lumber.

"We have to build a milk stand so you can start milking Maybelle tonight," he replied. My eyes widened as he continued, stating the obvious, "Without the kids, she needs someone to milk her."

What? Was I ready to commit to milking twice a day . . . every single day? There would be no sleeping in, no holidays, no nights and weekends off. No sick days, no snow days or even rain delays. It would be like having my time-consuming former client, Laura, back in my life. Having birds that were fairly self-sustaining had been relatively easy, but this was a whole new level of farm life, and I wasn't sure I was ready for it. Panic set in.

"I've never milked anything!" I shrieked. "What if I hurt her?"

"You won't," he said. "We'll show you how it's done."

It only took fifteen minutes for Brice to build the milk stand. It was an elevated platform about a foot off the ground. On one end there was a wooden bar placed at the goat's head-level to secure the feed bowl, with two movable bracing bars to keep the goat's head secure. I wondered how Maybelle would react to the new experience. All too soon, it was time for me to milk my first goat. Brice brought Maybelle into the barn and, with help from Danielle and a little goat food, lured her to the stand. Maybelle wasn't going without a fight, but Brice and Danielle were un-fazed. They expertly picked her up and plopped her onto the milk stand. The goat tried to struggle but, quickly realizing that food was involved, she put her head through the bracing boards and began gorging herself on the meal meant to keep her occupied during milking. I stayed back, preparing myself to—there was no other way to think about it—*fondle another woman's boobs.* I felt apprehensive. I felt very weird.

With Maybelle otherwise engaged, Danielle grabbed a stainless-steel bucket and an old metal milk crate she turned up-side down to use as a stool. She instructed me to sit on the stool and then showed me how to place the bucket under the doe and then she put her fingers around one teat. When she did this, it sent Maybelle into a stomping tizzy. She stopped eating and gave us a mean side-eye. I was totally intimidated, but Danielle wasn't one to take anyone's shit, especially a goat's.

"You may need to be stern with her until she gets the hang of being milked," Danielle said as she effortlessly squeezed off a couple streams of milk. The fresh milk made a loud, prolonged sound—*thud*—as it hit the metal bucket. I was amazed. May-belle, no longer occupied, continued stomping. She was pissed but Danielle ignored her, undeterred.

How was I supposed to be stern with her? I didn't feel confi-dent about this at all, but the thought of making cheese and caramels helped me muster the courage. I reached out and gently took hold of one of Maybelle's teats. I felt sheepish. My suspi-cions were confirmed. *Yep. Feels like a boob.*

In my head, I repeated *caramels and cheese, caramels and cheese* as I made my first attempt. Milk dribbled down my hand, spraying my other arm instead of the bucket. I already had terrible aim. With every stomp Maybelle made, I jumped. I couldn't blame her. If someone squeezed *my* nipple like this, I'd kick them, too. Another attempt got milk on my chin. *I suck so badly at this already,* I thought. *Aim down, aim down!* The Noonans were supportive but thoroughly amused. I could smell the warm milk as it ran down my arm. The cuff of my shirt was soaked. It took many tries, but finally I squeezed off one long stream of milk. It hit the bucket with a satisfying *splunk* and resulted in a resounding "YAY!" from both Noonans.

"I did it!" I said, smiling like a kid who had just hit a home run.

"Great job!" Brice chimed in. He patted me on the back, and said, "Now we have to get home to the kids and make dinner. Have fun!"

"Wait!" I whined. "You're just going to leave me here?! I still need to finish milking her and I need you here!"

They both laughed and ushered off Maybelle's two kids. There I was, all alone with an angry, childless doe and a nervous baby Valentina. I was able to get a couple more shots of milk into the bucket before Maybelle kicked its contents into my lap. Now we were both pissed. With no one to hold me accountable, I quit. I reasoned that she'd been nursing the twins all day, so her udder wasn't full, and I told myself I'd deal with her in the morning. Tomorrow, I would be a dairy farmer.

The next morning, though, Maybelle was still upset about losing her children, and I couldn't blame her. To make matters worse, her udder was tight with milk, which made it much more difficult to milk her, especially with my weak, untrained hands. We fought each other constantly. In the end, it would take two weeks just to strengthen the muscles in my hands and arms enough so that I didn't require constant breaks. Milking was a horrible, frustrating, stressful chore for both of us that usually left me with more milk on my clothes than in the bucket. The stainless-steel bucket the Noonans loaned me gave Maybelle too much surface area to kick, so I decided to switch to mason jars. They worked better, but even then I had entire jars kicked onto me more often than not. On the plus side, the milk was making my hands buttery soft. And I did love the smell, which was nothing like store-bought cow's milk. It had a sweet, rich fragrance and felt decadently creamy on my skin. Throughout the process, I completely understood why someone would cry over spilled milk. In fact, I had cried several times out of frustration after having milk thrown onto my crotch. I felt I was failing both of us. This was not how I envisioned my farm life.

One day I decided to research buying a milking machine, but I found that they were large and heavy, and cost thousands of dollars. I couldn't justify the expense even if I had several goats to milk. Dismayed, I took a break to check the mail. While I was at my mailbox, Farmer John pulled up in his old work truck and asked how my goat experience was coming along. I told him about my milk machine search and asked if he had any cheaper solutions. "Yeah!" he said. "I know a guy down the way who made his own battry (battery) powered tit milker. He loves it."

I'd heard what he said, but I couldn't get past the words *tit milker*. It made me immediately uncomfortable, but moreover, the way he said the word *tit*—with two syllables, like "ti-IT"—was hilarious. Oblivious, he continued: "He said you can use it to milk one ti-IT at a time, or two ti-ITs."

I was dying inside, trying my hardest not to laugh. Instead, I simply restated what he had said, using the word *teat* instead. We said our goodbyes and the entire way back up the driveway I repeatedly practiced my new favorite, countrified word: "Ti-IT."

In any case, I had to do *something* to make this twice-a-day process better for both of us. It seemed that everyone else's goats ate quietly while being milked. Not Maybelle. She was skilled at multitasking. Eat and kick. Eat and stomp. Eat and give me the evil eye. I was lucky to get three squirts off before she would stomp and angrily glance at me with her nasty side-eye. "I don't like you much either, girlfriend," I told her. It was awful. I needed a plan.

"What can I do to help Maybelle relax?" I said out loud to Kahuna, who Maybelle also disliked with a passion. Because of Maybelle's hatred of dogs, Kahuna was no longer free to roam the farm. My little dog was now the smallest creature on the farm; even the chickens had outgrown him. Kahuna looked up at me in silence and cocked his head to the side. Suddenly I had an idea. What self-respecting girl doesn't love a spa day? I decided to turn Maybelle's milk stand time into a full-on luxury spa treatment. It was worth a try.

That morning, when I set out to milk Maybelle, I brought along my iPhone, a Bluetooth speaker, warm, moist towels, and a good brush. I mixed fresh greens in with her grain and then turned on relaxing music. I found a couple fist-sized rocks and placed them in the bowl with her food. I was hoping the rocks would force her to slow down and not inhale her food, because she was always worse when her meal was finished. Feeling a surge of optimism and excitement, I pressed play on the spa music and threw open the barn doors to let her inside.

The gentle morning light streamed in through the open barn doors, illuminating the dust particles in the air. By now, Maybelle anticipated her meals and jumped onto the milk stand by herself. That was the only easy part. But today, instead of digging right in, she paused as she discovered the rocks and greens. She huffed and pushed the rocks around with her nose and inspected the greens with her lips. Clearly, she didn't trust what I was up to. Then, slowly, she started to eat.

Step one had worked. Next, I used the warm towel to simultaneously heat my hands while I applied it to her swollen morning udder. She paused eating for a moment, trying to decide if she would accept what I was doing or not. After a few seconds of motionless glances at me, she lowered her head again and fished around for more greens. I proceeded to milk her, gently and quietly, and stopped before she decided to fuss. Then I gave her a good brushing and rubdown. She balked at first, then suddenly leaned into the brushing. It worked. I had over half a jar of fresh milk and *none* in my lap! She had plenty more to give, but I didn't want to push my luck.

My old city-girl lifestyle had finally come in handy. I started calling the twice-daily milking our "mommy/Maybelle time." I would sing to her and chatter on about farm gossip. It took awhile, but we bonded, and it soon became my favorite time of day.

Eventually I had so much milk I could literally take baths in it. Even after making a big vat of caramel sauce, I still had a fridge full of the stuff. So, following Cleopatra's rumored milk bath rituals, I actually *did* take a bath in it. Eating freshly made caramel sauce straight from the jar while bathing in warm goat milk . . . It was the epitome of farm indulgence, and in that moment, I truly felt like I was living the dream.

With Maybelle under control, I could turn my attention to Valentina. My blue-eyed girl was everything I envisioned a baby goat should be: cute, cuddly, and loving. Valentina's sweetness broke down Maybelle's stubborn walls, too, and the three of us would often walk together around the property, foraging. The goats were like nature's vacuum cleaners, eating everything in sight. I helped by pulling spring vines down so they could reach them. They loved honeysuckle the most.

Maneuvering the vines and overgrown brush in the woods surrounding my property proved more challenging for me than the goats. The vines didn't always grow in the easiest to reach places. One day, while bent down trying to get through a particularly thick mess of vines, I heard a rip. Immediately, there was cool spring air infiltrating my butt cheeks. *Damn.* I looked down to find ancient barbed wire hidden in the vines. *Who cares, I'm the only person out here,* I reasoned, as I continued our forest journey with half my bum exposed.

Gia also joined our escapades. She'd travel from tree to tree like a jungle cat, never touching the ground. With regular meals she was putting on weight and looked more and more like an adult cat, if not a little rotund.

Unlike Maybelle, who was serious about vine hunting, Valentina was more interested in playing. The wet winter had produced a tiny stream at the bottom of a ravine on my property and the baby goat jumped back and forth over it like it was a game. Springtime had us all in good spirits. Sometimes Serafina, Rupert, and the other young turkeys would join us on our walks. I was like the Pied Piper, leading my eclectic entourage, and I was finally starting to feel truly connected to the land and my animals. Their trust in me and increasing affection felt like signs that I was on the right path.

But one day on a walk, my neck started to itch more and more violently. I absentmindedly scratched at it all day and when I finally looked in the mirror, I discovered an angry rash forming at my collarbone. It seemed to be spreading by the minute. I was about to head to the doctor when Farmer John pulled up my driveway. Seeing my flaming red neck, he commented, "You got poison oak?"

"I have no idea, but it itches to my bones. I'm heading to a clinic now," I said.

"Why are you going to a doctor?" he asked, looking at me like I wasn't the brightest bulb in the box. "You got it from your goats. Just drink their milk."

Not knowing what to say, I jumped in the car. "I'll have to try that!" I shouted out the window. "I have to go!"

Farmer John shook his head as I pulled away.

The doctor confirmed Farmer John's diagnosis of poison oak and that I had indeed gotten it from my goats. Goats love to dine on poison ivy and poison oak, which meant that their kisses became poisonous, because of the invisible oils on their mouths. The doctor said it was common for people to get it from their pets. *Ugh. How was I supposed to combat this?* On the plus side, the goat pen no longer had those awful vines. This would be a recurring rash, the doctor informed me, and it would only get worse year after year as my sensitivity to it increased. *Great. Something to look forward to.* I sheepishly inquired about drinking the goats' milk, and the doctor laughed. Here in Mississippi, he was used to hearing old wives' tales and home remedies, he said, but he stuck to modern science. One painful shot, several prescriptions, and a couple hundred dollars later, I left the clinic.

When I returned home from the doctor's visit and grocery shopping, I did my best to carry all the bags in at one time. None of my freely roaming animals were anywhere in sight. As I made my way down the long sidewalk to the front door, there was the slapping of little feet on the concrete behind me: Serafina. Over time I learned that she wasn't a young hen like the others. A farmer informed me she was older, based on her appearance and her giant eggs. Whomever I'd bought her from probably realized she was narcoleptic and at the end of her productive days.

Lugging my grocery bags, I realized Serafina was coming at me with speed. *What the heck is she up to?* I wondered. I was almost to the front door when she jumped up, grabbed the bottom of one of the plastic bags, and ripped it wide open. "What are you doing!?" I screeched as all my groceries tumbled out onto the ground. Serafina dove in like it was the Piccadilly buffet, pecking at everything as fast as she could. "No no no! That's not for you!" I yelled as I frantically tried to collect my hen-pecked vegetables. I grabbed a grape and threw it. Serafina took the bait and chased after it. I ran inside and slammed the door. Maybe it wasn't the narcolepsy that got her sold at a flea market . . . could it have been her grocery-grabbing ways? From now on, I'd have to keep my eye on her.

I spent the beautiful spring month of March swollen up like a balloon from the shot the clinic gave me, and I had to wear gloves to avoid scratching. I tried to protect my skin with long sleeves as best I could. But it wasn't long before the next rash showed up. Within minutes of the goats brushing their lips against any part of my body, I'd feel the familiar itchy tingle. I'd learned my lesson about scratching and ran straight to the kitchen to chug goat milk. It seems Farmer John was right. It made no sense, but the goat milk worked like a charm. Within an hour, the itching stopped and by the next day, the rash was nearly gone. That would be my last shot for poison oak.

The Concerto, the Diva, and the Trollop

Rising spring temperatures meant not only were vines and flowers awakening, but the bugs were, too. One warm evening, I turned off the TV to go to bed and heard what sounded like a muffled orchestra playing outside. I opened the door and listened. It was coming from the pond and surrounding woods. My property was alive with a symphony of insect songs and frog calls, and they were *loud*. I closed the door, but it barely muffled the raucous noise. After a dead-silent winter, I hadn't expected the flamboyant sounds of warmer weather.

Then, a movement on the floor caught my attention. There, dancing around on my new white carpet, was a spider. A big one.

I'd been afraid of spiders my entire life. I loathed them. The fear had been passed down from my mother. She could handle any creepy-crawly critter, except spiders. They were rare in my Florida houses, thanks to all the pesticides the landscapers and building managers used, but on the occasion that one happened to come inside, I'd always had a man to take care of business. Not anymore. Here I was, alone on my property, staring directly at my greatest phobia.

I couldn't deal. I was too afraid to kill it myself. As a kid living in the Philippines, we often heard scary stories of spiders laying eggs in people's faces. I had no intention of getting that close. *What was I supposed to do?* I couldn't go to sleep with this spider in the house, but I didn't know how to face this. The creature wasn't moving, it simply stared me down. I kept my eye on it as I logged on to my social media farm page and posted about my predicament and paralyzing fear. Right away, a woman commented, saying that when her husband is out of town during a bug emergency, she brings a chicken inside and lets it do what comes naturally. *Brilliant,* I thought.

Flashlight in hand, I made my way to the coop and collected Babette, one of my now-teenage babies, awaking her from her trancelike slumber. Babette was vocal, uninhibited, and fabulous. If she were human, she would surely have been an opera singer. Back inside the house, the spider hadn't gotten far. It was still plotting my demise, right in front of my face. I put Babette on the floor and waited to see if she would save me. At first, nothing happened. Babette cocked her head toward me with a curious look. Then the spider moved. That was all it took for Babette to jump into action and pounce on it, gobbling it up. Problem solved. And with that, chickens officially became my favorite animal. As I put Babette back to bed, lavishing her with love and praise for a job well done, I had a strange desire to sniff her feathers. To my surprise, unlike the unpleasant scent of a dog who comes inside after a bathroom break, she smelled of clothes dried by the sun on a clothesline. Not believing my own senses, I stuck my nose into her soft buttery feathers and deeply inhaled. Yep. Freshly sun-dried laundry. I made a mental note to look into chicken diapers. My marketing mind had visions of making house chickens the new fashion. "Chickens . . . the only pet that provides love, pest control, and breakfast!"

Even though my little diva had saved the day, I'd like to say I need to have words with whoever named brown recluse spiders. There is little *reclusive* about them. Over the next few days, I discovered them all over my house, and let me tell you, they are brazen little bastards. If they could have tap-danced in front of me, they would have. The ones with more reclusive personalities I would even find in my bed! My skin crawled, and I wanted to burn my house down. My chickens were too wild to keep bringing inside. It was time to call professional pest control.

The bug guy showed up to save the day. He was the typical Mississippi service guy, which meant he was impeccably well-dressed and courteous. When I commented about how nicely dressed he was, and how that had consistently been my experience since moving here, he looked dumbfounded. "Well, thank you, ma'am," he said. "But technically service people are guests in your home so I don't see why anyone would show up looking a mess. It's just disrespectful."

I thought about all the service people I'd had in my homes while living in Florida: plumbers, electricians, cable guys. Most of the time I felt unsafe in my own home. Many of these guys had propositioned me, and nearly all of them had creepy energy or looked utterly disheveled. I'd lost count of all the butt cracks I'd seen. One time I even had a cable installer finish my setup and ask if I'd like to take the rest of the day with him to go fishing and get high. *Um. I think I'll pass.* This new type of gentlemanly service was a pleasant change.

As the man was leaving, he noticed Gia in one of the rocking chairs on the porch. "When is your cat due?" he asked.

Huh? I thought.

That same night, I awoke to a horrible noise in the darkness. It sounded like the wail of a dying animal and it was too close for comfort. I sat straight up in bed and checked Kahuna. He was groggy but had clearly heard it, too. Then it came again. Kahuna growled a low growl. "What the hell is that?" It sounded like a wounded cat was howling.

Throwing on my clothes, I ran outside and listened. It was coming from the chicken coop.

I jumped over the deck railing and made it to the coop in seconds. There was my beautiful lavender pullet from the flea market, Francesca, standing in the middle of the coop . . . *crowing!* It was the awful, early, middle-of-the-night practice crowing of a young rooster. I'd finally understood the odd comments about my beautiful lavender girl. Francesca was a Francois. To make matters worse, his crowing was setting off the geese, who were reacting with their own loud honks. "HEY MAN! It's 4:45 A.M.!!!" I snapped at him.

I wondered if I'd ever sleep a full night again.

After the bug guy's comment about Gia, I called my neighbor Tricia over to get her opinion. To me, she was *the* supreme expert in feral and rescue animals.

"Would you mind stopping by to look at her?" I asked.

"Sure! I'm running down the road a piece, I'll come by after," she said.

"Did you just say 'a piece'?" I laughed. I still wasn't entirely used to some of the vocabulary out here.

When Tricia arrived and inspected my cat, it took her all of thirty seconds to give her assessment. "Yep. She's already got milk plugs on her nipples. She's expecting, and soon." Gia lay there, letting Tricia stroke her giant baby belly. "I can feel the babies. There's at least a few."

My original spreadsheet didn't have *any* cats, and now they were multiplying. My babies were having babies, and I wasn't ready for it. "How is that possible? I don't have a male cat!" I said. Tricia laughed at me. "Girl, I have a male cat running around our place, Bob, and he's intact. If he's the father, we'll know when they're born. You said you wanted to live in the country. Unwanted animals are an unavoidable part of it."

Count Your Chickens

I had seen Bria, one of my flea market hens, sitting in a catatonic state for weeks and knew she was experiencing something called "broodiness." Apparently, I had learned, when a hen wants to have babies they "go broody." It's a biological instinct, the same as nesting in women. One telltale sign of a hen going broody is that she starts to pluck the soft feathers off her belly, so she can pad her nest with them. This also allows her warm, bare skin to have direct contact with the eggs, which keeps moisture inside them and also helps the hen better detect development and movement inside the shell.

To be honest, I wasn't even sure Francois was fertilizing the eggs. From internet information, I knew there was no way to tell if the eggs were fertilized without cracking them open. I did know that most likely, if a rooster was present, the eggs should, theoretically, be fertilized. Since Bria had a terrible habit of biting me, it meant I couldn't use a flashlight to inspect development inside the eggs. Other farmers advised me that hens tend to kick unfertilized eggs out of the nest once they realize there's no development inside. I had to have faith and let nature take its course. Within a few weeks, my first chicks from my own chicken hatched, and the next generation of life on my farm began.

On one unseasonably warm day, I sprawled out on top of a large fallen oak tree, enjoying the light breeze and a little chicken TV. Bria was one of the oldest and meanest of the flea market chickens and, in true Bria fashion, she had stolen eggs from the other girls and was now proudly marching around with chicks of varying sizes and colors, none of whom were her own, biologically. She was the very definition of a tough old broad, and having newborns didn't soften her bitchiness one bit. She fussed at them just like she fussed at me. If I even *looked* in her direction, she'd respond with a stink eye and a growl. Still, she and her little ones were incredibly entertaining. The tiny, fluffy chicks scurried frantically around their mother as she taught them to scratch for bits of food.

Then, Bria turned her demonstration from scratching at the dust to the fine art of bathing in it (dust baths serve as pest control, keeping mites and ticks at bay). The chicks joined in, mimicking their mother by throwing themselves on their sides. They thrashed their legs and tiny T. Rex arms, creating little dust clouds. The chicks reminded me of Pig-Pen from the *Peanuts* comics, each of them wallowing in their own dusty haze. I was utterly charmed by the scene.

During my observation, it hit me that afternoon, in a sudden and powerful way, that this was my life now. This wasn't a temporary lark, despite the doubts of Kelly and my mother. I was attached to this land, and these animals, in a way that was finally starting to feel very real. It was no longer so foreign, and it wasn't a prolonged vacation; it was my own version of paradise, what I'd dreamed about during my last years in the city. I'd always wanted to be self-sufficient, and now that finally felt attainable. I still didn't understand why I was driven to this lifestyle, but for now, I was content easing into it—even if I wasn't ready to own it out in the world.

It was a gorgeous day. My eyes closed for longer and longer as I drifted in and out of sleep on the oak tree, feeling the light breeze blow my hair around, listening to the sweet sounds of bustling chickens, baby peeps, and munching goats. Then an unfamiliar movement caught my eye and shocked me out of my hazy contentment. What happened next made me remember that, for all her beauty and loveliness, you should never take your eye off Mother Nature.

I held my breath as, from under the fallen oak tree, right below where I was lying, slithered a very large rat snake, still groggy from its winter hibernation. I'd heard of these bastards from other chicken people. They're not venomous, but they can destroy an entire flock overnight. When a snake attacks, it attempts to gorge itself on its prey, and then regurgitates the suffocated animal because it can't get past its shoulders. The bodies remain uneaten. The head and neck are a wet, half-chewed, matted-down mess, and you're left with a flock of birds who died the most grisly, horrific deaths. It surprised me that, just like humans, nature could also be surprisingly wasteful.

Frozen, I didn't know what to do. The snake poured out from under the tree, its thick body seemingly endless, like a clown car from which clowns never stop coming out. As I watched, I could feel the blood drain from my face. It was a fear response, the foreboding of what I knew was to come. The snake paused in a patch of sun, much of its body still hidden under the tree. Its long tongue flicked at the air and it raised its head slightly. Only a few feet away, Bria and her chicks were oblivious, merrily scratching at the ground and playing in the dust. I could tell that this predator had its sights on my newborns. A switch flipped deep inside me. *Not on my watch.* I was scared, but I knew I had to act.

My mind raced, considering any weapons I had on hand. My guns were far away inside the house and I was still uncomfortable using them anyway. There was no time to waste. I would have to find something else, and fast.

The only option in view was a rusty old shovel in the barnyard. I slowly slid off the back of the fallen tree trunk and quickly grabbed my weapon. When I turned back, the big snake had slithered closer to my preoccupied hen. It was now just a foot away from my babies. The snake was so focused that it didn't seem to notice me coming from behind. My heart raced. I wanted to cry out for help—the thought of what I was about to do made me feel sick—but who would come? The threat was immediate. I raised the shovel over my head and with all my strength, pushed past my fear and heartbreak, and slammed it down on the snake's head. I couldn't believe what I was doing. It was almost as if it was someone else doing this brutal act.

Shocked by my actions, the chickens and goats rushed away in a flurry of hooves, feathers, and squawks. I'd been shaking so hard that I missed the snake's head and hit its big body. The shovel simply bounced off. This was not how I envisioned this going. The predator didn't flee. It pulled itself into a protective bunch, head aimed at me. Now it would be much more difficult to deliver a killing blow. Its enormous size meant it could easily strike within the distance of the short shovel handle. Having the serpent's attention solely focused on me scared me even more. Now I was at risk of being bitten. We stared each other down.

My heart raced, fueled by adrenaline. I had to make a move; I had never killed anything besides insects before, but now I had to commit to taking a life. Gripped with fear and guilt, with tears streaming down my face, I flew into a crazed frenzy, beating the snake repeatedly with the heavy old shovel. It fought back, lunging and striking. Somehow I was able to jump out of the way and took my chances to deliver more blows. But it wouldn't die. I could feel two people inside me—one who wanted to run away screaming and the other intent on finishing what I'd started. In that moment of realization I hesitated and the snake struck again. This time I was able to pin its head to the ground. I tried to decapitate it with the shovel but the edges were dulled from rust and time, and the snake was much stronger than I predicted. What I thought would be quick and easy wasn't. For what seemed like an eternity, I banged away, crying and yelling, "JUST FUCK-ING DIE!" The predator struck at me repeatedly. I heard myself squeal each time it came at me, but now I was an insane person committed to the fight. I couldn't just let it go, knowing it would come back for my babies. It took almost an hour for the snake's body to stop moving. Even then, I didn't trust that it was dead. By now, all my animals had gathered around me, silently watching the entire event. Using the shovel, I scooped up the body and, after several failed attempts, finally hoisted it over the fence. It was much heavier than I expected.

Miserable, shaken over what I had done and the way I had done it, I sat in the coop and cried. I needed comfort, but there was no one around to give it to me. My solitude on the farm was double-edged; in the best moments, I had it all to myself, but in the worst, I had no one with whom to share my burdens. I cradled Mae Mae, one of my adolescent chickens. The other young chickens seemed to sense what I needed and one by one, they flew up to perch on top of my lap, jockeying for the best spot. I smiled as I wiped away tears. At least they would be safe—for now. That snake had been an imminent threat to my babies, and yet it tore me apart that I was directly responsible for taking a life. I wasn't sure how I could live with myself. Danger and death had arrived so suddenly, so out of the blue. The violence haunted me, playing on a loop in my head for days.

Hoping for a Hero

That spring I'd acquired baby quail to go with my chickens, turkeys, geese, and goats. They were just days away from laying their first beautiful, speckled eggs, and with the warmer weather, I was finally able to move them out of my garage. They went into the small, elevated coop I'd used for the flea market chickens and turkeys early on. The quail behaved a lot like my chickens, only they were excellent flyers. They seemed to appreciate being outside with the natural light and breezes and made sweet, happy sounds throughout the day. I was proud of myself for raising them without incident, and their precious calls gave me a joyous feeling.

The next morning, excited at the prospect of being greeted by my adorable singing birds, I bounded out of the house only to be met with an eerie silence. Before I even made it to the quail enclosure, I saw feathers on the ground. *Lots* of feathers.

The only thing left of my ten babies were their severed heads and little angel-like wings. *Who or what could have done such a thing?* The doors to the coop were still secured tightly, just as I'd left them the night before. The coop was several feet above the ground and seemed unharmed. What animal could climb and get inside a locked coop without opening the doors?

Then it dawned on me: raccoons. One small section of the coop had a different type of hardwire, with one-inch holes. The raccoon was able to get its arms inside and scare the quail into blindly flying around. In their panic, they were easily captured and pulled through the wire. This raccoon had picked my babies off, one by one. Blood drained from my face. I couldn't take these brutal deaths anymore.

This was the third devastating predator attack in short order. I felt sick, but I knew it was time to invest in a twenty-four-seven security system for my animals: I needed to get a livestock guardian dog. Like the cat, geese, and quail, a dog wasn't part of my original plan, but my spreadsheets had officially become obsolete awhile ago.

Kahuna wouldn't be able to protect anything; he was only a seven-pound purse dog. I needed a big farm dog that would know what to do. The food and vet bills alone would be painful, but I was out of options.

I spent hours online researching dog breeds. Before going the breeder route, and hoping to save an abandoned dog's life, I visited shelters and rescues. At a nearby shelter, I found a beautiful two-year-old female Great Pyrenees. We bonded, and she seemed like a perfect fit, until I asked if the shelter knew why she was there. The previous owner turned her in after the young dog, fueled by pack mentality with other dogs, killed all their chickens. Unfortunately, this story line kept repeating itself with other shelter and rescue dogs, and ultimately, I had to turn my focus on finding a decent breeder.

There was a Great Pyrenees breeder in Tennessee with working livestock guardians. Their puppies were raised with the very animals they were intended to guard. When the breeder sent a picture of a male puppy, my heart melted. He was tiny and had that puffy-eyed, smashed-nose newborn look—more like an oversized cotton ball than a puppy. I was going to name him Luca, Italian for Luke, and I'd bring him home in a few weeks. While most of my farm decisions had come fairly easily, this one made me incredibly nervous. As the anxiety settled in, I realized that even more than having geese or dairy goats, a farm dog was the biggest commitment. Everyone was willing to buy or take farm animals that produced food, but dogs were a commitment for their entire life span. I knew this was the last nail in the coffin of my former life. Like it or not, I was locked in.

Gia's kittens were due any day now. I seemed more nervous than she was. I worried about recognizing the signs, but when I found her hiding in the barn one day, it was obvious. I got a cozy old beach towel and put it in a box for her, but she had other ideas.

Gia chose the cold hard concrete floor of the barn to give birth, and I sat down to try to comfort her. She started panting. When the pushing started, she let out a screech. This was the first time I'd witnessed an animal giving birth, and I felt completely unprepared. The act of birth had always made me feel as if death was lurking nearby. It seemed like a huge risk, like spinning the wheel of fortune—win or lose, life or death. Between my own losses and having had a friend who had died in childbirth, I had my own deep issues surrounding labor and birth. Now, here I was, feeling helpless and worried again, suffering flashbacks to my past while trying to act as doula to a cat.

As the first kitten emerged, Gia stood with the baby halfway out and pushed until it fell on the floor. She began cleaning it as the other kittens started coming out.

By the fourth kitten, I still had no clue who the father was.

Each one looked like a carbon copy of Gia. I put the kittens in the box with the beach towel and she joined them. Finally, she seemed to be in a more relaxed state. Then another one started coming. "Geez, Gia, how many babies do you have in there?" I asked.

The last kitten was a bobtail tabby—an exact duplicate of its father, the cat around Tricia's house, Bob.

Over the next few weeks, Gia moved her babies from hiding place to hiding place. At one point she stuffed them inside the fallen oak tree, where the giant snake had been living. That was it. I didn't trust her safe spots anymore. I moved Gia and her kittens to the garage. Maybe I was being a helicopter grandparent, but I didn't want to risk anything hurting them.

Luca weaned himself early, at seven weeks, which should have been my first clue to his independent streak. On my way to pick him up from the breeder, I was hesitant the entire drive. As I pulled up, I saw a woman holding what appeared to be a big white bear cub. Luca was huge. *That couldn't possibly be my puppy,* I thought. He looked more like a baby polar bear with his little eyes, coal black nose, and white cottony fluff. At only seven weeks old, he was well over half my body length. His thick fur added to his bulk. I was intimidated—intimidated by a *puppy*—and intimidated by the commitment to my new lifestyle. I quickly processed the emotion. This wasn't just about a dog; it was about the survival of my fledgling farm. There was a lot riding on this puppy's shoulders and there was no going back now.

I slipped into autopilot and placed Luca next to me in the passenger seat, which he filled completely. He put his head on the center console and quietly watched me the entire hour's drive home. I wondered what he was thinking. Did he know I had no idea what the hell I was doing? Even at his young age, his eyes reflected a kind of universal knowing. This didn't help my nervousness. Once we returned home, I put his crate in the chicken coop, where I'd decided he'd sleep. There would be no house time; he was meant to immediately bond with his livestock. There were strict methods for raising a guardian dog, and I intended to follow them.

If I was nervous, Luca was the opposite. He was the most laidback puppy I'd ever seen. At first, Maybelle wanted to kill him and tried to pummel him into the ground every chance she got. Luca didn't care. It was a game to him. Nothing seemed to faze him, not even physical reprimands from the large doe. He acted as if her headbutts, ramming, and biting attempts were forms of play. When I put him in the coop with the chickens at night, he never protested. He quietly ate his dinner, then curled up with his stuffed monkey. Unlike most puppies, he didn't pay much attention to food or treats and he never destroyed his toys.

Great Pyrenees are known for their profuse, loud barks. It's their offensive strike, a way of warning predators away. But Luca was always quiet. I wondered how long it would take before he had any effect on the barrage of predators, which seemed to be lurking everywhere.

I didn't have to wait long. Luca was barely four months old when he experienced his first predator attack. One evening, two juvenile chickens refused to go into the coop. I put the other animals up for the night and prayed that the mere scent of a dog would keep any would-be chicken killers at bay. It didn't. The next morning every animal, including Luca, was traumatized. He was whining and utterly distraught. When I let him out of his crate, he ran straight to the perimeter fence, where he paced and barked. There, on the other side, were the remains of my two girls. Only their heads and feathers were left. The killing had happened in full view of all my animals. Luca sniffed the air and ran around. I took him over to the remains, to let him smell any scent the predator had left behind. He sniffed and whined and looked at me. I felt defeated. I was failing my animals in the most important way. I couldn't keep my own human babies alive, and now this. I took several deep breaths to center myself and stop the spiral into anxiety. Now, I worried about the emotional health of the very animal I had gotten to protect the others. In our short time together, we had bonded in such a particular way. Unlike Kahuna, who was like my child, Luca had the weight of purpose and real farm responsibility on his puppy shoulders. Most people get dogs as companions, but this dog had a full-time job he was literally growing into. Our relationship was complex and evolving, but I already loved him dearly and *needed* him, and yet I didn't completely understand him. *Was I supposed to teach him how to guard?*

On my social media farm page, I posted about the attack and Luca's behavior. Several people responded, all of them saying that there had been one particular traumatic event that seemed to trigger the guardian instinct in their dogs. Everyone said there was no need to teach him, which I found hard to believe.

As they predicted, it took a few days for Luca to recover emotionally from the experience. After three days of whining and cowering, he suddenly snapped out of his worried state and started practicing his bark. He refused to go into his crate or the coop at night. He paced the perimeter of the pen, and I decided to honor his desire to freely roam. He seemed to be practicing his guardian skills, and I wanted to have faith in his instincts, and his ability to deal with Maybelle. Within days, his bark graduated from novice to expert level. He was turning into a big dog, but his bark still far extended his body size. Now he barked all night long, roaming to each corner of the pen to put all predators on notice, reminding them that he was present and in charge. His incessant barking would mean sleepless nights for me, of course, for well over a year as I learned to decipher their various meanings. But from that first night on, I knew the only kills on my land would be if Luca made them himself, or if he couldn't physically reach the predator.

Luca was a large beast of a juvenile dog. With each passing day, it was painfully obvious that I needed help training him. Farm dogs have specific tasks, and there was no one in the area with expertise in the Great Pyrenees breed. The more I read, the more I realized I had made every mistake in the book. I didn't even know there was a difference between guarding and herding. Apparently, Great Pyrenees don't herd, they guard, and they're bred to be independent-minded so they're not particularly into human guidance.

I had wanted the smartest, cutest puppy I could find. I didn't know I wasn't supposed to buy the alpha (which Luca was). I didn't know I wasn't *supposed* to get the smartest puppy (which Luca was). I didn't know a livestock guardian dog was supposed to be from a big litter (which Luca was not). Having siblings teaches the puppy when rough play hurts. At one point, someone sent me a quote from a dog trainer: "With lots of time, patience and effort you can train a Great Pyrenees to do exactly what *they* want to do." That pretty much summed up my Luca.

The more he grew, the more of a pain in the ass he became, and not just to me. No amount of headbutting from Maybelle and Valentina could correct his rough-and-tumble nature. Even Gia joined in, reprimanding him regularly. But while the goats loathed their annoying new roommate, Gia seemed to genuinely adore him, despite her powerful, claw-extending blows. One swipe she gave him was so strong that her claw hooked into Luca's oversized droopy lips. It looked painful, but didn't seem to bother him. As soon as I unhooked her from him, he immediately started doing the next annoying thing. Gia allowed him to play with her increasingly active kittens, who loved their big white play toy. Now that they were big enough to fight back, he was more gentle with them.

Luca was unlike any puppy I'd ever met. He had absolutely no interest in playing fetch. He didn't lick faces or chew things. His favorite thing seemed to be staring into my eyes. He needed constant eye contact. Everything was on his terms. I'd definitely dated guys like that. It never ended well.

When I brought Luca home, I thought it would be the end of senseless death on the farm. But his size meant that he could accidentally kill an animal by just putting one of his big paws on it, and this often resulted in broken chicken backs. The frail, hollow bones of my birds couldn't support the heavy weight of a playful Pyrenees puppy. Animal after animal died by the paws of the protector brought in to keep them safe. I tried everything I could to correct his behaviors, but he didn't care about food or treats, and anger and punishment only escalated his outbursts. He didn't *mean* to kill his friends. He simply didn't understand his own size and strength.

It was an ironic nightmare. I had twice as much to worry about now, trying to guard my feathered babies (who could fly out of their protective pen) from the very dog I got to keep them alive. When Luca accidentally killed three of my beloved turkeys, I was so furious that for a split second I contemplated shooting him. Then, horrified that I was capable of even *having* such a thought, I was beside myself with grief and anger. Every moment of every day I worried he would strike again. The serenity of the farm had vanished. Every time I heard an animal screech, I'd leap from my chair and rush outside. Most of the time, I'd find Luca with one of my babies in his mouth. He was a giant, out-of-control toddler, and I was disgusted with him, and with myself and my ineptitude. How was it possible to feel so much animosity toward *a puppy*? I was losing track of how many times I'd cried in frustration over his behavior. Now I could see why there were so many adolescent Great Pyrenees in the shelters. I loved him, but I hated almost everything he did. As long as I was by his side, he was an amazing dog, but I couldn't trust him for five minutes alone with the animals. Nothing the experts suggested worked. One person recommended beating him with a dead bird, then tying it to his collar until it rotted off. *Um, no thanks.*

One day, when Luca broke free from his harness and ran away, I was strangely relieved. I hoped he wouldn't return. But fifteen minutes later, he did. He was a problem I would have to learn to live with. The Noonans commiserated with me. Their livestock guardian dog, Raina, had displayed similar behavior as a puppy. They assured me repeatedly that Luca would grow out of this as he reached his adult stage . . . which, apparently, could take three *years*. It had taken that much time before Raina stopped killing their animals, they said, but now the Noonans couldn't imagine their farm life without their guard dog. Danielle tried to console me. "I know it's hard, but stick with it. Luca will be the best thing you've done for the farm and your animals. One day, he will just get it and he'll be worth his weight in gold. I promise. We all go through it."

How could I punish him when he simply didn't *understand*? He was listening to his instincts, and doing what came naturally to him. He seemed to genuinely love the other animals and was visibly upset whenever he realized he'd killed them. He made no attempt to eat them. He wasn't *trying* to be bad . . . but he was breaking my heart, and wearing me down. Of all things, a *puppy* was becoming my biggest farm failure.

Gia's kittens, while utterly adorable, were like five wild monkeys, climbing on everything. They even annoyed the chickens by trying to play with their tail feathers. They liked to hide and ambush me as I walked by. My legs were covered in scratches, but I didn't mind. When they ambushed Maybelle, she retaliated with a swift headbutt, sending the kittens flying, which didn't deter them in the least.

I wanted Gia to have a playmate, so I decided I'd keep one kitten on my farm. One of my nieces chose a sweet female and named her Merigold. Then I had to find homes for the others, and that proved far more difficult than I'd expected.

Around this time, my stepmother invited me to dinner with friends in Oxford, about twenty-five minutes from the farm. During dinner, one of the women mentioned a man named Morgan who lived nearby. He loved cats, apparently, and was about to get more for his ranch from a shelter. My ears perked up. I told her I had kittens that were about ready to go to new homes. She said she would love to show pictures of the kittens to Morgan and get his thoughts.

I sent her some photos and held my breath. She wrote back and told me Morgan would love to take them, and that he was going to name them "Ike" and "Tina."

"Morgan" turned out to be Morgan Freeman, the actor. My stepmother's friend was his assistant. And so a couple weeks later I found myself delivering the two kittens, Tricia's bobtail cat's mini-me and one of Gia's look-alikes, to Morgan Freeman's home.

"*Huh*, who knew!?" I said as I arrived at the big iron gates of his beautiful Mississippi ranch, which was about thirty minutes from my little place. The gates, which had big *M*s on them, opened onto a long winding drive. I drove slowly down the road, passing busy ranch hands, every one of them smiling and waving.

Kitten carrier in hand, I tentatively knocked at the large front door. Unfortunately, Mr. Freeman wasn't around. He was, it turned out, in a meeting with Johnny Depp.

"Umm, okay, um, I'm delivering kittens," I said, unsure of what protocol to follow. A celebrity experience of any kind was the last thing I expected in rural Mississippi.

I was taken to his assistant, and she invited me to bring the kittens inside. The housekeeper prepared bowls of food and water for Ike and Tina. I followed along as the assistant took them to check out their new digs. Outside, there was a fabulous pool area, which looked more like a tropical resort than a ranch in Mississippi.

The kittens wasted no time getting into everything. It was like I'd released Tasmanian devils. Tina made herself at home by jumping into a large potted plant and immediately digging into the soil, spilling it over the side. Ike took to pawing, biting, and tearing at the landscaping with a wild look in his eyes. I laughed nervously and said, "They were clearly raised in a barn." After one last goodbye to the wildly frisky kittens and a quick tour of the beautiful house, I was on my way, feeling that I couldn't have asked for a better home (or estate) for Gia's kittens.

It turned out Mississippi was a small world. A few months later, while I was having cocktails in Oxford, I met Mr. Freeman's girlfriend. She made a comment about how he had gotten a pair of kittens that were "CRAZY." They were always climbing the window screens to look into the house. A bit embarrassed, I didn't say anything. As I was learning, it wasn't just human kids who could be a challenge. Juveniles of all species had a knack for driving their parents insane.

My Double Life

Most of the year in Tampa, the weather was too hot and humid for my taste. Summer storms were a welcome reprieve, and I tended to come alive during the winter months, when the humidity and temperatures were lower. But it had been years since I'd experienced true changing seasons, and in Mississippi, I was loving every minute of it. What I didn't expect was the weather switching back and forth from winter to spring for months on end. But by late April, spring had burst forth, and winter was slowly releasing its grip. Delicate shades of green were everywhere. One morning I noticed that the animals had gathered around a large old tree, one that had looked dead for months. The tree was now clearly alive, and it had produced beautiful soft, almost velvety leaves that were much larger than my hand.

I walked toward the tree and saw that all around it, thumb-sized berries, ranging from red to deep purple, covered the ground. They looked like elongated raspberries or blackberries, and all the animals except Luca were gorging themselves on them. Looking up in the canopy, I saw that there were thousands of berries in varying stages of ripeness. It was an old mulberry tree. Visions of smoothies and pies filled my mind as I scrambled to beat my animals to the fallen fruit.

Jumping up, I was able to grasp the lowest branch. I pulled it down to my eye level and plucked a pristine ripe berry. The thought of squirrel pee crossed my mind. *Screw it,* I thought and popped it in my mouth. My taste buds exploded. It was, hands down, the best berry I'd ever eaten. I stared up into the canopy at all the beautiful fruit, just there for the taking. The tree had to be about fifty years old, ancient for the species, and appeared to be barely hanging on. It was far too tall to climb and set in a precarious position on a natural incline, which made a ladder unsafe. If I waited for the berries to fall, I'd never be able to compete with my animals, who had stationed themselves beneath the tree. Then it dawned on me: *If there's one old mulberry tree . . . maybe I have more.* As I walked my property, looking at everything with fresh eyes, I was amazed to find more food growing—wild blackberries, a peach tree, a plum tree, a fledgling persimmon tree—without any human intervention.

My property had six mulberry trees of various ages, two of which the animals had yet to find and had berries I could reach with a ladder. I got a frilly, white apron from the house and filled the pockets with bite-sized sweetness until my hands (and apron pockets) were stained watercolor pinks and purples.

With my berry bounty safely inside the apron pockets, and the clear blue sky above me, I climbed on top of the old fallen oak tree in the pen and fed myself mulberries as if I were Roman royalty. In moments like these, I felt truly enamored with my secret farm life. The anxiety I'd had in the city was still present, but it was slowly easing its grip on me as the months passed. Still, I wondered why it was taking *so* long to undo the stresses of my old life. Could someone have PTSD from simply living a stressful—but normally stressful—city life? What exactly *was* this anxiety anyway? My type A personality wanted to get rid of the discomfort immediately. Back in Tampa, I functioned on adrenaline, running from obligation to obligation. Here, with the exception of the headaches with Luca, things were relatively much less stressful on a daily basis. But the farm wasn't the total quick fix I'd hoped it would be—there was something that remained unsettled, something I couldn't quite grasp, lurking deep inside—but the more I allowed myself to let go of my old life, the more I became focused on creating my new one. And I had hope that, with more time, soon I'd be emotionally free. There were already some significant changes; I had stopped loathing Mondays and had even begun to enjoy Sundays. And I was starting to let go of the desperation for more time. In my city life, time was ever present and important. Time was money. In the country, it passed in a different way. Other than scheduled conference calls for my business, my life was no longer being run by a clock. I slept until the sun woke me, or until my bigmouthed rooster did. I no longer had to be on time, or fight rush hour traffic. The natural by-product of these changes was a release of a knot of anxiety in my chest I hadn't been aware I'd been living with, and yet my impatient personality was still anxious to purge *all* the remaining anxiety immediately. All I wanted was to feel the sense of freedom my animals seemed to have, and I wanted it *right now*. I longed for the day where my phone dinging from a text or email didn't immediately trigger my anxiety to respond right away.

Deep in thought, I had the strange realization that I was a person splitting in two. One part of me was trying to rise into freedom, the other part desperately trying to not get sucked down into an abyss. It felt like one woman was awakening, and another was dying. I wanted to be a new me, badly. But instinctively, I knew that to do that, I'd have to deal with all that plagued me, and I had no idea how to do that or even if I had the courage to.

On the tree that day, my mind continued wandering. In the last several months, after tasting the difference of kale fresh from the ground or a just-picked berry, I'd decided I was ready to plant my own garden. It crossed my mind that I needed to build up my compost with different types of manure. This was the country, so rather than buy manure, I was hoping Farmer John would let me scoop some out of his cow pastures. I pulled my phone out and shot off a text to him.

"Do you mind if I come get manure out of your fields?"

My phone rang immediately. "You're not going to put it in your house, are you?" Farmer John asked with a concerned tone.

"Uhhh, nooo? It's for my compost pile. Why would anyone want to bring poop in their house?" I asked, incredulously.

"Well, you never know about you city people. Sure, help your-self."

From my perch on the fallen oak log, my animals had started slowly gathering around me and settling into their afternoon naps. In the tree canopy above, several white winged bugs fluttered around in a giddy manner. They reminded me of fairies. More of them appeared. They had an awkward flight pattern, but an almost magical quality. Then, all of a sudden, there were *hundreds*.

I sat up to get a closer look. The hundreds started to multiply. Then I realized they were streaming from the giant dead oak I was lounging on. *Oh my god, I know these creatures*, I realized. They were the bane of Florida homeowners: a termite swarm!

Jumping off the tree, I woke the animals and called their attention to the swarm streaming from their winter hidey-hole in the tree, hoping they would be interested in the airborne meal. The ducks sprang to action first and absolutely lost their minds, quacking in delight as they rapidly picked off the bugs one by one. The chickens and turkeys busied themselves running around, bumping into one another as they plucked the termites from the air. It was an all-out feeding frenzy. In my head, the theme song from the old TV show *The Benny Hill Show* started playing. (Bet you haven't heard that in a long time!) My animals were going berserk over the flying meal. Most of the termites barely made it out of the hole in the tree. Delia, one of my new ducks, was the smartest and positioned herself directly at the exit hole. As the termites came out, she plucked them off like bonbons. My birds saved the day. I stood back, proudly and smugly watching the strange comedy around me. Maybe, just maybe, I was starting to become a natural at this lifestyle.

Once the bug-eating show was over, I made my way to the chicken coop to check the nest boxes for eggs. The older flea market hens had been laying for a while and my younger, fancy girls were just starting to lay. Anticipation of the new eggs had me checking the coop throughout the day. It wasn't uncommon to collect up to six eggs a day. I was learning each girl's egg style—short and fat, long and skinny, speckled or colored. There were even eggs that varied in color from one end to the other—ombré eggs! Of course my girls were down with the trends. The way Bubba talked about shrimp in the movie *Forrest Gump*, I could talk about eggs: *eggs Benedict, egg salad, poached eggs, deviled eggs* . . . With so many eggs to keep track of, I started marking each one, noting the date it was laid with the hen's name, accenting it with hearts and stars.

Passing through the door to the coop, I noticed that red wasps were making a nest above the door, less than two feet from my head. Since my new mantra was to be one with Mother Nature and live and let live, I didn't pay it much attention. The wasps had been working on their nest for days and they had left me alone.

So I'd leave them alone, too. At this point, I figured we were cool with each other.

From the nest boxes, I collected a large brown egg and two ivory-colored eggs. I had seen my beautiful black-and-white Coco Chanel loitering around the nest boxes all morning. Sure enough, when I got to the last nest box there was the cutest little mint-green egg, with the telltale blood smear that often happens the first time a pullet lays an egg. I carefully placed it in my berry-stained apron with the other eggs.

Not wanting to break my new green egg, I walked out of the coop more slowly than usual. Suddenly, something struck me on the top of my head. It felt as if I'd been shot with a high-powered BB gun. "OWWW!" I yelled, and felt the back of my head. I looked up and saw the red wasps, all in a row, aimed at me like little fighter jets.

My head and my feelings were hurt. I launched into a screaming tirade: "I'm going to kill you! I'm going to kill *all* of you! I'm going to kill your entire family!" It felt good to let off some steam, but the humiliation sank in when I realized my neighbors could probably hear me screaming like a crazy person.

My head throbbed. I sat down on the ground outside the coop, careful to not jostle my apron of eggs. As I sat there, fuming and plotting the wasps' imminent destruction, there was another sudden, searing pain on my lower back near my spine. It hurt to the bone. I turned to see Francois, running from the scene of the crime. My once prized girl, now an angry young rooster, had flogged me with his spurs and ripped through my shirt. Spurs are hard, sharp extensions located above the foot on the inside of a chicken's leg. They were usually smaller, or nonexistent, on females, but roosters could have big ones, and they used them for fighting. "You sucker punched me and ran?!" I bellowed.

Francois had been increasingly aggressive since he started

crowing. Frankly, he horrified me. Crazy eyes aren't cool in people and, it turns out, they're pretty disturbing in animals as well.
Every time I let my guard down, he attacked. At one point, he
cornered me in the coop and came at me. I threw my foot up to
fend off his impending attack. That was a mistake. Throwing your
foot up to a rooster is like putting your dukes up and saying *Let's
do this, bitch!* I had unwillingly invited him to rumble and he
lunged at me full force, kung fu style. Anyone who's been terror-
ized by a butthole rooster knows the kung fu moves—and it's
horrifying. I screamed as I tried to escape while he elegantly elevated off the ground and whipped me repeatedly. Shrieking, I
ran back to the house with Francois in hot pursuit. You may have
seen the rooster attack videos on YouTube—it's definitely hilarious until you're the one running for your life. And let me tell you,
roosters can run faster than you think. I reached the door to
safety and slammed it behind me. From the window, I could see
my angry rooster pacing near the door, waiting for me, plotting.
In all the fury, I even managed to have the thought that dealing
with an asshole rooster was *still* far better than having a micro-
managing client with an overinflated ego. At least I could carry a
broom or water gun to ward off attacks. By the way, a broom
works better than a water gun for roosters, but the thought of
using either on an annoying client made me smile.

One day, after verifying that the coast was clear of roosters and
wasps, I picked up the phone for a business call I had scheduled.
This conference call was an important one. Cell service in the
country was sketchy at best, so I usually took calls by a window
for decent reception, although I had to be careful—noisy animals
could interrupt at any time and blow my cover. It was the end of
spring, and I had been in Mississippi for the bulk of a year now,

but I still hadn't changed my social media "location" status. Most of my clients, and many friends, still had no idea that I'd left Tampa. When it came to my business, I was concerned that if I told people, it would change everything. They wanted to think a well-heeled, well-connected city girl was guiding their endeavors. I was happy to remain deep inside my private world for as long as I could.

At that time, I was working on a celebrity sports event: generating publicity, building a website, and creating graphic assets like ads and banners. My client was a large private golf course. Several other parties involved in the tournament would be on the call. I assumed my usual position by the window for optimal cell service and dialed in. While others were talking, I gazed out the window to admire my animals roaming the property. A couple of hens saw me in the window and ran over, looking for a handout. I gave an obligatory "Uh-huh" so the call participants knew I was listening. What I was really doing was showing the hens my open palms to prove that I was not, in fact, hiding their treats.

As the call dragged on, the bright red comb of a chicken emerged from behind the woodpile. As the comb approached the house, the theme song to the movie *Jaws* started playing in my head. I'd recognize that big red comb anywhere. It was . . . *Francois*. I now said his name with contempt. The accidental rooster had become my nemesis. Lately, I had been forced to carry protection, in the form of a broom, anytime I left the house.

Francois emerged from the woodpile and froze. He had seen me, too. Our eyes locked. The music in my head changed to an old western theme. He sashayed over to the window and squared off to me like it was high noon. With protective glass between us, I felt comfortable staring at him with my best Clint Eastwood squinty eyes. Francois's pupils became creepy pinpoints as he focused on me. He took two steps closer and cocked his head to the side with a distrustful, judgmental look. Maybe he couldn't reach me physically, but I swear the wheels were turning in his puny brain. I shook my head slowly and silently mouthed, *DON'T YOU DARE DO IT!*

Francois inhaled deeply. I scrambled to mute the call but it was too late. The rooster proceeded to belt out an ear-piercing crow, four feet from my phone. He was so close I could hear the wheeze at the end of his crow even through the windowpane. Everyone on the call went silent. I felt the blood drain from my face. I put my hand over the receiver and mouthed through the thin pane of glass, *SHUT UP! SHUT UP!* Francois rebalanced himself, looked me directly in the eyes, then crowed two more times for good measure.

I was mortified. Finally, someone on the call hesitantly spoke up, "Was . . . was that a . . . *rooster*?!" I heard a few chuckles. All I could muster was a nervous laugh. I said, "I heard it, too. That was *weird*." Francois, satisfied with himself, moved on. I breathed a hesitant sigh of relief: My secret life was still intact—barely.

Holding the phone between my shoulder and my ear, I went to pour myself a cup of tea, no longer caring if I dropped cell service. My nerves were shot. I muted the call as I tried to shake it off and refocus, and then I glanced up to see a chicken glide by the window. My windows were several feet off the ground, so this seemed impossible. *How did a chicken just glide by?* I craned my neck and saw that the chicken was riding Maybelle around the backyard. Kahuna started running around, yapping. His hatred of the goats was growing. Was my hen so lazy that she needed a goat Uber? How did they even decide to do this?

I surveyed my animals and noticed my sweet doeling, Valentina, actively in a fight with one of the male ducks. He was biting at her, and she was attempting to stomp and headbutt him but he wasn't backing down. Out of nowhere, Rupert, my young tom turkey, arrived on the scene. He puffed up and dutifully strutted over to separate the fighting baby goat and her irritating waterfowl suitor. Rupert despised all forms of shenanigans. He was becoming a very serious turkey and was the only poult who had survived playtime with Luca. He was now large enough to inflict major damage on my big puppy.

As I watched my menagerie of animals, someone on the other end of the phone said, "Well, that's about it. Thank you for your time."

My farm life seemed a whole lot like running a daycare—or maybe a college bar. There was fussing and fighting, flirting and fun, puke and poop. Was this normal? How could I manage all this while still working as a full-time professional? Would I ever be able to fit in, in Tampa Bay again? Could anyone relate to me now that I was a fledgling farmer? My life was diverging drastically from the lives of my friends and family. I could count on one hand the people I knew who had ever milked a goat or killed a snake with a rusty shovel.

Around this time, other questions began to plague me. I'd been on the farm for a while—were people starting to figure out the truth? Would I ever be able to fit into society again? Did I even want to? Before moving to Mississippi, I'd had a certain vision of what farm life would be. In some ways, it was much better than I could have ever imagined. A life in nature suited me well. My brain seemed to expand; I learned, experienced, and evolved, and my nervous system was starting to feel entirely different, calmer. In other ways, this life was starkly challenging. I had no idea I would become so reclusive. At times, I dreaded even leaving my farm for errands. Other people's energy began to feel overwhelming. I had family nearby, and with the move I'd originally hoped to spend more time with, and become closer to, them. But my need for seclusion grew more intense as time went on, and it felt like an indicator that deep and unfamiliar things were stirring inside me. I couldn't put my finger on what was happening and I didn't really want to; I just wanted the feelings to go away. Some people are brave enough to invite their demons in for tea. Not me, I slammed the door in their faces, never desiring to entertain them. If I purposely pushed them away, I reasoned, they would eventually get the hint and leave forever. And yet, on the other hand, it's impossible to solve a problem when you never really face and identify it. So I remained in a perpetual state of fighting an uneasy feeling. It reminded me of my experiences with morning sickness: I was happily creating a new life and yet there was an ever-present sense of discomfort, and the feeling that I could throw up at any moment. But at least with my pregnancies, I had known the cause. . . .

In Florida, I had fit seamlessly into society. I received social invitations, hosted parties, and was very much a cog in the wheel. But now, I was seeing behind the veil, realizing that many social interactions were inauthentic. Participating in small talk was becoming increasingly difficult. When most people asked how I was doing, my new internal reaction was *Why are you asking when I know you really don't care?* It wasn't a judgment; I did it, too. I was starting to question and reject social norms and yet I didn't have any ideas about how to do it any better. More and more, I felt like I had no clue how to straddle both worlds.

Word had gotten out among locals in the farm community that a woman with farming interests had moved into the area. I was contacted by a guy who was starting an organization for sustainable agriculture in Mississippi. He wanted to know if I'd meet with him to discuss a possible board position. Since I was becoming increasingly socially distant, and starting to worry about it, his timing seemed perfect. I needed to spend more time around people.

We met at a local coffee and pastry shop. After hearing what he had to say, I was excited about not only the organization's mission of sustainability but also the prospect of meeting new people. And I wouldn't have to wait long—midmeeting, a woman breezed through the door and made a beeline over to us. "Hi! I'm Kathryn. I'm so sorry I'm early, I can wait until you're finished talking," she said.

"We were just finishing, and I'm glad you're here, this is Jake," the sustainability guy said, gesturing to me. "I'm talking to her about a board position as well."

Kathryn was petite and had a southern accent with the animated mannerisms to match. A lot of southern women tended to naturally use "jazz hands" to accentuate their words, and Kathryn was no exception. I listened as they chatted and learned she had two kids who had graduated from high school early and were now enrolled at Ole Miss.

I could tell Kathryn was smart. She had a strong energy about her, and, as is often the case with strong women . . . she annoyed me at first. But, as is *also* often the case, feelings of competition quickly turned to respect. Soon, we would discover how much we had in common—especially our feelings of isolation—and we'd become close friends.

Shortly after meeting Kathryn, another new friend came into my life. Brooke was imported from California by her husband. The importation of spouses seemed common in small-town USA. With limited "resources" in the area, it made sense that people would leave their hometowns to find a partner to bring back home . . . sometimes for better, sometimes for worse (it's not always easy to acclimate to a different culture and adhere to other people's beliefs about how you should conduct your life).

Unlike with Kathryn, I loved Brooke from the moment we met. With Brooke, there were no feelings of competition. Instead, she was so similar to my city friends that I loved her immediately, partly due to nostalgia. We bonded over stories of our past, the parties, the travel, music, men.

Brooke was tall, slender, brunette, stunningly beautiful, and impossibly kind, and yet she didn't take shit from anyone. Years of solo international travel and independence meant she was solidly secure in her own being, which was more than I could say for myself.

Brooke was the youngest in her family, Kathryn was the oldest. Brooke had a bohemian upbringing. Kathryn, whose mother was British, lived a much more formal life. Brooke was a little younger than me and had her kids at an older age. Kathryn was a little older and had her children shortly after college. My two new friends couldn't have been less alike, with one exception: They both freely and generously shared their families with me. And both women seemed to mirror my emerging needs for different types of relationships—ones with a lack of small talk, brutal honesty, and the freedom to grow emotionally, without judgment. That freedom of growth, I recognized, was becoming more precious to me each day.

Food and Fancies

As midsummer rolled around, I was excited to finally enjoy my garden bounty. I'd had a hell of a time keeping the goats out of my organic asparagus patch. The other vegetables were on one of my elevated porches, away from goat lips and bird beaks. A farmer who told me that "goats are a force of nature" had been correct. Like tornadoes or typhoons, goats could demolish gardens, landscaping, trees . . . anything not cemented to the ground. Their world revolved around two things: eating and playing.

On the side of my property was an expansive patch of wild blackberries. At the edge of the patch, my personal bodyguard, Rupert, joined me. As I collected a few berries to throw to my giant turkey, my arms and legs showed the telltale cuts and scrapes from blackberry thorns. "Worth it," I said to Rupert. I was still in awe that I could actually pick real fruit straight from my yard; it just never got old. As I gathered the blackberries—food I hadn't even planted, food that had arrived on its own—more inspiration hit.

I'd read somewhere that kudzu leaves were edible and had nutrition similar to spinach. The invasive vine was overtaking part of my property so, I figured, why not try eating it?

Fighting off the goats, who were equally interested in the vines, I collected a bunch of young leaves in a colander. "Butter makes everything better!" I said to Kahuna in my best Julia Child voice. Kahuna ignored me, too busy nosing around the kitchen floor for potential fallen food. I plopped a dollop of butter into the pan and washed the kudzu's delicate green leaves.

After flavoring the melted butter with a bit of fresh garlic, I sautéed the kudzu as I would spinach. The kudzu wilted quickly in the hot butter, and the smell made my mouth water. I took it off the heat and pulled one of my nice plates down from the cupboard—why not celebrate trying something new with fancy dinnerware? Just because I lived alone didn't mean I shouldn't use my nice things, I decided. My new life was a celebration in itself, with or without someone to share it.

The sautéed kudzu looked beautiful on my fancy plate. But with the first mouthful, I realized this was a mistake. While the flavor was somewhat similar to spinach, there were fibrous veins in the leaf that made it texturally unpleasant to eat. Imagine if spinach and celery had a baby. "Oh man. *That* was unsatisfying," I said to Kahuna. *Bummer.* From then on, I'd leave the kudzu-eating to the goats.

But I was still in inspiration mode. I walked back out to the garden and saw that my tomatoes were red on the vine. I'd been talking to the plants and nurturing them like children for months. They just *looked* like summer. My friend Kathryn was coming to visit from Indiana, and I wanted to do a tomato tasting with her, so I decided to wait to pick them. I moved on to my organic asparagus. I had purposely bought three-year-old crowns so I wouldn't have to wait the two years or so for the plants to establish themselves. When the crowns first arrived, they didn't look like anything special, just long, dried, gray roots. Now, despite some early losses (courtesy of the goats, of course), the asparagus was growing like a weed in the strong Mississippi sun. One day there had been nothing, the next a three-inch spear. I plucked one from the ground and bit into it. Just like Farmer Bradley's kale, the asparagus was amazing. It tasted like the earth, not like dirt . . . more like pure minerals. Even without seasoning, it was perfect. I announced to the animals, "Your mom is an incredible gardener!" I left the rest of the growing spears alone; I'd still have to wait a year to fully enjoy them.

After collecting mint from the garden, I made my way back to my kitchen lab. I had a local watermelon and fresh lemons on the counter. This was something I couldn't mess up. It took over thirty minutes of cutting and juicing the watermelon and lemons, making the simple syrup, and combining the ingredients. I couldn't wait for it to chill, so I shook it with ice in a martini shaker. I mashed in the mint leaves and voilà: fresh watermelon mint lemonade.

Part of what makes slow cooking so delicious is the loving effort that goes into it. It's the opposite of the instant gratification you get from takeout or ordering in a restaurant: With these raw materials, I had to *work* to create something, and in the end, that made it taste so much better.

"Fancy goblet or mason jar?" I asked Kahuna. "Yes, definitely the goblet." Sitting on my porch swing, the first sip tasted like ambrosia, the food of the gods. It was the perfect cooling afternoon beverage. Holding my drink, I walked out to the porch to watch the animals sunning themselves in the summer rays.

In moments like these, when I made self-nourishment and silence a priority, I could see how drastically my life had changed. I had a new understanding of the differences between relationships that gave me inspiration and energy and relationships that drained me. My new friends, Kathryn and Brooke, were setting high bars while many old business relationships were becoming increasingly exhausting. Having the audacity to put myself first and be deliberate about quiet time had led me to consider and finally understand my own needs. I could now distinguish between what I truly loved and what I did merely because it was the "popular" thing. Back in Tampa, my life had been full of activities I did just to fill the time, things I tricked myself into thinking I liked. Yoga, for instance, in our current culture, now seemed a lot like an attempt at monetizing Zen. I was all for being mindful and fit, but the work of the farm now gave me that. Also, wine: With the exception of a couple wines I'd had in Spain, I usually had to choke it down in the name of being social. I much preferred other beverages, so why had I always agreed to drink wine when, to my supertaster taste buds, it tasted like chemical vomit?

Why, I began to ask myself, had I done so many things I disliked, or stayed in unfulfilling relationships far beyond their expiration dates? Was it fear? Like Chad, was I also afraid of being alone? I considered the PR profession I now loathed and remembered the tactics of Edward Bernays. His methods, which had permeated the modern world, undoubtedly had a hold on me, as they did on everyone. But how to break free? How did someone find out who they really are underneath the layers of what had been sold to them? In the name of not being a fraud in my own life, I continued down my mental list. Reevaluating each person, activity, or behavior, I started crossing items off, disconnecting from anything that didn't feel like it served me or simply wasn't truly *satisfying*. At first, it triggered my anxiety to think of having to let anything go . . . and then, it became an exercise that was delightfully fun. Soon, I found myself considering the concept of consumerism. Even the way I shopped was shifting. In the city, my shopping habits revolved around how others perceived me. Now, my choices were more about making investments in *myself.* The shift made sense, considering that the core of a farming lifestyle was really about *nourishment,* about *life itself.*

The quietness of this life was actually allowing me to learn about who I really was, and who I wanted to be. Running down the mental evaluation felt like I was dropping one heavy emotional brick after another, freeing myself a little more with each item. There was no judgment toward myself or others, just excitement to get rid of all that was unfulfilling. As the farm became my home, I sensed that I was changing fundamentally, but I wasn't sure whether it was actually a whole new transformation— maybe, I realized, it was more like a simplification. Maybe it was a return to who I really was, to who I had been all along.

It was a slow process, extricating myself from the beliefs and habits formed while living in the rat race, but it was gradually getting easier. My life of seclusion helped me avoid most interpersonal dramas with friends, co-workers, and even road ragers. I was truly becoming the focus of my own life. I realized the busyness of my previous life may have been common, but it wasn't normal. True presence felt like something new to me. Truth be told, *I* felt new to me. I found it ironic that a place with few humans was far more humanizing than the places where they are ubiquitous. Without constant bustling and distractions, I noticed more of what was around me. And the more present I was in observing nature and the animals, the more I saw parallels between the animal kingdom and the human world. Animal personalities varied so much, even within the same species. Some of my animals were fiercely independent, others wanted cuddles every chance they got. It seemed the alpha types were the ones who generally sought out my company, and oddly, that had been true of people as well.

Among my animals, there were great parents and there were terrible parents, and then there were those who had zero desire to parent at all. I developed intense interest in this observation, undoubtedly due to my own experiences with motherhood. Two of my hens preferred to jointly raise their chicks as same-sex co-parents. Another was a child abductor and egg thief. I constantly had to remove stolen babies from (*ahem, not to name any names*) Bria. Once, I even caught her singing the egg song to claim another girl's egg. "Uh. Bria. I know you don't lay green eggs. You can't take credit for that!" I chastised. But it didn't seem to faze her. Had she been human, no doubt she would have been a great politician or titan of industry.

Some of the hens seemed to want to be mothers, but they simply couldn't sit still on the eggs long enough. Others would sit on eggs forever but didn't tend to them properly. Hens are supposed to keep turning and inspecting the eggs lovingly, which helps with air circulation, regulates the temperature throughout the egg, and keeps the yolks and babies from sticking to one side of the shell, so they have an easier time hatching. Some mothers, as soon as the chicks hatched, would abandon them. If I couldn't get another hen to accept the neglected chicks, I had to raise them myself as a foster parent. It was exasperating and heart-wrenching to see the confused chicks running from hen to hen, being rebuffed repeatedly. I was learning how difficult and delicate parenthood was, even for animals. Contemplating my animals' varied experiences, I was able to push aside the hatred for my own body's failures and the thought that maybe I would never be a mother, never have anything to contribute to the world, never leave a legacy.

I guess I always expected perfection in nature regarding

motherhood. But as I would come to learn, even the animals were often far from perfect parents. There were the ones, like me, who couldn't produce a healthy child. Some even abandoned their young when danger presented itself. Then there were other types of moms, like Bria, who missed their calling as a mountain lion and would fight off any person or animal to save their babies. She seemed to raise very healthy offspring and stick with them well into their adulthood. As much as she hated me, I admired her. She didn't take any of it lightly and could easily hatch twenty eggs and devote herself to every chick. Most of the girls were lucky to hatch and raise as few as two or three chicks. Some animals were wonderfully sweet to their little ones, but Bria was always frazzled and fussing. She ran her family like a drill sergeant and was in constant need of a spa day. She showed me that it was possible for animals to be helicopter parents, too.

That day on the porch, while I was enjoying my watermelon mint lemonade, Rupert came and positioned himself next to me, silently standing guard. I couldn't believe how much I had fallen in love with a turkey. He was huge, almost twice the size of the others. His face had a menacing appearance, but he had a big, loving heart. "Hi, sweetheart, how's my big, brave boy?" I said to him, quietly. His head turned turquoise, a sign that he was relaxed and happy. "I wonder if there are any other girls in the world, sitting on their porches, talking to their turkey?" I said. This gentle giant made me feel special beyond belief. The way he always sought me out for attention—he followed me *everywhere*—was different from the other birds. His commitment to me was sustained, it wasn't treat-based, it felt like companionship and respect.

I let my leg dangle off the side of the porch swing and rocked myself slowly back and forth. The old wood and metal chimes played gently in the breeze. Everyone except Rupert was deep into their afternoon naps. All was right in my little private world . . . when suddenly I felt a searing pain, like a hammer had dropped on my big toe. Expletives spewed from my mouth like a volcanic eruption. Rupert, clearly thinking my toes with red polish were berries, had pecked my big toe . . . hard.

The birds had been noticing my red toenails for days. I shooed them away several times, not thinking they would actually mistake my toes for fruit. Walking around with bare feet or even open-toed shoes was a rookie mistake on my part, I'll admit. After I shrieked, the bumpy, featherless skin of Rupert's head that changed colors based on his emotional state—the equivalent of a mood ring for turkeys—turned bright red in upset, but my toe hurt too badly for me to care about his feelings. I would make up with him later. I shot off an apology text to my neighbors for my "*fowl* mouth" and went inside to doctor my aching toe.

In late July, it was finally time to harvest the tomatoes I'd been waiting so anxiously for. Kathryn was arriving soon to share in the results of my first gardening attempt.

Plucking my very first tomatoes from their vines, I inspected and admired each one. Their smell was heavenly; they were the embodiment of the sunny season. While I was oversmelling my prized creations, I saw Luca intently watching a mother hen and her newly hatched chicks. Motherhood is contagious among chickens—not unlike how it is among women—and I now had several mothers with babies running around. The hen was calling her straying babies back when one toddled past Luca. Seeing the chick, he picked up his giant paw and put it on top of the baby, covering it completely. "LUCA, NO!" I yelled. He looked at me, his paw still on the chick, which I could no longer see. The mother hen was frantic.

At that moment, a light bulb went off in my head. Instead of screaming at him, I calmly and sweetly called out, "Let it go, baby." Luca sighed heavily and lifted his paw. I braced to see a smushed chick. But instead, the baby—a malleable newborn, saved by its softness—ran to its mom as if nothing had happened, nuzzling into her feather skirt. It was a miracle both that the chick wasn't injured and that Luca had listened for the first time *ever*. "GOOD BOY!" I said in a high-pitched tone. He ran to me and I showered him with love and praise.

It took an extreme amount of self-control to not flip out on Luca in a moment of danger, but I found that it paid off in dividends. For a dog who couldn't care less about treats or avoiding my anger, it turned out that the key to getting good behavior from him was calmness and praise from me. This meant I'd have to exercise incredible control over my quick temper in the midst of his troubling antics.

I went back to collecting my cherished tomatoes. But as I plucked one from the vine, suddenly a wild and unwelcome thought entered my mind. Several times, I had witnessed my birds eat small, quiet animals, such as snakes, lizards, and frogs. It had always disturbed me to see the chase ensue only to end in the traumatized, mute animal being torn apart or even swallowed alive. None had been delivered a polite or easy death. The way nature nourished itself horrified me at times. Suddenly, I looked at the tomatoes, feeling as if I'd just ripped a baby from its mother. Like the silent animals, the plant's life was in danger; did it, too, suffer in silence? It couldn't verbalize fear or pain. And like the quiet snake, I wondered, could plants *feel*? Had these tomatoes spent months growing happily, wanting to thrive and procreate, only to be ripped away and eaten? Thinking these things made me feel like a crazy person and yet, I was genuinely disturbed. All those small animals, eaten alive, stuck in my mind. I wished I could unsee them. I had no idea how to come to terms with it. *Is all of life just about injuring or consuming other life? Was my garden just another kind of factory farm?* No wonder Native Americans and other cultures close to nature give thanks and honor the food they intake.

For a long time, well before my farm days, I'd been increasingly sympathetic to the vegan lifestyle. It seemed a natural progression for someone who loved animals. While I already ate less of it, eventually, I thought I might forgo meat altogether. But now, I just felt guilty no matter what I ingested. I had a direct and more thoughtful relationship with my food in a way that I hadn't had in the city. With no middleman, I was becoming very aware that there was nothing that held life—neither animal or plant—about which I wouldn't feel guilt when eating. As my love of food and cooking was growing, I developed a fierce reverence for all the ingredients that went into a recipe. I now believed that plants were as sentient as any of my animals. Ultimately, I decided the best I could do was give everything on my farm a loving and respectful life, while it lasted.

Later that day, Kathryn arrived. After slicing the tomatoes I'd picked earlier that morning, I arranged them in a circle on a plate. Then I ceremoniously drizzled olive oil from my last trip to Greece over the slices. I love olive oil the way most people love wine. It amazes me how each year's yield can be so vastly different from the last. This oil seemed like the perfect complement to the newly ripened fruit. Finally, I sprinkled on a bit of salt. The tomatoes were ready to try.

Pushing my earlier thoughts from my mind, I speared a

perfect-looking bite and lifted it to my mouth. Even with my residual plant-killing guilt, my mouth still watered at the scent. And then, after all my monthslong anticipation for this first bite of summer, it was . . . *awful.* Truly the worst tomato I'd ever tasted. The flavor was similar to the way dirt smells. *How can this be?* I thought to myself.

Kathryn looked at me expectantly. "Well?" she asked.

"This is the most disgusting tomato I've ever tasted."

"What?! Maybe the oil is rancid?" she suggested. But we both tried the oil, and it was phenomenal.

"Kathryn, this tomato is disgusting. Try it." I shoved the plate closer to her.

She tried the tomato. Her nose wrinkled. "I can't believe it. You're right, it's terrible. Maybe it's just this one. Try another one," she said. Not wanting to waste any more nice olive oil, we tried the next tomato without condiments. It was the same. *Awful.* I'd grown the worst tomatoes in the world, from organic seeds and soil, with zero pesticides. I couldn't understand it. Had it been my singing that turned them to shit?

Later that evening, Kathryn and I took our usual positions on the porch rocking chairs. After the experience I'd had earlier with the tomato and thoughts of chickens eating the silent animals, I wanted to process it with someone else. "I have to tell you what happened to me before you got here today."

She listened intently in the darkness as I continued, "I really don't know what to think, but it's sort of messed me up. I'm not really sure how to reconcile this in my head."

"I don't have an answer for you," she said, "but I do know that research is actually being done along those lines. I recently watched a documentary about this subject. And, well, this isn't going to make you feel better . . ."

"What did they say?" I braced myself for her response.

"That the smell of fresh-cut grass is the scent of the grass blood. It's their chemical scream. That plants are very much alive, that they feel and just communicate differently than we do."

Chills ran up my arms.

"Yeah. That doesn't help at all. That just makes me never want to cut my grass again."

The Rainbow Salesman

Toward the end of my first year of almost total rural reclusiveness, I was developing something approaching basic farm competency. I could start a fire, shoot a gun, trap predators, and keep my animals alive . . . well, for the most part I could keep my animals alive. My property seemed to have a magical, healing energy, and I was very much starting to enjoy the seclusion in my country cocoon. So, of course, it was around this time that I received a text from an old flame in Tampa.

I'd known Paul for years. We met at the famous Gasparilla parade after our respective divorces and had had an instant connection. At the time, I chalked it up to alcohol consumption, but over the years, we would circle back to each other again and again, never quite getting anything off the ground. Still, this slow burn also gave us time to get to know each other.

Paul was different from most guys I knew in Tampa. It was rare to meet anyone who was as at home in a bustling city as he was in the forest, hunting for dinner. But he had mastered both worlds—city and country. This was endlessly appealing. He was almost exactly my age, just six days older than me. After a string of relationships with much younger guys, it was a refreshing change to be courted by someone I could relate to on so many levels.

Our yearslong flirtation had always been thwarted by one of us being taken while the other was single. There was a constant magnetism between us, like we were orbiting each other, sensing our unfinished business even though nothing had ever really started. After years of being with much younger people, it seemed we were both ready for something solid, reliable, and honest. So when he reached out in August just before my first full year on the farm, I was surprised, but completely receptive.

Paul had never kept his desire for me secret. It was one of the things I adored about him. Toward the end of my relationship with Chad, Paul (whom I'd known for years at that point) had even publicly proclaimed (drunkenly and loudly) in front of a large group of people: "She will be *MY* girl and I *WILL* marry her!" (Fortunately, Chad was too inebriated to realize what had just transpired twenty feet from him.)

Paul's behavior was arrogant, boastful, and embarrassing—but there was something appealing about his certainty about life, and, of course, his certainty about me. Over the years, I watched him go through girl after girl, every one an exact duplicate of the last: young, pretty, petite, brunette (usually), and spoiled. And yet, he always said I was the one he wanted. Two different girls he dated told me how he would tell them, in a matter-of-fact way, that I was his number one and that he was just passing time with them. At the time, I thought this was insane but also romantic.

His loyalty from afar was mesmerizing. This kind of blatant interest had always piqued my curiosity. Guys who played the waiting game never held my attention for long. There were a lot of traits I didn't like about myself, but this was one I loved; I wouldn't settle for a man who wasn't direct or played games. It takes courage to put one's heart or intentions on the table; there's nothing impressive about hiding behind walls. Some people find walls mysterious. To me, walls are boring.

Once I had finally broken up with Chad, my timing with Paul was off, yet again; he was newly committed to yet another carbon-copy girl. His choice in women was the only thing I couldn't wrap my head around. I was slender but not petite, and I certainly wasn't young anymore. The trophy-style wife seemed to be his type, and that wasn't me.

But now, after two years with his latest girl, he wanted to talk. As usual, our conversation was oddly direct.

"I'm in the process of leaving her and I want you to know I have thought of you every single day. Would you be willing to see me and see how things go?" I was floored but honored by his honesty. "I moved to Mississippi almost a year ago but you're welcome to visit me here." One final statement made his intentions clear: "I'm telling you now, you will be the last woman I'm with, even if we don't work out. And even if it means I have to buy a farm for you, I want you back in Tampa with me."

Considering his past dating habits of girls on rotation, I wondered if he was codependent like Chad. But somehow it felt more like Paul was trying women on for size, looking for his match. He'd never struck me as the needy type. After his blunt words, how could I resist this? Every man I've ever dated had one thing in common; they came at me guns blazing, without hesitation. Presuming there was attraction, certainty of self and certainty of desire was what turned my head. Even after all this time, I was attracted to Paul and excited to see him, but I worried about his visit. My life here was drastically different, and very quiet. What if he judged that? I had become fiercely protective of my private world. It took mustering all the courage I had to accept his visit and allow myself this vulnerability.

When Paul arrived in Mississippi, he was relaxed and happy in a way I had never seen him before, and I was cautiously hopeful. He smiled and laughed easily. We were both a bit nervous, but he seemed genuinely relieved to see me. I wondered what was going through his head, if maybe he didn't fully trust that his feelings for me would still exist. Honestly, I had wondered if I'd still feel chemistry, too. But like most people with unfinished business, our connection was still very much intact.

I watched as he took in the scene at my house. From the front of my property, it wasn't obvious that the back held a bustling animal menagerie. Even though the animals had free range, they often stayed behind the house, near the barnyard. As we walked around, they heard us coming and started running, walking, and sashaying over to greet us. There were over forty animals of several different species parading to meet us. I suddenly felt nervous; here was another big test . . . would he run?

Paul's eyes widened, and a big grin slowly spread across his face. He laughed in disbelief. "This is so cool. I can't believe you're doing this," he said. Watching all my animals enthusiastically run toward me was one of the best experiences of my daily life, and now someone special from my former life was equally as moved by it as I was. The smile on his face meant the world to me and I felt myself exhale in relief. "So you don't think I'm a nutjob for doing this?"

"Not at all. I love it. I just wish it were in Tampa," he said, still smiling.

Later, we settled in for one of our famous heart-to-heart talks; although we seemed to intellectualize our feelings, we communicated exceptionally well with each other. "What do you want from life, Paul?" I asked. A distant look crossed his face as he considered his answer. "I just want to be happy." I nodded in agreement and decided not to push further. I wanted to give him a break from his life in Tampa. Our conversations had always been focused on the future and, for now, I wanted to stay in the present as best I could. Fortunately, he changed the subject. "Hey, our fortieth birthdays are coming up in a few months. I've been thinking we should do something fun. I want to take a trip together, what do you think?" Of course, I agreed, and it was exciting to have something to look forward to.

There was a compatibility between us that made things feel easy; it's like I had no guard up whatsoever. I felt relaxed around him, and with his constant attention, I found myself fantasizing once again about creating a family.

On the way back to the airport at the end of his visit, we decided to take a tour of Graceland, Elvis's home. Walking through the pristine 1970s throwback decor made both of us feel like we were revisiting our childhood. There was such a peaceful, relatable feeling about being with someone my own age. When it was time for Paul's flight, we agreed that I would fly to see him in Tampa a couple weeks later, and we planned to stay in touch daily. His trip had put me in the blissful, hopeful state that only a potential new love can.

After Paul left, I went to check the mail. Heading back up my driveway, I discovered my animal parade behind me. Gia, Luca, the goats, the ducks, several chickens, the geese, and the turkeys—they had all accompanied me all the way down to the mailbox. Of course, I scolded them with baby talk and chased them back up the driveway.

Back in the house, I saw I had a text from Tricia.

"Gurrl, I just watched you walk down to check the mail and all your animals followed you! I laughed so hard. It was adorable."

I smiled. I could now hear her southern accent through her text messages.

Fall was in the air when I was on my way to Paul's house in Tampa. It was my first time leaving the farm and my first time leaving the animals. To say I was apprehensive was an understatement. Kathryn's daughter, Hayden, who was in college at Ole Miss, had volunteered to be my farm sitter. I was nervous but had to trust that everything would run smoothly while I was away, even with my naughty puppy. The thought crossed my mind that, even if things worked out with Paul, I was in no way ready to give up my new life. But I quickly told myself that we were nowhere near that level of commitment yet.

When I arrived, he was standing at his front door with a concerned look on his face. Walking in, I understood why. He told me that his latest ex-girlfriend had broken into his email and found out I was coming. She let herself into his house and placed pictures all over his living room, pictures from every event they'd attended together, every trip they'd ever taken. There were desperate notes she'd written, citing their time investment and all the reasons they should be together. She'd put her toothbrush and razor next to his. His bedroom closet still held some of her clothes. What the hell had I walked into? This was crazy town. I considered the options. Was she, in fact, still living there? Was all this planted, or was the truth somewhere in between?

Paul was shaken. "I should have changed the locks," he said quietly. *Well, no shit,* I thought, but I held my tongue. I was starting to wonder if this seemingly strong guy actually had no backbone at all. He hastily collected the photos and notes and handed them to me saying, "Look, you can dump them all in the trash."

Instead of throwing them away, I placed them on his TV console. This was between them and I wanted to see how he handled things going forward. He was so shaken that I contemplated leaving.

But I stayed. I told myself their breakup was recent and the dust would settle soon enough. Fortunately, he calmed down and we talked for hours. The next morning, trying to start fresh, Paul told me he had a surprise. He took me out back to the pool area and showed me how he'd turned his yard into a giant edible garden, something that was frowned upon in his gated yacht club community. I had inspired him, he said, as he showed me his papaya trees and pepper plants. I held one hand over my mouth, hiding my disbelieving grin, and the other over my heart. It was deeply touching. Everything was flourishing under his attention. The farmer in me envied his green thumb. As we walked around his little Garden of Eden, he was as happy as a kid excited to show off an art project. I loved that the same things could bring both of us satisfaction: a small seedling, a carefully tended life, marveling at the fruits of our labor.

Paul wanted to show me his life. We drove around in his open Jeep talking and enjoying the warm Gulf air. After the drama of the night before, the affection between us had returned. I was reminded of why we'd been doing this for so long, why this connection between us kept persisting.

The next day, he introduced me to his father and brother. We all piled into the car and headed to Gainesville to see the Florida Gators take on the Tennessee Volunteers. Since football was involved, the family meeting didn't feel like a big deal, more like dipping our toes in the water of commitment rather than a full-blown formal introduction.

I was excited to run into some of my Tampa friends at the tailgate. Most of these people I only saw about once a year, anyway, so they presumed I had never left the city. After the game, Paul and I walked the campus and toured his old fraternity house. It was interesting to see him in his old stomping grounds, reminiscing about the past, immersed in nostalgia. On the return home, we sat in the back seat. He laid his head in my lap and I stroked his hair listening to the conversation with his father and brother. Periodically he would squeeze my hand. It wasn't like the fiery, passionate relationships of my past but we felt good, solid.

Upon my return to Mississippi, we spoke daily and continued talking about the future. And even though the days grew darker as fall set in, Paul seemed as if he were offering me the rainbow life, and now I dreamed in Technicolor.

Lock Up Your Husbands

Fall was finally in the air and I received a rare invitation to a party. Thankful for a reason to get dressed up, I put on one of my old go-to little black dresses, one I'd worn in Tampa but never had use for on the farm. I'd forgotten how much I loved dressing up. I blew the dust off my favorite Gucci shoes, which still fit like Cinderella's slippers.

Maybe I'd been naive, but my first year in Mississippi had brought changes that I certainly hadn't anticipated. Unfortunately, it turned out that my uncle had been prescient; the marketing and PR business I'd worked for years to build was tanking. Not being able to take in-person meetings with potential clients in Tampa meant few sizable projects in the pipeline. And the small budgets of many local businesses I met with in Oxford weren't producing the same financial results I'd had in Florida. Social events in Florida had always produced excellent business connections, but it wasn't nearly as easy here. For so long, my success in PR had required a demeaning life of no boundaries, bending over backward to cater to clients' whims regardless of nights, weekends, or holidays. But after almost a year on the farm, I was growing stronger. I was beginning to no longer recognize the woman who had fallen over herself to make clients happy. On conference calls, I found myself cutting right to the point, just like the Noonans and other country folk. It was easier than ever to sniff out the crap. I would also no longer put up with married clients attempting to cross the line sexually. It had been a common experience and their behavior disgusted me—and so did my own history of tolerating it.

I was starting to wonder if my abusive past caused me to have little in the way of setting boundaries. My exterior was tough as nails, but I was never able to say no to clients who made ridiculous requests. On the farm, I'd begun to realize that I always felt like a little girl when people tried to exert power over me, and in the end, I'd always submitted. And I just couldn't stomach it anymore. Now, there were things I could no longer accept: calls and texts after business hours, inappropriate propositions, off-color jokes. I hadn't had the guts to tell clients off before. I knew it was because I always feared losing my job—so I stayed in my golden handcuffs, because they paid the bills. Financial success had always been more important than self-respect to me . . . but all that was changing.

As I set firmer boundaries, I noticed nearly all my male clients falling away. The first man who suddenly proclaimed "You're just not doing your job well anymore" worked for a large private golf course. After several rebuffs and turning down his gross advances, he told me they were hiring someone else. This wasn't a surprise. He was part of a well-established pattern. The golf course employed a string of pompous, sexist men to oversee the club's marketing and sales, men who always seemed to be getting them quietly sued. Now I wished I hadn't kept quiet, putting up with douchebag after douchebag. The owner who kept hiring these jerks was a good man, but I had been too afraid to tell him of my experiences, and like so many women, I'd stayed silent.

Arriving in my little black dress to the party, hosted by someone I knew from childhood, it was clear the partygoers were predominantly couples. In typical southern fashion, everyone was well dressed and southern belle accents permeated the house. I knew that as a single woman in small-town USA, I was walking through a social minefield. Had I not known the hostess, I would have left immediately. I kept my head down, making sure not to make eye contact with any men who were taken, and made a beeline for the bar, determined to shake the negative vibes. There was no bartender, so I started to mix my own drink. And then, out of nowhere, a man hopped behind the counter—the bartender, apparently. We chatted as he mixed my cocktail. He was funny but not flirtatious, and I didn't find him attractive.

"Hey there!" the guy said in an animated tone. "Let me help you with that, what did you want to drink?" Relieved to have someone friendly to talk to, even briefly, I smiled. "I'm not sure, I was just about to see what my options are."

"Let me make something I think you'll like?"

I agreed and watched him whip up my cocktail in a theatrical way. He was silly and seemed as if he'd been drinking a little himself. I was grateful for this kind interaction, but when I turned to walk away, drink in hand, I almost bumped into a wall of four women, all of them giving me hard stares, in *full* Bitch Mode. Before I could say excuse me, one of them cut in, "That's her husband you were talking to."

Great. I had run into the mean girls of Mississippi.

Apparently, the guy who jumped behind the bar to make my

drink wasn't the bartender. He was a married man just joking around at a party and now I had to deal with the fallout of his insecure spouse. *Ugh.*

But I also felt pity for that woman. I knew, very powerfully, that I would rather be single than trapped in a bad, distrustful marriage. I remembered, years ago, when I found my ex-husband out in a bar without his ring on. I was pregnant at the time, housebound and racked with nausea, and a friend offered to take me on a short drive for some fresh air. As we drove past a bar, she noticed his car in the parking lot. When we stopped in to say hi, he seemed nervous and not at all happy to see his wife. As we left the bar, my friend asked, "Why wasn't he wearing his wedding ring?" I stopped in my tracks. I hadn't even noticed. I returned to see for myself and ask him where his ring was. "It's in my pocket, it hurts my finger sometimes," he said. *I'll bet it does,* I thought. Shortly after the wedding, my husband's main form of communication was yelling. Remembering his drunken spells, lack of intimacy, and constant threats of divorce sent a shudder through my body. That relationship was a defining moment in my life. I knew then that if I ever became a parent, I would always ask myself, "Is this the kind of marriage I'd want for my children?" I never again wanted to feel trapped, and I certainly didn't want anyone else to ever feel trapped by me.

I knew how important it was, being able to leave a relationship that wasn't working. When I was seven years old, while we were living in Oxford, my parents divorced. It was difficult at the time, and took readjustments for all of us, but it has been the biggest blessing of my life. Their twenty-year marriage wasn't working, but when it ended, I got to see both my parents in happy, respectful relationships for the first time. It gave me an excellent example of what relationships could and should be. And when they found *their* happiness, it raised my own bar. I made romantic mistakes like everyone else, and I had to find my own way, but seeing what was possible—real, respectful contentment—helped me to wake up from bad situations.

At the party, I tried to shrug off these mean girls, but the miserable women wouldn't let me through without a response.

So I said, "You don't have to worry about me. There's literally *nothing* I find attractive about *any* of your husbands." I pushed past them and heard their guffaws. Animals weren't the only ones with pack mentality.

I left the party deflated and a bit disgusted. But the truth is, on some level I understood why the women were protective. It wasn't so much their husbands as it was their financial stability and perceived social status that they were protecting. As I'd come to find out, it wasn't particularly easy to make a decent living in small-town USA. And I'd come to realize that, regardless of sexual preference or location (city or country), people loved to say the words *husband* or *wife*—even if they despised the person they were married to. There was something about being hitched that seemed to give people a false sense of superiority. I understood it, because I felt the same when I was married, too, but deep down, it always felt programmed, inauthentic.

In an effort to get out of my head, I called Kelly on the drive home, ready for some honest girl talk. After telling her the story and sharing a generous amount of indignation, my cell service abruptly cut out. And there I was again, all alone.

Somehow, it was really just dawning on me that I'd moved to the Bible Belt as a single woman in her sexual prime. In the South, single women over the age of twenty-five are viewed as villains by many married women. Moving to Mississippi probably wasn't the best decision for my love or sex life, but I was determined to keep an open mind. Life wouldn't have led me here if love couldn't find me, right? At least now I had hope with Paul.

Only weeks after visiting him in Tampa, my daily communication with Paul was quickly lessening, turning into every-other-day texts, but I understood—we were both busy. One day I picked up the phone and actually called him, craving that human connection, but the call was brief. He was preoccupied with other things, struggling with managing his mother and his ex-girlfriend, who was, apparently, still inserting herself into his life. I, meanwhile, was having difficulty understanding how someone so strong in the business world could let other people dictate his private life. For someone who successfully managed financial clients and had an array of business interests, it surprised me that he wasn't firmer about setting boundaries in his personal relationships. I decided it was something to pay attention to.

Paul wanted a family, too. That's part of what had always connected us. But his ex-girlfriend knew how to twist this to her advantage. "I have to tell you something," he said cautiously, then plunged forward. "She said you are too old to have a healthy baby, that any kids we had would have problems. I have to tell you that scares me . . . a lot." With those words, I felt as if all the air went out of my lungs. It was as if everything I'd ever lost was suddenly front and center, all my greatest insecurities confirmed. I could actually *feel* the ache in my heart. I had no defense—against either my ghosts or this girl's psychological blow. It was emotional manipulation at its finest and had eaten away at Paul until he decided to tell me, so we could discuss *his* insecurities around it.

It was cruel, but effective. How could I fight for a future with him? What if I did "win," and it only ended in a string of more miscarriages? How would he react? Would I end up ruining his chances of parenthood as well? Most women give birth to life. All I'd ever given birth to was death.

The ego and biological desire for offspring could be equally as strong in men as in women. If his primary desire was to have children, it was true that there were no guarantees with me. And to make matters worse, his mother worked on him as well. He couldn't stop talking about it. "I saw my mother again today. She's still angry with me. She said I wasted a young girl's life and I should have married her." He seemed utterly distraught. I was incredulous that anyone would pressure their child into marrying someone. The emotional barriers piling up in front of us were starting to seem insurmountable.

I soon decided I wanted no part in the games and manipulations of Paul's mother and his ex-girlfriend, the women who claimed to love him. I wouldn't fight or defend myself in any way. I had lost faith in him as a man and potential partner and I knew I never wanted to feel I had to control or manipulate someone to keep them with me. Not long after I expressed all this, he decided, unsurprisingly, to get back together with his ex. He cited his time investment with her and his mother's desire as his reasons. Not love: *time and pressure. And now, there would be no fortieth-birthday celebration.*

Falling Short

If you've ever had a broken dream, you know that one of the hardest parts is the way you can encounter painful reminders of it in daily life. In Tampa, so many of my friends had gotten married and started families. I was happy for them, but seeing all these people with solid partners and growing bellies just exacerbated my own losses and reminded me of my long-standing desire to be a wife and mother. To be a part of something real. Had it felt like regular ole selfishness, it would have been easier to deal with, but this emotion ran much deeper. I felt like I was falling short not only of societal expectation, but also of an intense biological desire.

This, I knew, was part of the reason I now found myself living in rural Mississippi. I was doing my best to outrun those painful reminders, but after the breakup with Paul, I realized that even here, even in the middle of nowhere and even with the distractions of my rapidly growing farm, my broken dreams were reflected everywhere I looked. Holidays were the worst. Social media was chock-full of happy families, and adorable kids dressed in their fanciest clothes. Even though I knew that social media never told the full story, it felt like being kicked when I was already down: What I had struggled and failed to do seemed to come so easily to everyone else. This hurt wasn't passing or temporary; it existed in my very core. Maybe I had squandered my fertility by taking my time in the romance department. Maybe I should have settled for Chad or fought for Paul. But that didn't feel right either.

There was a gaping hole in my heart, and I feared it would be there forever; that when I was eighty years old, I'd still be carrying it around. After Paul and I broke things off, a darkness began to creep into my thoughts, but I pushed it away. I wasn't ready to let go. I wasn't willing to accept that my motherhood was lost. I couldn't. The thought of being a biological failure tore at my ego, and my heart. The passing months and years didn't seem to make it any easier. The burden only grew heavier. I could do nothing except try to ignore it and hope it would all go away. In a strange and terrible way, the ticking of my biological clock was becoming increasingly quiet.

My sister Jenifer called to ask if I'd like to come into town for Halloween. She and her ex-husband wanted to take my niece Andie trick-or-treating one last time before she was officially too cool to be chaperoned by her parents, and they asked me to be on candy duty at their house.

Upon my arrival, we enjoyed a cocktail while my niece finished putting on her unicorn costume. Shortly after they left, the first kids arrived and rang the doorbell. I heard the rustling of costumes and tiny voices on the other side of the door. Hearing the sweet voices made my heart melt and sink at the same time. With the candy bowl in hand, I opened the door repeatedly to the same scene: princesses, Power Rangers, zombies, all sorts of cute and creative creatures. The littlest ones were accompanied by their parents, who encouraged "pleases" and "thank yous." The parents of the older kids, mostly dads drinking beers or moms carrying cups of wine, stood off to the side enjoying their parental comradery. I noticed grandparents were often in tow as well. It's like they were in a club I didn't belong to. I so desperately wanted to enjoy this holiday with my parents, to see my own mother fuss over my kids' costumes. How wonderful it must be to connect with your own parents as a parent yourself. The thought felt like a stab. I inhaled deeply in an attempt to steady my emotions, but I couldn't help but wonder, *would I ever be part of their club?*

I'd always loved Halloween, and I'd been happy to help out my sister. I refused to let my grief rob me of a holiday like this—but the thing is, I couldn't tell grief what to do, when to be quiet, when not to rear its ugly head. So there I was, answering the door and doing my best to keep my composure as my heart ached with each "trick or treat!" Over and over again, I smiled and handed out candy and cooed over the costumes. Over and over again, I closed the door and broke down in hopelessness. It was like being trapped in a glass box filled with water, suspended in emotion. I could see those on the outside, but they couldn't really see me. I was losing my connection to the outside world as I reached grasping for everything I had lost and feared I would never have.

The next day, Brooke invited me over to visit. She was easy to talk to, and we were becoming close friends. No subject was off-limits.

"How was your Halloween?" she asked, knowing about my past.

"Not great. It was hard seeing all the families."

"I'm so sorry, girl. I know it must be difficult."

The sympathy in her bright green eyes was apparent. I nodded and we moved on to less heavy topics. As usual, our conversation jumped from subject to subject, with many thoughts left unfinished.

"I'm going to head home now, I need a nap," I said.

Brooke sighed.

"You have no idea how lucky you are. I love my life, and I love my family, but I miss the freedom to nap or go places whenever I want," she said.

I thought about the idea of freedom the entire drive home.

Naughty Animals

The bulk of my business dealings ran on conference calls. Usually, things went smoothly. But one day, the cell service inside my house dropped to zero bars. I had no time to run to town, so I had no choice but to take the call outside. I had to be where I could focus, away from distractions and noise interference, *especially* from farm animals. My car didn't have the space I needed to spread out, plus the sound from opening and closing the door would alert the animals to my presence. I would have to take the call on my porch, speak softly, and pray for privacy.

Seeing none of my animals, like a ninja, I crept out, quietly closing the door behind me. *So far so good.* With my trusty broom weapon next to me, I arranged my notes, pen, and morning tea and then dialed into the call. Everything went well for the first several minutes. Then, much to my horror, a series of extremely unfortunate events ensued.

At this point, I had several young roosters, courtesy of Francois and his hens. Francois was the first to arrive on the scene. *Crap.* I reached for my protective broom and waved it at him as the call began. Francois, knowing I meant business, puffed up his chest in defiance but kept his distance. Then the entire gang of four young roosters walked around the corner. Like teenage boys, they started tussling with one another.

It was my turn to lead the call. I was trying to sound professional while the young boys squared off with one another. They were all a foot apart, in an almost perfect square, and decided this was an excellent time to belt out their song at each other's faces— repeatedly, and all at the same time.

I silently mouthed death threats and attempted to shut down the crowing as I apologized profusely to the call participants, all of whom believed I was merely *visiting* a farm. When I turned back to my workspace, I caught Valentina nosing around. As I shooed her, she grabbed my notes and took off. I was able to snatch my notes back, but not before she had eaten a corner off. Then I turned to see Maybelle helping herself to my morning tea. She sipped it dry and, staring directly at me, smacked her lips. *Deep breaths. Deep breaths*, I told myself, trying to stay focused.

I calmly escorted the goats away from my workstation and sat back down on the porch swing to resume my attention to the call. That was when Valentina raised the stakes. She must have walked around to the other side of the porch because suddenly she was behind me, chewing at my hair. I yanked it out of her mouth and gave her a dirty look. I tried to ignore her, keeping my back to her and guarding my papers. As I took notes, she proceeded to rub her face on my arm as if it were her personal scratching post. Maybelle joined in on the other arm, causing my hand to slip, marking up my notes. *Sigh. This must be what it's like to have toddlers.*

I shooed them away again and kept talking when suddenly . . . *God, I'm so embarrassed to even write this* . . . there was a loud *farting* sound right behind me. Valentina had snorted. If you've never heard a goat snort, they are shockingly loud and sound like an enormous poot. There was zero chance the others on the conference call didn't hear it. Cell phones are like noise funnels for interference.

Everyone was silent, sitting in their city high-rise offices far away. I wanted to drop the phone and run, but it was too late. My face grew hot and my eyes teared up from utter embarrassment and frustration. I scrambled to explain myself, every ounce of professionalism gone. High-pitched words tumbled out: "Oh my god, um, animals make awful noises all the time . . . I swear I didn't just poot, that was a goat snorting!" No doubt I'd made all of us superuncomfortable, but they were kind enough to laugh. One man on the call was laughing so hard it sounded like he was crying.

At this point, embarrassed and sweating profusely, I extricated myself from the commotion, silently cursing my animals. I grabbed my notes and made my way to the driveway to hide behind my car and continue the call, out of sight of the animals.

Just as I was finally regaining my footing, one of the young roosters I was particularly fond of crept up behind me. Standing silently behind my back, only inches from the phone, he let out one hell of a crow, aimed directly at me. He put so much effort and volume into it that it hurt my ears. *How is this happening?* Content that his message had been delivered, he marched off, leaving me to deal with the mini heart attack I'd just had. I wondered if this was what parents who work from home dealt with constantly. The humiliation was complete.

It was an early morning in late fall and the sun was casting its lovely rays over the pond. I had already fed the animals and was just finishing cleaning my morning dishes; there was a low but distinct knock at the front door. "Are you expecting someone I don't know about?" I asked Kahuna lightheartedly. There was no car in the driveway, so I looked out the window of the front door. Still no one. I opened the door, expecting to see a child or a package. Instead, it was my geese.

The geese backed away and let out a collective, surprised *honk!* They looked at one another, then back at me. I don't know what was more astonishing: the fact that the geese had knocked on the door, or that animals could actually look surprised. From the expressions on their faces, I knew right away that I'd made a very bad error and I immediately shut the door. These birds were smart, smarter than some people I'd known. A few seconds later, I heard another distinct knock at the door. My suspicions were confirmed. I had fallen for it the first time, and now they were trying it again. *DAMMIT.* They now knew how to summon their human at will; they wouldn't simply *forget* that. I knew this wouldn't be the last time I answered a knock on my door to find my geese standing there.

My cute little Luca had quickly outgrown me. Even before he was considered fully grown, he was large, protective, and unruly, like a rough-and-tumble teenage boy. I noticed that when he was around Farmer John, Brice Noonan, and other men, he was a relaxed, happy puppy and listened fairly well. But with me and any other female, he was on constant high alert. If I was in the front yard and a car came by, Luca would chase it—not to play, but to protect me. He only relaxed when there were no possible threats around me or his animals.

I remembered the question a Karakachan breeder had asked me when I was searching for livestock guard dogs: "Do you have a husband?" I was offended at the time but soon realized that he wasn't being sexist, he was trying to help. The truth was that without a man around, Luca was hardwired to protect. He simply treated estrogen differently from testosterone. I saw this tendency in my other male animals as well, especially the turkeys. Around female turkeys or human women, the skin on a male turkey's head would turn a beautiful turquoise color. Around men, and especially traditionally hypermasculine men, their heads turned red. I could always tell what mood my male turkeys were in, or even if they approved of someone, by their head color. If their head was nearly white, it was an indication that they weren't feeling well. Ultimately, I found that all my animals constantly altered their behavior depending on the gender and energy of who was around them. They approved or disapproved of people all the time—just like humans do. We don't have to hear someone speak a word in order to make a snap decision about them. The difference is, animals don't have the social constraint to behave in a civilized manner. Animals don't lie about how they feel. My big puppy was just doing what came naturally.

Luca was also growing into an insufferable kleptomaniac. So far he had stolen several pairs of shoes, and various items from the neighborhood kids, such as scissors, vegetables, and even a welcome mat. Was he building a fort I didn't know about? At least he stole *pairs* of shoes rather than just one. Whenever a neighbor was missing something, they texted me. The kids learned to take their toys inside or risk losing them. I usually found these stolen things in Luca's hidey-holes, which he kept around the property. His goods would be neatly placed in the holes, covered in dirt and leaves. If I didn't watch him while he buried things, I'd never find them; he covered his holes that well. I also learned never to chase him when I caught him stealing. Pursuing him only made him run faster, and I could never keep up.

One crisp fall day, Luca brought home yet another neighbor's pumpkin decorations, acting perfectly innocent about it. "Stop stealing everybody's shit!" I barked at him. He just looked up at me and continued eating, his face stained orange. "Dogs don't even eat pumpkins! That's not a thing!" (Actually, it is.) I continued, exasperated. I'd already had to replace several pumpkins he'd stolen. He didn't go for the small decor. Luca subscribed to the "go big and take it home" philosophy.

Another day, a workman came out to tend to something on the property. Before he started, he placed his large hard hat and boots on the ground. I warned him: "Hey, my dog is a thief, I wouldn't leave anything on the ground if I were you." He looked at me like I was dumb and said, "Thanks, this stuff is heavy, it'll be fine." I shrugged my shoulders. "Suit yourself."

I sat in one of the rocking chairs on the front porch sipping a fresh cup of tea and waited for the show to begin. It was the first time I'd ever been excited to see my klepto dog take anything. The way the guy had dismissed me on my own property . . . I figured he deserved it.

As if on cue, Luca arrived. Like a stealth bomber, he trotted over and nonchalantly scooped up the helmet, then kept going without breaking his stride. I smiled from behind my teacup. The guy yelled "HEY! Come back here!" and took off after Luca. I called out, "If you chase him, you'll never see your helmet again!" But the man couldn't hear me over his own shouting.

He ran as fast as he could, but Luca, in total delight that someone was playing his favorite game, was quickly out of sight. "I tried to warn you," I said, even though the workman was too far gone to hear me.

Fortunately, the neighbors were cool about the embarrassing crap Luca pulled. "Gurrrl," Tricia had said, laughing, "this is country living. Dealing with naughty animals is just part of it!"

As I returned home on the day that I had sheepishly replaced my neighbor's pumpkins, I saw Luca trotting by, head held high, looking *quite* satisfied with himself. He was carrying a machete in his mouth. *A machete.* This long puppy phase might literally be the death of me.

Despite her old age and narcolepsy, Serafina was the ring leader of the flock and always commanded the charge for my groceries. As I exited the car one particular day, thankfully there was no sign of the animals. They usually had a group nap around this time. I removed the grocery bags as quickly and quietly as I could and made my way to the front door in a rapid tiptoe. Then I heard the distinct sound of little dinosaur feet slapping the pavement behind me. *Shit.*

I took off in a full waddle run, weighted down by too many bags. The animals easily caught up to me. Serafina was the first to jump up and tear the bottom of a bag. Somehow, she always seemed to know which one held the good stuff. The groceries fell to the ground and a zucchini rolled away. Luca was there to collect it and he swiftly ran off with his treat.

The chickens pecked as fast as they could at my raw vegetables. I opened a bag of peas and threw them to distract them from everything else. The birds ran to catch the flying peas and I made it inside. Before slamming the door, I shouted, "You guys are *ASSHOLES!*"

No Kidding Around

The holidays went by mostly unnoticed by me. But by February, Maybelle and Valentina were due to kid (i.e., give birth) at any time. In the fall, I had borrowed a beautiful buck from the Noonans to court my girls. We named him Rhett Butler, thanks to his black tuxedo coloring and prolific pouf of curly bangs between his ears. Both does were waddling around the property, heavy with babies. It was Valentina's first pregnancy and she was nervous, pacing and pawing at the ground continuously. There was amber-colored discharge coming from her vulva, and her udder was full and tight. I tried comparing her symptoms with Maybelle's, but this was Maybelle's second kidding and she showed zero signs of impending labor. It was business as usual for her.

My niece Krissy, who was staying with me at the time, was as nervous as I was. Krissy had moved from Colorado to attend Ole Miss, and after spending time on my farm, she was interested in veterinary school.

Trying to come to these labors as prepared as possible, I'd armed myself with internet knowledge about goat births, but truthfully, neither Krissy nor I had a clue what we were doing.

Worried about Valentina, I called the Noonans. This wasn't their first rodeo with birthing goats and Danielle was a vet tech. They were more than happy to visit and, hopefully, assist if needed.

Brice and Danielle checked both does over. They confirmed that Maybelle was acting normally and that Valentina was ready to drop her kids any moment. We set up shop in the barn with lawn chairs, music, and drinks and settled in for baby goat watch. Several hours passed and Valentina's body contractions produced nothing. Her ever-increasing stress wasn't helped by having so many people around, so Danielle and Brice decided to leave and give the laboring doe her space. By early evening, Valentina lay down and appeared to push. Maybelle, sensing her weakness, charged at the younger doe and landed a hard blow right to her baby belly. "Krissy!" I yelled. "Get Maybelle out of the barn!"

Maybelle had been out of the barn less than a minute when I heard a distinct sound. "Did you hear that?! It sounded like a baby goat!" Krissy and I both checked Valentina over, but there was no change. "What the hell?" I said. "I know I heard a baby goat! Did you check Maybelle when you put her outside?" Krissy shook her head no, grabbed a flashlight, and we both went outside.

Maybelle was standing there, looking normal. Then she turned to look at her side and perfectly mimicked the sound of a baby goat. Our eyes widened. She was talking to the babies inside her belly. Krissy aimed the flashlight at her. "Oh my god!" she said. "There's a baby coming out!"

Maybelle let out one long scream. Out of surprise, disgust, and solidarity, Krissy and I screamed with her. Then she pushed out one giant, jet-black kid. Luca, hearing three screaming women, came flying around the barn barking, not sure what the hell was going on. Maybelle had become a mother figure to Luca, and in a total panic, he tried to get inside the fence, pawing and whining frantically. Krissy and I did our best to comfort the animals as Maybelle tended to her giant buckling. But we were full of too much adrenaline, and, to be honest, a bit freaked out by the birth; we just kept repeating "it's okay, it's okay" in rapid, high-pitched tones. Our attempts to reassure and soothe Luca (and ourselves) had the opposite effect. We took Maybelle and the buckling back into the barn with Valentina. Maybelle, preoccupied with her newborn, would now leave the laboring young doe alone.

Just as Maybelle finished cleaning her buckling, she squatted briefly. With hardly a push, another baby fell out onto the floor in a rush of goo. This kid was tiny, but very much alive. Maybelle switched her attention to her fairylike doeling. The little cream-colored girl was so dainty and beautiful, and we couldn't wait for her to dry so we could cuddle her. Meanwhile, we tended to the big buckling, and poor Valentina's labor was still no further along. Valentina seemed to be content resting so, exhausted, we went to bed. I slept lightly, hoping Valentina would alert me if she needed help.

It was three A.M. when I heard Valentina scream. I jumped out of bed so fast that Kahuna went tumbling to the floor. I ran to the barn, barely noticing the brisk night air on my bare arms and legs. Maybelle was curled up with her now fluffed newborn twins. At first, I couldn't find Valentina. Then I saw she had crawled under a heavy, unmovable workbench. Some animals hide during labor, but, considering her condition, I didn't think hiding was a good sign. I crawled under the bench with her. She let out another scream that sounded just like a wailing woman. I tried to encourage her, but a strange sense of doom filled my heart.

The first kid was fighting to emerge, but Valentina seemed to be passing out or dying. Her scream was so piercing it felt like my ears were going to bleed. Her body contracted again, and finally a beautiful baby came sliding out. It was a sable-brown buckling with adorable ivory legs that looked like knee-high boots. He seemed to be a textbook birth, so I couldn't figure out why she had labored for so long. Valentina looked at her baby but made no efforts to clean him, as Maybelle had done with her twins. Completely saturated in birthing goo, he started shaking from the cold night air.

Now that one kid was out, I presumed that if Valentina had a second baby, like Maybelle's, it would be much easier. There appeared to be another baby coming, but Valentina had given up. She was just lying there, ignoring her baby boy, ignoring the warm molasses water I put in front of her for hydration and energy. I grabbed clean towels and hurriedly wiped the buckling's face and made sure he was breathing. He coughed and let out a loud baby cry. I placed him next to Valentina's head, hoping to encourage her to keep going and clean her baby, but she ignored the shivering newborn.

Valentina was exhausted. She had nothing left to give. She lay flat on her side, her eyes glassed over. There was blood and birthing goo everywhere. Perched on my elbows, wedged under a cramped bench, I was covered in slime and couldn't reach my phone to call for help. It was useless to yell for Krissy, who was sleeping at the far end of the house; with the heater on full blast, she would never hear me. I was desperate and alone with my paltry farm knowledge and couldn't hold myself together. Crying, praying out loud, terrified, I knew that three lives depended on me. I was quickly growing hysterical. With tears and snot running down my face, I begged Valentina to keep going. None of my book reading, YouTube watching, or city logic could help me out here. I felt utterly helpless. *What the hell was I even doing on a farm?* Leaving the city was a foolish fantasy, and now my ignorance was going to cost innocent lives. Just when I thought

I had this farm thing figured out, nature called my bluff. *You're a stupid, stupid girl!* I told myself, feeling horribly selfish and hating myself in the midst of a life-or-death crisis for which I was responsible. The results of my ignorance were lying on the cold, bloodied floor in front of me. *Who was I to ever think I was good enough to be a mother, I couldn't even keep a goat alive.*

Between my bouts of ugly crying and prayers, suddenly, the sack holding a second baby burst. The liquid drenched me, but by now, I was well beyond caring. Another contraction produced the appearance of a tiny, velvety nose, quivering like a rabbit's. It was alive! I could clearly see little pink lips. The next contraction exposed the baby's head. It opened its eyes. They were bright blue. The kid let out a weak, high-pitched whimper. That sound, coming from a bodyless head sticking out of a goat vagina, was unnerving.

Then my blood went cold. The feet should be first, *not the head.* SHIT! *No, no, no!* From the videos and diagrams I'd studied to prepare for the births, I knew that headfirst could mean trouble. After hours of labor, Valentina couldn't do this on her own. This was up to me.

I needed to push the baby back inside its mother, but I was scared I would suffocate it in the process, or hurt Valentina further. But I had to act. I took a deep breath and committed to following through, no matter what happened. Cupping the baby's little face to close its eyes, I gently pushed it back inside. "I'm sorry, I'm sorry, I'm sorry," I said in rapid succession, apologizing to Valentina and the baby repeatedly for my lack of experience. Valentina let out a weak cry. I knew I was hurting her.

The birthing goo made it easier to reach inside the doe. I slid my fingers down the baby's body to feel for front legs. First, I found an ear, then I followed along its neck and body and, somehow, I was able to find a tiny shoulder. I gently hooked my finger underneath the first leg. Slowly, I pulled that leg out. I repeated the action on the other side. Then, holding both little legs firmly, I watched Valentina's body for signs of the next contraction. Now in the right position, the baby slid out easily. It immediately started coughing and snorting, shaking its little head to get the goo out of its ears, nose, and mouth.

Valentina lifted her head and suddenly sprang to life. She sat up and immediately drank deeply from the warm molasses water. It seemed to give her the strength to clean her shivering first-born. Unfortunately, it meant I had to attend to his twin.

I was shaking from nerves, weepy, and still very unsure of what I was doing. I wrapped the second baby in a clean towel. It coughed and made a phlegmy, throat-clearing sound. I was afraid the act of pushing it back inside had put fluid in its lungs. All the while, Maybelle was watching the whole scene intently. She stood up and, leaving her own newborns, walked over to us. After her earlier attempt to hurt Valentina, I was concerned she was coming to deliver more blows. Instead, Maybelle sniffed Valentina but made no effort to hurt her. Then she turned her attention to me and the coughing baby. She gently sniffed my teary face. She seemed to want to see the baby I had swaddled. I was concerned she might be aggressive, but I held open the towel, exposing the newborn to the inquiring doe.

I would never have guessed that Maybelle, my mean and stubborn goat, who incessantly bullied Valentina, was capable of the tenderness and generosity of what happened next. Maybelle proceeded to clean Valentina's secondborn. She licked its little mouth and head dry, consuming all the birthing goo off the baby. I was stunned. As the magnitude of Maybelle's gesture sank in, I ugly cried again—only this time it was from relief, love, appreciation, and awe. Every part of me knew I was witnessing a miracle.

Knowing time was still of the essence, using the towel, I started mimicking Maybelle's licking motion with my hand over the rest of the baby's body. When Maybelle was satisfied that the baby was going to be okay, she allowed me to take over. She sniffed my face again, and I kissed her velvet nose in gratitude. I watched as she made her way back to her own twins, who were snuggled up together in a corner, already clean and soft with full bellies. I held Valentina's baby close—she was a girl, it turned out—threw my head back, and thanked the universe, hot tears pouring down my face. So many variables had come together, and everyone had survived.

Valentina was now on her feet, nursing her wobbly firstborn. His little tail wagged like a puppy's. I was relieved she was doting over her buckling, but I knew the secondborn doeling needed colostrum, quickly. Colostrum is a thick, yellowish precursor to milk, full of the nutrients newborns need to start a healthy life. When I presented Valentina with the doeling, she wanted nothing to do with her bright-eyed little girl. I ran to the house to wake Krissy. I needed a baby bottle right away (something I should have had on hand already!). Krissy got up and rushed to the only place open at three A.M.—Walmart. I worked on forcing Valentina to let her doeling nurse. It took forty-five minutes before she finally let her. "*Thank god!*" I said, when at last I saw the doeling latch on. Krissy returned and the bottle was, fortunately, not needed.

The little doeling was a miracle. She had unusually baby-soft, black fur with tan "boots" and ears and muzzle. Her blue eyes sparkled with life and she had perfect, smiling pink lips. Looking at her I realized she was my dream goat—the exact one I envisioned back in Tampa, before I ever thought a farm life was possible. "I think I'll call you Gemma Jane," I cooed.

I wanted to share my joy with some of my city friends. That

morning, when the rest of the world was awake, I texted them a series of adorable photographs. Kelly wrote back, "Why are you sending me pictures of rabbits?"

The trauma of Valentina's labor stayed with me for a long time. Fortunately, for her and the twins, everything ended well. For me, the entire event was a reminder of an old wound—my pregnancy losses, my own inability to make it to labor. My mind wandered back in time. The memories were still fresh, the pain more accessible than ever.

Broken Toys and Ghosts
of the Past

My second winter on the farm was a little easier. Simply due to staying power, I was getting a bit of credibility with my neighbors. This winter, I ordered firewood early and wouldn't let my well freeze due to rookie mistakes.

The best part of my house was the fireplace. I could sit by its warm glow all day and night, losing myself in the sounds, flickers, and shadows. All year, I found myself looking forward to fire season and its early darkness. I could burn through a cord of wood quickly, and I loved using my bonfire pit just as much. My hair constantly smelled of hardwood smoke. Each day I walked my little kingdom in search of things to burn, from sticks and paper to pine cones.

I had various people tell me, repeatedly, to make sure I bought seasoned wood. Seasoned wood is wood that has been allowed to dry over a long period of time. With less moisture, the wood is lighter and much easier to ignite. I always thought, *Duh, who would buy anything else?* Apparently, though, I would.

The first two orders I made, I just presumed the wood was

seasoned. After I used up those orders, a neighbor told me about another source for firewood. It was less expensive than what I had been buying. *Great!*

When this new vendor delivered the wood, I helped unload it. Carrying and lifting things around the farm was my replacement for the gym. But after the first few armloads, I realized how lightweight this particular load of wood was. I could carry much more than my usual limit. Surely, I hadn't gotten that much stronger from my farm chores. "This wood sure is light!" I commented as I merrily reloaded my arms again, feeling like Wonder Woman. The man gave me a weird look and with a thick, country accent replied, "What kinna wood you been buyin?" I thought about it for a second and said, "Um, hardwood . . . looks just like this, only it's much heavier." Shaking his head, chuckling, he responded, "Guuuurrlllll, you *are* from the city, aren't ya? I'll bet you've had a heck of a time g'ttin' fires goin."

Truthfully, when I thought about it, with those first two orders of wood, it did take me a long time to get my fire going and keep it going every day. Without a gas starter, I'd spent a lot of time tending to my fires. The wood had been very difficult to light. It popped and produced a lot of steam and had to be watched constantly. I just figured that was the way it was. I did find the pop and fizz of the wood to be highly entertaining, but it had been superannoying to have to repeatedly get up to stoke the fire. Evidently, the wood I'd been buying previously was green, fresh from the forest, and not at all ideal for burning.

Sure enough, the seasoned wood lit quickly and stayed lit. This was life changing. And to make it even better, I mixed in unseasoned wood. Now I had the pop and fizz I loved AND a lasting, easy-to-light fire.

I had a community of neighbors and fellow farmers, but life was still quite solitary. Sometimes weeks would go by and I wouldn't speak to or see another person. It surprised me how little this bothered me—in fact, how much I was completely okay with it. Had I gone a few days in the city without human interaction, it would have freaked me out. Now, it felt like the only thing I needed were my fur and feather babies.

It was easy to get lost in farm life with four baby goats around. I could—and did—cuddle them for hours. Their fur was like long velvet and their little faces smelled like fresh cream. I couldn't stop kissing them and inhaling their baby scent. I discovered my goats were a lot like cats without claws. They were soft and clean, they hated water, and they were always trying to climb things. And, like cats, their curiosity often got them into trouble.

Gemma Jane had become an adorably rambunctious addition to the farm. She seemed to be developing an odd habit of eating spiderwebs, but that was fine; the fewer spiders, the better, I figured. She and the other kids liked to chase and pluck tail feathers from the roosters and they loved playing on the giant fallen oak tree. Their favorite game was King of the Mountain. Anytime I bent over, they jumped onto my back, sometimes all four of them at the same time. I was a living toy, and I loved every minute of it.

I often kept my mind occupied in the kitchen. I'd loved cooking in Tampa, but having greater access to local foods and an abundance of time in the country fueled my experiments much further. It wasn't unusual to spend the whole day cooking. I would start with cinnamon rolls and by the end of the day have French bread, homemade chocolate, and roast chicken with fresh herbs.

After one of my kitchen days, I opened the back door to find Luca with something in his mouth. He dropped it at the foot of the stairs. It was a six-inch-tall Lego toy. Children had lived in this house before me, and their old toys were buried around the property. By this point, many of them had been unearthed by the chickens and squirreled away by Luca. The toys were bleached, dirty, and broken, and yet I couldn't bring myself to throw them away. In some cases, I couldn't bear to touch them at all.

The most enchanting toy was an old soccer ball. After Luca dug it up, it became his favorite thing to play with. Each day it moved to a new location around the property. One windy day I watched it roll across the grass, touched only by the invisible hands of the air. These were the moments when my mind traveled back, taking me far away from the farm.

The night before my first miscarriage, I had a prophetic dream. In it, I had a curly-haired, blue-eyed little boy. The toddler was partially hiding behind the railing of the staircase. He looked at me, waving his little hand, and said, "Bye-bye, Mommy." I bent over and sweetly asked, "Where are you going?" He simply smiled at me, then turned and disappeared. I woke up feeling strangely alone, and that was when I knew that something very real was wrong.

After that first miscarriage, I had desperately wanted to fill the void in my heart and arms. That was when I decided to get Kahuna. He was a puppy when I got him, and each birthday he had marked what would have been the age of my first child.

Thinking of Kahuna's tie to my first child sent chills bursting throughout my body as I watched the abandoned soccer ball silently moving across the property. The scene brought back that dream and the barren heartache, the devastating feeling of emptiness that followed. As the ball moved slowly across the ground, I hugged my little Kahuna tightly to my chest.

It took time, but the ghosts of my past finally caught up to me in Mississippi. The little toys appearing everywhere, thanks to Luca, were a reminder of the sorrow I didn't care to face. Paul was gone, and there were no other prospects around. I was now in my forties, but I kept telling myself that I still had a chance at a family. I had wanted children for so long, and I wasn't going to give that up. How do you let go of a dream like that? Why would I keep being presented with signs of what I didn't have, if I wasn't entitled to it?

But brushing off those nagging reminders of the past didn't make me stronger; it only made me feel delicate, breakable. After Luca proudly presented the Lego toy, I was frozen, afraid to move. My body felt like glass that would shatter into a billion shards if I even breathed.

By spring, the spastic southern weather was unseasonably warm. My little hilltop property started to green up and the daffodils and other bulb plants bloomed early. Daffodils symbolize new beginnings, rebirth. Looking at the clusters of these flowers coming up everywhere, it dawned on me what the name of my farm would be: *Daffodil Hill.*

With these signs of new life, I made it my mission to leave behind the stagnancy and darkness of winter and reconnect with society. The spring peepers, awoken early from their winter slumber, resumed their raucous party on the pond. I left the windows and doors open to the fresh air. This year, I would enjoy their music.

It was time, I knew, to stretch my own legs in the dating world. Jenifer had told me that my standards were too high, that

I was way too picky. It was annoying to hear, but I figured it couldn't hurt to see if she was right. I signed up for various dating sites and apps, including Match.com, Tinder, and, yes . . . FarmersOnly.com, a dating site geared toward people living (and farming) rurally.

I received over one hundred messages in less than a day, with not one interesting match. After a thorough search of its offerings, I quickly removed my profile from FarmersOnly. I decided that I was more of the "gentleman farmer" type, desiring a bit more sophistication and worldliness than what I was finding. Match.com wasn't much different, but definitely less authentic. Many of the people were creepy, trying to communicate with faceless profiles that felt predatory, or they seemed to have been on the site an extraordinarily long time. One thing was for sure, there were a lot of lonely guys out there. I felt sorry for all of us.

Being on Tinder in a college town was no picnic. The primary options were college guys seeking sugar mommas and divorcées desperately trying to recapture their lost youth or repair injured egos. The one man I connected with was in town for an upcoming college football game. We chatted for a bit until he asked me, "Are you married?" *Ummm.* I fired off a response, "No. Why would I be on a dating app if I were married? But now I suspect you are."

He denied it, but the dumbass had told me enough about his life that I was able to find out his wife's and kid's names with a thirty-second Google search. "If you contact me again, I will tell your wife. Remember her?" I wrote. After that, I deleted Tinder. No way was I risking getting into a relationship with a guy like that. Anytime a man mentioned only being able to communicate during the workday, never on nights and weekends, it was the telltale sign that he was married. I quickly lost all faith in online dating tactics. The initial rush of attention, while a nice ego boost, was diminished the moment I actually did a deep (or even a shallow) dive into the "suitors."

Eventually, my sister gave my number to a guy who lived in town, and she and several other people encouraged me to go on a date with him. She said he was outgoing, attractive, and successful. In the name of not having overly high standards, I accepted the date when he asked me out over text.

He offered to pick me up, but I thought better of it and told him I was happy to meet at his house. He responded with his address, followed by a picture of his large house for "visual reference." I recoiled at the obvious bragging, but since so many women had vouched for him, I was going to give him the benefit of the doubt.

When I pulled up to his house, there were so many cars in the driveway it looked like he was hosting a small party. He greeted me at the door. "Why do you have so many cars parked in your driveway?" I asked.

"Oh, one is my maid's, these are mine," he said, gesturing to a Range Rover and another car. "And that one belongs to my butler."

"You have a butler?" I asked, incredulous.

"Well, he's a friend of mine who fell on hard times. I'm letting him stay with me and help out."

Good lord, this guy is calling his poor friend his *butler* AND telling his business to a stranger? Another warning sign. "He's going to drive us in my Rover. We can sit in back and have cocktails while he drives."

"Okay. Well, I'd definitely love a cocktail." That was the best response I could give. In fact, I wanted several cocktails. I wasn't sure how I could fit in the back seat with this guy's ego getting larger by the moment. But again, in the name of being agreeable, I stayed.

We got to the restaurant, his "butler" in tow, and after a couple drinks, I relaxed a bit. Maybe I'd misread him. Maybe he really had a good heart. I didn't feel any physical attraction, but he seemed friendly enough . . . *until* he looked me in the eye and said with a completely straight face, "You know, you'd be really pretty if you wore more makeup, got your teeth fixed, and wore high heels." I laughed, thinking he was joking. Then he repeated himself. "I'm serious. You would be hot if you did those things."

I resisted the urge to throat punch this clueless cad. After chugging one more drink, I couldn't get home fast enough. I'd rather be alone than ever go out again with someone I didn't respect and wasn't attracted to. *Score one for my high standards,* I thought. Of course, my sister and the others who encouraged me to go out with him were also appalled by his behavior. It goes to show that social status is no indicator of good character. I vowed never to do that to myself again. Chemistry was important. Just because a man was single didn't mean he was right for me. And just because *I* was single didn't mean I was on the market for anyone. From then on, anytime another woman tried to set me up with a man, my first question to her was, "Would *you* have sex with him?" If not, why would they think I would want to?

The next morning, trying to put the horrible date behind me, I went to the barn and was surprised to find that one of my new does, gifted to me from a friend, had delivered a beautiful blue-eyed doeling. The baby was barely dried from birth, staring at me with large dilated pupils. The doe busily fussed over her new baby, ignoring everything else around her, including me as I tried to check on her. One of the teenage goats seemed utterly traumatized over witnessing the birth. The teenager kept yelling at me in her shrill little voice, as if I could do something about it. "I hear ya, sister. I feel the same," I shot back.

Maybelle and the other does were unfazed. They'd seen this before. Having a kid wasn't interesting to them when they weren't involved. After calming the traumatized teen, I slipped into the pen to inspect the new arrival. She was a perfect chubby single-ton and already had the nursing thing down. I was grateful that there seemed to be no complications. My animal family had grown as rapidly as my old handbag addiction.

My birthing duties were soon interrupted by a call from an old friend. He wanted to know if I would help chaperone a fraternity outing at Ole Miss. He was the fraternity adviser and often served as a confidant to the young men. A group from the frat and their dates were heading to a concert in Tupelo, and they needed someone over the age of twenty-five to ride in the van and attend the event. In exchange for chaperoning, they'd pay for my ticket and drinks, and I wouldn't even have to drive the van. It wasn't my ideal social situation, but college kids could be fun, and I needed to get out of the house, so I accepted.

When I arrived at the pickup point, my friend greeted me. "Jake! I want you to meet someone." A tall, well-dressed guy got out of the van and walked toward me. My friend introduced him as Gunnar.

I had to consciously close my mouth. Gunnar was nothing like the usual college guys I'd seen all over town with their long, swept-back bangs and concert tees or preppy appearances. He still looked young, but his style, wild curly brown hair, confident physical manner, and charm gave him a worldly air well beyond his years. His eyes were kind, bright, and focused intently on me. His physique and features were—I'm not kidding—as if Michel-angelo's statue of David had come to life. Few men my own age had sophisticated style or gentle but confident energy like his. He would stand out in any city, in any crowd, regardless of his age.

Gunnar shook my hand. Smiling and looking me in the eye, he said, "Hi, Jake! I've heard so much about you." Just then, an adorable young woman bounced over. Gunnar introduced her as his date, and, oddly, I felt relieved.

We piled into the van and the guys made drinks out of the little coolers they'd packed for the short trip to Tupelo. Gunnar sat behind me and asked what I wanted to drink. We chatted the entire way to the venue. His attention made me uncomfortable, but at the same time, I liked it. I hadn't casually chatted with a cute guy—or anyone—for a while. But I could feel his date staring at the back of my head. I couldn't imagine what it must feel like to watch your date become enamored with a woman twice your age. That would suck.

As the drive went on, our chatting turned to barely veiled flirting. When we arrived at the venue, I did my best to stay away from him. Strangely, his date befriended me and asked for dating advice: How could she make Gunnar be more interested in her? *This can't be happening*, I thought. I laughed nervously at the ridiculousness of the scenario and said, "If you don't think you're holding a man's attention, then maybe he isn't worth yours."

Toward the middle of the night, Gunnar caught me on the dance floor. "I'm not usually rude to my dates, but now that I met you I don't want to stop talking to you. You're not like the other girls I know or anyone I've ever met." I couldn't recall anything in particular that made our conversation in the van *that* interesting but the shy feeling I had made it obvious, if only to me, that there was chemistry.

I could barely look him in the eye. "Gunnar! I'm not like the other girls because I'm a woman twice their age!" I felt incredibly old and silly. *But man, if he were twenty years older,* I thought, *it would be ON.*

"What does that have to do with anything?" he asked. "Look, I need to deal with my date tonight, but I'm taking you out next week."

I laughed. "Gunnar! You're not listening to me! You can't be older than . . . ?"

"I'm twenty-two. And, no. I'm not listening to you," he said, giving me a serious look. "I'll call you next week."

Later that week, I went to a bar in town for a drink and ran into Gunnar. His face lit up when our eyes locked. He made a beeline and gave me a big bear hug, then he said, "I have a confession to make." I braced myself, and he continued, "I'm not twenty-two." *Oh no, this can't get worse.* But it did.

"I'm twenty."

I wanted to melt into the floor and slink away in total humiliation. But, of course, I didn't. Instead, I began a completely unexpected romance with twenty-year-old Gunnar.

The Birds and the Breeze

Of the many things I was too naive to understand before moving to the farm, I didn't expect so much backbreaking work and I didn't realize that I would never, ever have a day off. Inclement weather and illness weren't excuses. Eventually, though, I did discover a solution. As time went on, and my second year led into my third, I started being careful about the manual labor I took on by myself. If I hurt myself, I'd be screwed and my animals would suffer. So I began to find ways to outsource.

Ole Miss made kids who got in trouble complete community service hours. This program became a lifesaver for my farm. I started saving big projects for these kids and kept a running list of things they could do. So many kids started reaching out that I had to refer them to other farms. It made me even more grateful to be near a university. Need my barn painted? Chicken coop cleaned out? Debris removal after storms? Check, check, check! Some of the college students were utterly worthless at farmwork, but many gave me renewed hope in humanity.

At one point, a group of kids came to help me clear a large pile of old trash left from the previous owners. "If you see a snake, don't touch it, just let me know and I'll come get it," I instructed. Five minutes into their project, I heard a collective *GASP!* "*Miss Jake, Miss Jake!* There's a snake!"

As I ran toward them I yelled, "What kind?!" A girl answered, "We don't know, but it's blue!" *Wait. What?* Blue? Surely it was an old hose they uncovered, I thought. All six kids were standing away from the pile. "Where is it?" I asked, and they pointed at a small lizard, about five inches in length. It was black and had an electric blue tail. The lizard, apparently aware of its effect on the students, stood at the top of the pile, bowed up, facing them defensively. "Guys, that's a blue-tailed skink; it's a *lizard*," I said with a laugh.

I reached down and the lizard immediately ran away. "Everyone okay now?" I asked the group. They nodded. Then I heard yet another student yelling for me from behind the barn about fifty feet away. "Ma'am! Come here! I found one of your goat's horns on the ground!" When I found him by the goat pen, the kid opened his hand to reveal a small piece of pine cone. *Sheesh.* "Where are you from?" I asked him. "Boston," he replied. I nodded. "What's your major here?" I continued. "Theater," he said. I made a habit of asking where kids were from. Depending upon their answers, I found it increasingly interesting to see how they interacted with nature and my animals.

I had favorites among the college kids. One of them wanted to get in his work hours at night. The barn was trashed from the animals, but it was the only place he could work, since the rest of the property had no lights. I felt embarrassed by the state of it, and I tried to explain: "I'm so sorry about this mess but I haven't had time to deal with it. If you could tidy up a bit, that would be great." The kid's face lit up as he looked over the messy barn. Wheels were turning in his head. A few seconds later, he said, beaming, "Ma'am, I'm OCD. Cleaning this barn would be my pleasure."

"Umm, okay, great! I'm going to bed early so I won't be back out until morning but text if you need anything."

The next morning I woke up to a text from the kid that had come in around midnight. He said he had finished and was leaving and he thanked me for the hours. Opening the barn door, I was amazed. The place was *flawless*. Even the floor appeared to be scrubbed clean. All the feed was in proper bins, everything was put in order. He had organized everything better than I had ever thought to. All the tools were hanging neatly on the wall. Then I noticed the baling twine, which I saved off every bale of hay and straw. Baling twine is like gold, as useful as duct tape. This kid had not only untangled the twine, he *color-coordinated* it and hung it on the wall. Somehow he had even gotten the kinks out of the individual strands. I kind of hoped he would get in trouble again.

During Luca's first year, he still had a baby coat that was easily brushed and maintained. But the adult coat that grew in proved to be very different. This adult coat created mats at the end of his fur like crazy and he was forever rolling in vile things. To make matters worse, after he was neutered, he no longer let me get anywhere near his backside. My once-fluffy, beautiful boy was starting to look like the other ratty farm dogs I'd seen. Not wanting to be an irresponsible dog owner, I took him to the groomer to have him bathed and the mats cut out. Fortunately none of the mats were touching his skin, they just sort of hung in a mess. I knew not to shave him, because shaving removes a dog's natural air-conditioning and makes them several degrees hotter, which could prove deadly in southern summers. It also exposes their delicate pink skin to a much greater possibility of sunburn.

After his grooming, Luca was a changed dog. He was fluffy and smelled good for once, but he refused to interact with me or look at me at all. I tried bribing him with his favorite frozen meat treat but he ignored it. I was so dumbfounded by his behavior that I took pictures and posted them to my farm Facebook page. On the page shortly after, I received a message from a dog trainer:

"I know you think Luca looks better now but the reason he's acting this way is because you removed his coat of armor. He knows he can't defend himself well in a fight now. It's your vanity you need to worry about, not his. The loose mats and dirt on your dog not only assist in controlling pests, they also get caught in predators' mouths and disable attacks. Where he's getting the mats evolved naturally around sensitive areas as protection for the skin underneath. Working guard dogs need their coats intact. I know you didn't mean to hurt him but the next time you see him engage in a fight take the time to observe what's happening and how they fight and defend themselves."

Ouch. At first I was pissed about the verbal smackdown. I thought I was getting a handle on farm life after the first years, but things like this cropped up all the time—topics about which I just had no idea. So I decided to put my butthurt aside and do as the dog trainer suggested.

Fortunately, Luca had made himself sufficiently gross again by the time I did see him in a fight, against three German shepherd dogs who ran up onto the property. Rupert was the first to alert Luca to the threat. Maybelle, who had basically raised Luca and now loved him like one of her own, was developing a bad habit of facing off to strange dogs, or any predator that got Luca's attention. While the other goats would run to safety, Maybelle always backed Luca up in skirmishes. For this reason, I usually tried to intervene, chasing the other dogs off. But there would be times when I wouldn't be around to help. I had to let this play out, at least to a point, and the last thing I wanted to do was distract him.

It wasn't easy to fight the instinct to get involved. I prepared myself to jump in at the first sign of real trouble. Maybelle followed Luca's lead and started to run after him. Gemma and the other goats, now on high alert, bolted from the scene to watch at a safe distance. I ran after Maybelle and grabbed her by the collar. She pulled against me and cried out for Luca. "I know, baby, I'm scared, too," I said, white-knuckling her collar.

Luca chased the two smaller German shepherds, biting at their butts. Both dogs turned to bite back and received mouthfuls of hair and god only knows what else. Luca's hairy knots released easily with their bites and stuck to their mouths and faces like Velcro. The first two dogs ran away, trying desperately to get the filth and fur out of their mouths. They didn't even bark. With the two smaller dogs out of the way, Luca could engage the largest one. I held my breath. Maybelle pulled hard against my restraint, crying for her puppy.

And then, a strange feeling came over me: Despite what was happening, I knew everything was going to be okay. Luca's transformation was instant. My giant, fun-loving puppy had turned into a rabid wolf, a killer. The two large dogs connected for only a few seconds. In a flurry of hair and teeth the alpha shepherd, his weapon disarmed thanks to the mats of hair in his mouth, ran for his life. Maybelle screamed for Luca but he stayed hot on the disruptive dog's trail and refused to stop his attack. I watched as Luca grabbed the dog and, propelled by their momentum, they tumbled down a small ravine in a spiral of tails and teeth. As they disappeared from sight I held my breath and my panicked doe. I heard the shepherd cry out, then saw him fleeing the ravine,

Luca chasing him down the road. A minute later Luca returned, strutting about like he hadn't even broken a sweat.

I released Maybelle and we both ran to our hero like his personal cheerleaders welcoming him home from the winning championship game. I checked him over for wounds. There were none. Luca had handled three marauding dogs beautifully and quickly. My eyes were opened. I had a completely new respect for my dog and a breed bred to guard independently of human intervention. I'd been faithfully observing my other animals—the chickens, geese, and goats—but I hadn't brought that same loving curiosity to Luca's behaviors, because I thought I already knew dogs. I had always had companion dogs, though. Now, I held working dogs in much higher regard. When it came to Luca, I'd always seen his habits as more of a stinky nuisance. How wrong I was. Those three dogs, which I had tried repeatedly to keep off my property in the months before, never returned.

While farm life wasn't exactly what I expected, it was also becoming everything I didn't know I needed. Even though I was completely tethered to my farm, which I hadn't anticipated, I felt that I had so much more freedom than I had in Tampa, and I felt much more present in my daily life. I could breathe easier and be more creative with the way I lived. In fact, farm life *demanded* creativity. If something broke, I had to make it work with what I had on hand. I loved conquering those small challenges. Instead of dealing with the anxiety of possibly running late for meetings, my morning routine consisted of sitting on the porch, soaking in a little sunshine and fresh country air, while taking mental notes of all the chores and work duties I needed to do that day.

Most of the chores doubled as fresh-air gym workouts with the added benefit of making things tidy, if only for a few moments. Nearly all the tasks were in service to the animals, and each day my physical exertion was truly a labor of love. But there were some things I still thought of as "men's work"—basically anything that made me sweat too much or could ruin my nail polish. I still had *some* vanity left. One such chore was cleaning the gutters. The large oak tree that hung over my house tended to drop leaves directly into them.

When my oldest brother, Mark, visited from Colorado the previous spring, he went to clear out the gutters for me. But two minutes later, he was back in the house; there was no way he could have cleaned them that quickly.

Surprised, I asked, "Is something wrong? Do you need me?" He responded, "The gutters are already clean." *How is that possible?* I had never cleaned them. "I guess it was the gutter fairy," I said. At the time, I shrugged it off.

The following fall, as I sat on the porch one morning, a shower of dead, wet leaves suddenly rained down from the roof. Luca didn't appear alarmed. Every few seconds, the debris seemed to propel itself out of the gutter. Occasionally it would stop for a couple minutes, then start again. I couldn't see anything from my viewpoint and none of the animals seemed to care. If it were a rat or squirrel, Luca would have reacted. But he just lay there, looking bored. *Just what was going on here?* The leaves appeared to be actually jumping out of my gutters.

Then I saw a blue jay fly away with a rotten acorn in his mouth. A minute later, he returned and resumed his dutiful exploration of my gutters, searching for food. He swept the entire gutter trail and kicked out loads of heavy dead leaves with his little stick legs. *That's one lucky female blue jay who has that guy for a mate,* I thought. *He's smart, strong, and resourceful . . .*

Thinking of the blue jay triggered a childhood memory. When I was five, my parents sent me to a Montessori school that often hosted a Native American chief. He was an old man, with a heavily lined face and dark, kind eyes. The last time I saw him, he said he wanted to tell us each what our animal spirits were. This got all the children excited and we quieted down quickly to hear what he had to say. When it was finally my turn, he put me in his lap and said, "Your animal spirit is the jay bird." My dismay and response were immediate:"But I don't want it to be a jay bird!" He smiled patiently. "It's a jay bird for now but one day it will become a jaguar." That answer made me beam. In my kid's mind, I had just gone from the worst animal to one of the coolest.

Watching that resourceful bird digging deeply through muck only to be rewarded by finding treasure resonated somehow. In her own way, nature had delivered on my Disney-style farm fantasy, in which animals sang to me and helped me with chores. Of course it wasn't exactly what I'd envisioned, but I suppose a wild bird rummaging through my gutters was close enough. As I watched this little bird end his search and finally fly away, I marveled that its own weight didn't stop it from flying.

One thing about farm life that was *not* out of a Disney movie and for which I wasn't prepared was the sheer amount of sex.

Farm fornicating doesn't just occur in springtime. It's year-round, with an increase in spring. Depending on the species, animal sex can be noisy and downright obscene. Animals have no shame—they don't care who sees them going at it. It was endlessly embarrassing on occasions when I had farm visitors.

When the goats are interested in mating, their behavior is particularly disgusting. I had decided to keep one of Maybelle's bucklings from the following spring, and now Valentino was a big, beautiful buck with a black and gray coat accenting his striking blue eyes. He acted more like a dog than anything; in fact, he became fast friends with Luca. They played *hard*, running around the property like wild kids. Luca would bite at Valentino's legs and Valentino would rear up and headbutt Luca. They regularly just beat the hell out of each other. It wasn't unusual to see cars stopped at the edge of my property, the passersby watching the animal antics on my front lawn. Valentino was as naughty as Luca and impossible to keep penned. Each night I would put him to bed in the pen and each morning I would wake up to find him on the front porch, lounging with Luca as if he were just another dog. He could jump most of the fences on my property. And if he couldn't jump them, he often bullied himself right through the wire. While the male animals tended to be the most entertaining, they also gave me the biggest headaches and did the grossest things.

It was officially fall-mating time; Valentino turned his attention to the does. He reeked to high heaven—I could always smell him before I saw him. Bucks have a disgusting habit of peeing on their faces and—I'm not kidding—*in their own mouths* to attract the does. What would seem like an impossible feat for most males is easy for goats; they simply extend their very long, skinny penis and put their face toward it, then they spray their urine. *It is disgusting.* And you know those goat videos and commercials that feature bucks yelling and wagging their tongues, spewing spittle at the camera? That's real, too. During rut (periods of time when love is in the air) my sweet Valentino would become a sex machine. I could barely deal with him. I started entertaining myself by blasting the Bee Gees' "Stayin' Alive" in the barnyard while he paraded and bounced around the property in all his stinky glory. Valentino made the perfect John Travolta as he strutted to the music. (I often found myself making up songs, creating playlists or setting the animal behavior to music . . . after a few slow years in Mississippi, I'd officially replaced the bar scene with the barn scene.) The does could be equally obscene. They transformed from my affectionate fur babies into noisy, tail-wagging little humpers. Often, I opted to stay inside during the full-on goat orgies.

I'm not sure what disturbed me most about goat sex: the smells, the uncomfortable courting rituals, or the actual act itself. Goats have penises that look a little like long pencils. The sex lasts about two seconds, then the buck throws his head back in ecstasy and disengages. *Figures.* I don't know why the does give bucks the time of day.

Usually, animal sex is preceded by courting. With poultry sex, for instance, there's lots of dancing involved. Roosters lure the girls in with offers of food or bravado, then dance around them. Some girls love time with their man; others not so much. Some hens, like Bria, angrily beat the crap out of the rooster afterward. I now totally get the term "henpecked." The girls who don't like roosters tend to steer clear of them and won't go into the coop at night.

Geese have a beautiful water dance and make haunting sounds. Since my geese had some privacy on the pond, I didn't have to witness the graphic details. I could simply enjoy the water dance from afar.

Male turkeys have "beards," which is a small bunch of wire-haired whiskers protruding from their chests. It's just chest hair, basically, and it tends to grow longer as they age. Like many women who grew up during the Tom Selleck era, turkey hens seem to really love chest hair. They will walk up to the male of their choice and grab it, pull on it, put their face in it, even motorboat it. It's the turkey hen equivalent of a flirty butt smack. *My kinda girls!* The toms seem to enjoy this attention and puff their chests out as much as they can. Beyond that, turkeys have the most awkward sex imaginable. The hen crouches on the ground while the male dances around her before finally—again, I'm not kidding—*standing on her back* to *eventually* do the deed. Sometimes this lasts for quite a while. He stands on her back, making every effort not to slip off, while the female lifts her tail. It's incredibly awkward and painful to witness. I have no idea how we have baby turkeys.

Then there are the ducks. Male ducks, called drakes, are the Casanovas of the waterfowl world. My drakes were driving every female crazy. And I mean *every* female on the farm. They had no standards. Sure, they preferred a nice female duck, but ultimately, species was of no consequence. To make matters worse, drakes have obnoxiously large private parts and often have the attitude to go with it. They do it on land, in the water, anytime the mood strikes, year-round. Drakes were some of the most annoying animals on my farm.

Maybe I was buoyed by this farmwide rush of hormones, but on hot days, I also started taking certain liberties—such as dropping trou whenever I felt like it. One early fall afternoon, overheated from my chores, I whipped my pants off and threw them into the grass down by the pond. I would never strip down in the city, but in rural life, on my own property, it was no biggie. There was no one to see me, so I did it all the time. This time, of course, while I was wearing nothing but a flimsy tee shirt and lacey thong panties, I heard a loud motor revving up the road. It's unusual for people to drop by unannounced in the country, so I didn't think much of it. I craned my neck to see who was coming over the hill.

It was Farmer John. I ducked and presumed he was just passing by. Then he turned up my driveway. *Shit.*

I looked frantically for my discarded pants. It was too late. If I ran to them, I'd show my bare bum to this very religious man and embarrass us both. I decided to yank down the front of my shirt, act like everything was normal, and hope the ever-present breeze didn't expose my panty predicament.

I kept one hand nonchalantly over my crotch region as I greeted him, realizing with horror that by tugging on the front of my shirt, I was exposing my bum even more in the back. Either Farmer John was being superpolite or was completely oblivious, because he stayed to chat. We made our way over to the goat pen I'd recently added. I carefully walked behind him, holding my shirt down.

There's something about new fencing that all farmers are drawn to. Since installing it I had seen several of them pull up and get out of their trucks just to inspect my fence. I would watch from the window as they tested it for sturdiness and then nodded to themselves in approval. I felt proud, like I'd finally arrived. It was as if I had a hot new Ferrari in my driveway and they felt compelled to kick the tires.

Soon, we looked up to see another truck driving by—Farmer Alfred. To my absolute horror, Farmer John waved him over to us. *Shit. Shit. Shit.*

I greeted Farmer Alfred with my free hand and we all started chatting. There I was, having farm talk with two legit farmers, like I was part of their clan. One small breeze would reveal my lace thong, but I couldn't turn and walk away because my ass was showing. I stayed frozen in place, starting to sweat from anxiety while the two men discussed this year's cotton yield and then moved on to debating the best watermelon varieties to plant. I felt just like one of the boys, talking farm while in my panties. Did you know there's a particular variety to plant if you want watermelons to survive shipping and another kind that's just plain old good eatin'? Mississippi is *really* into its watermelon growing.

When the guys finally departed, I stood in the driveway, smiling like a moron and waving goodbye with my free hand. Slowly, I backed up until they were safely out of sight before turning to run and retrieve my pants.

Meanwhile, Gunnar and I were getting a good thing going. It certainly didn't hurt that he looked like a Greek god and treated me like a queen. We saw each other when we could, going out for dinners or occasional concerts. Still feeling sheepish about the age difference, I preferred to keep things low-key. We had deep, honest conversations and a pressure-free relationship, since we both knew this had an expiration date. I vowed that I wouldn't limit the rest of his college experience in any way and knew that, ultimately, I wanted someone I could better relate to in terms of life experience.

At one point while we were dating, Gunnar needed a ride back to his place. He directed me toward his house. As we got closer to campus, I started to get nervous. "Where *exactly* is your house?"

"It's on campus. I live in the Pike house for now."

"I'm dropping you off at a frat house?!" I shrieked. I should have known. When we talked previously about our "houses," I naively presumed he was talking about an actual single-family home. Mortified, I resisted the urge to slump down as far as I could into the driver's seat. I'd never been more grateful for oversized sunglasses and couldn't get him out of the car fast enough.

But on the drive back to the farm, I reasoned that men date much younger girls all the time. In fact, they often act entitled to it. I'd briefly dated a man twenty years older than me, and no one around us batted an eye; so why was *this* twenty-year age gap so embarrassing? I decided I wasn't going to let my insecurities ruin a good thing.

I hadn't yet introduced Gunnar to any of my Oxford friends, but in the fall, I decided to take the plunge. The plan was to have dinner with Brooke at a local restaurant on the busy town square. I figured most people would look at us and just think Gunnar was my son, anyway, so I wasn't too stressed about being out in the open.

Dinner went well. Gunnar held his own with worldly Brooke, who seemed amused by us as a couple. When he excused himself for a bathroom break, she looked at me with her devilish grin and said, "I can see what you see in him. He's a little hottie!" Later, he put his hand on my leg under the table. My own self-consciousness aside, I loved that our age difference didn't seem to faze him.

As dinner wrapped up, I checked my phone and saw that I'd missed a text. It was my friend Kathryn's daughter, Hayden, who watched my farm on the rare occasions I had to be away. She knew I was on the square and invited our little group to a house party a block away. When I told her I was with Gunnar, she responded, "Bring him, too!" The thought of all of us arriving together at this college party was just too much for me to handle. (The last time I stopped by one of Hayden's house parties, I got hit on by a twenty-one-year-old guy. I didn't realize we had an audience until I turned him down and laughter erupted behind us. One kid announced, "DUDE! YOU JUST GOT TURNED DOWN BY A FORTY-YEAR-OLD WOMAN!" Ugh.) Fortunately, Gunnar had other plans, so Brooke and I would say goodbye to him, stop by the party just to say "hi," and promptly leave. I could handle that.

But when we left the restaurant, Gunnar insisted on escorting us to the party. The streets were bustling with college kids, and Gunnar grabbed my hand. *So much for keeping things on the down low,* I thought. Brooke's eyes shot to our hands. Sensing my discomfort, she raised her perfect eyebrows and slyly grinned. *Shut up,* I mouthed.

As we approached the house party, I told Gunnar to head on to his event, hoping no one would see us together. It was too late. As he dropped my hand, he gave me a kiss and hug goodbye. Of course, every college kid at the party was standing in the front yard to witness the display. To make matters more embarrassing, Gunnar waved to several of the smirking frat boys. "Hey, guys, what's up?" he called out.

As Gunnar and I parted ways, both of Kathryn's kids, who in many ways felt like my own children, saw me and burst out, "Jake! Did you just walk up holding the Pike president's hand?!"

I smiled and said, "Actually, he was holding *my* hand."

Might as well own it, I thought.

The Noonans were always hosting get-togethers, so I felt it was time to host my own. Kathryn was in town for the weekend, and the fall weather was perfect for a bonfire. While I was busy preparing for the festivities, I was contacted by a group organization for families with children with special needs who had heard about my farm. They asked if they could come out to see the animals. It wasn't the most convenient time, but I agreed to the visit.

They arrived with kids of all ages, who were quickly running everywhere. One kid kept chasing the chickens. Chasing chickens (or any animal) is a big no-no. I gathered the kids to explain the farm rules and why chasing animals frightens them and makes them distrustful of humans. I encouraged simply being still and allowing the animals to come to them, to build trust.

While I was bent over, answering questions from the kids, one of my young goats, Ellie, walked behind me, brushing her little head against my backside. Ellie and her needle-sharp horns had been a challenge for me. She'd already accidentally given me a black eye and punctured my lower jaw with her spastic movements. She was like a baby who barely had head control.

Despite Ellie's sharp horns, the kids loved her. She was adorable, with the most vivid blue eyes. Then, she started pooping. This triggered the chickens to come running to the poop buffet. Some of the kids looked horrified, others were laughing.

At this point, I knew I had to explain what was happening. All I could think to say was, "We recycle everything here." A couple parents chuckled, but the kids actually seemed to accept the explanation. Then our attention was drawn to Luca and Valentino, my male goat. At the time, Luca was minding his own business, more interested in human interaction than his goat friend. But Valentino wanted to play and wasn't accepting Luca ignoring him, so he pawed at the dog's back. Luca swatted him away.

Nothing is more stubborn than a goat. Valentino, undeterred, simply put his head down, pulled out a big chunk of Luca's hair, and proceeded to eat it. This was always the buck's way of goading Luca into a fight. To the delight of the bystanders, it worked. An interspecies fight was always interesting and could get rough at times. The pair ran around leaping, headbutting, biting, and pawing each other—when suddenly Luca jumped on the buck's back and started humping him enthusiastically. I could feel the blood light up my cheeks.

The young kids were wide-eyed. The older ones, and the parents, were smirking. Mortified, I spoke up, "Yeahh, they like to play rough sometimes and Luca really enjoys hugging." One dad with a huge grin piped up: "It's obvious he really gets into *hugging*. I'm a *hugger,* too." I nodded and grinned in embarrassment, feeling my cheeks growing brighter.

Two of the older boys, probably around eleven or twelve, had been prowling around in the woods. When they emerged, they started chasing each other and fighting with large fallen branches. This got Luca's attention, so the boys started playing chase with him. Alarmed, I told the parents: "The older kids are welcome to play with Luca, but if they run from him, he *will* take them down." The parents called the boys over and I explained Luca's trigger. "He doesn't do it to hurt you, but he's so big he can accidentally hurt you. AND he's too fast to run away from. I'm giving you fair warning that if you don't want to go face-first into the ground, don't run around the farm."

For some reason, to a boy's mind, that warning actually sounded like an invitation, or a challenge. The father recognized the frisky look in his son's eyes and said, "You heard her, you're asking for it if you play chase with the dog." The kid took off running anyway. Luca, seemingly on the exact same wavelength, gave him a good head start, then raced after him in hot pursuit. "This isn't going to end well," I told the father. He responded, "Well, we can enjoy the entertainment in the meantime. My son always has to learn the hard way."

The kid was in a full sprint toward the pond, grinning from ear to ear. The smile disappeared, though, when he looked over his shoulder to realize the large dog had nearly caught up with him. Just as the kid reached the basin of the pond, Luca leapt high and effortlessly took down his prey. They disappeared into the basin and we all heard a loud splash. There was silence, then a few seconds later the pair emerged from the pond, soaking wet. The kid looked defeated, but not hurt, thank god. Luca was panting, supersatisfied with himself. "Man, I wish I would have videoed that!" his dad said.

Seeing the attention the older boy was getting, the younger one took off running. Luca, not one to miss an opportunity, followed suit. The younger one was easier to take down, and this time it happened in full view of everyone. As soon as the kid was on the ground, Luca proceeded to start humping him wildly. "Oh god, I'm so sorry!" I said to the parents, and ran to rescue the boy, but not before I heard the little sister say, "Daddy, they're hugging!"

When the visit was finally over, I got back to my tasks for the cookout. While cleaning the house, I passed a mirror and something white on my butt caught my attention. "Please tell me I haven't been walking around with chicken crap on my butt . . ." I said. I backed up to discover a two-inch hole in my pants. The white was part of my exposed butt cheeks . . . and my crack. Cheek is one thing, but butt crack is quite another. With surgical precision, Ellie's little razor-sharp horns had struck again, and there was no way the families hadn't seen it.

The cookout guests, including the Noonans, family, friends, and some college kids who helped on the farm, arrived. My bonfire was in full swing. The animals were put up for the evening except for the turkeys, who liked to be front and center with their gobbling commentary. Since the turkeys were decent short-distance flyers, I had no choice but to give them free range; no pen could keep them and they roosted high in the trees at night anyway. None of my adult males were aggressive. Most were shy, except for Rupert, who was gentle with everyone and loved children, often letting them pet and hug him.

I saw Danielle eyeballing Rupert. Then she asked, "Do you ever burp him?"

"Come again?" I said. Surely, I thought, I had misunderstood her question.

"Do you ever burp Rupert?" she said again, smiling. This made everyone laugh.

"No. Can't say that I have. How and why would one burp a turkey?"

Danielle had everyone's full attention as she sauntered over to Rupert, straddled the big bird and put her arms around him in a bear hug. She pressed into his overblown chest as if she were doing the Heimlich maneuver. To everyone's surprise, Rupert let out an enormous belch. The spectators roared with laughter. Rupert, who was a very dignified turkey, was none too happy with what had just transpired. He quickly inhaled deeply to refill his air sac.

"Oh my god!" I exclaimed. "I had no idea you could do that! What? . . . Why? . . . *How?*"

"Turkeys use their big air pouches to puff out their chests and make that drumming sound. It's just a fun party trick, it doesn't hurt them," she explained.

After Rupert regained his composure, his head started turning red. He was annoyed. Several guests wanted to see the burp again. Danielle obliged. This time, Rupert retaliated. He craned his long neck and turned to grab Danielle's hair, shaking it violently. Danielle quickly let him go. He didn't hurt her, but he did effectively communicate that he didn't enjoy the uncivilized behavior. Rupert was a turkey with boundaries. Sometimes I thought I could learn a few things from him.

Later that evening, when the guests departed and the bonfire was nearly out, Kathryn and I were finally able to sit on the porch and catch up on life. Earlier in the day, I had noticed her new shoes. They were ultrapadded sandals in a drab putty color that looked like something Fred Flintstone would have worn. Even though I'd lived on a farm for a while, I still had standards, and these shoes were atrocious, so, unlike my city self, I refrained from commenting on them. But she brought them up. "Did you notice my new shoes? They're so comfortable, I love them!" Well, she *asked*.

"I noticed them. They're ugly as hell. You can't wear those if you go anywhere with me," I said. There are some women who prefer their friends to *not* look fabulous. I wasn't one of them. In my mind, the better my friends looked, the higher my stock went, too. And with my closest friends, like Kathryn, I didn't see any point in being dishonest.

Kathryn laughed. "I knew you'd have something to say about them."

"And yet you wore them anyway. Are they orthotics?" I said, unable to stop myself.

"No, but they *are* incredibly comfortable," she responded, kicking them off next to her rocking chair.

We continued to stare off into the night sky. On cooler nights like this, the stars were brilliant and abundant. We gabbed about life, drank cocktails, and received visits from the cats. Both girls loved Kathryn; she was a cat person and they knew it. Luca decided to swing by and lay down next to us for a brief stint. I put my bare feet into his thick, warm coat, like he was a bearskin rug.

When we were finally ready to go to bed, Kathryn put her feet down to search for her awful new shoes. "I can't find my shoes . . . did you move them?" she asked, a bit alarmed.

"I can't take credit for that. They must be there," I said, turning on the porch light.

The shoes were not there. "OMG, did Luca steal them!?" she asked, knowing Luca's penchant for theft. "Surely not. I'd like to think he has better standards," I responded. But she was right—the shoes were missing and Luca was the prime suspect. I got a headlamp and we made our way out to one of his hidey-holes.

I didn't have to dig far to unearth her shoes. There they were, dusty but still perfectly intact, side by side in his hole. "I can't believe you knew right where to find them!" she said, surprised.

"We got lucky, this is a new hole I saw him covering earlier today."

Back inside the house as we readied ourselves for bed, Kathryn popped her head into my room.

"Hey, I wanted to thank you for taking care of Hayden while she was sick. It means a lot to know she has someone here since I moved away." Hayden had started reaching out and dropping by to see me often. When she had been admitted to the hospital for an allergic reaction, I visited her and then took her in during her recovery.

"No need to thank me. I'm happy to do it. And besides, I love spending time with her."

As I fell asleep I recalled a day Hayden had come over just to watch cartoons and eat cereal. For a brief moment, I'd felt like a mom. She had started referring to me as "Som," which she told me meant "second mom." I always had to stop myself from getting misty-eyed each time she said it.

The Rainbow Salesman Returns

On the morning of my forty-second birthday, I woke up to several texts. I stared at my phone, blinking and bleary-eyed from sleep and disbelief. Paul had texted me birthday sentiments early in the morning from his deer-hunting camp in West Virginia. It was a place he visited annually to get away. At this point, I was still happily seeing Gunnar and had given up on Paul and the dream he had been selling me for some time. I responded casually, thanking him for the well wishes.

During my morning farm chores, I left my phone in the house. When I checked it later, there was a book-length text from Paul. He told me that he still thought about me every day, that I had no idea how many times he'd checked my status on Facebook. He said that whenever anyone asked why he wasn't married, he told them about me. He lamented his current situation with the same girl we'd had issues with previously and explained how disappointed he was in himself that he let it get this far and wasted so much time. He said that even if I never wanted to speak to him again, he knew she wasn't for him and never had been—he'd succumbed to outside pressure. On and on he poured his heart out and somehow made the text feel intimate. When he described how hard it had been to think of me every day and not be able to tell me . . . it hit me like Cupid's arrow.

I was floored. I reread his text several times before responding. This was everything I could have wanted him to say to me. He had put it all out there, and I knew the courage it took to be this honest. He was taking a big chance knowing that I might reject him. Whenever someone was vulnerable and communicated their heart, without filter, it immediately got my attention.

Soon after, we spoke briefly over the phone. He said he no longer cared about having children. If we couldn't have them, that was fine with him; he just wanted to be happy and see things through with me. He informed me that he had yet to end things completely with the girl but assured me he'd have her out of his house and life by the new year. That single text and subsequent conversation rekindled what I thought was dead forever. And that rainbow life appeared again.

With winter and the cold weather arriving in December, I brought my recently acquired baby chicks into the house for warmth. I'd received them as a gift from a farm friend. Most mornings the chicks were up before me, playing and chattering to one another. Their incessant chitchat was cute, but also annoying, since I didn't have to get up that early. Chickens are hardcore early risers and can perceive daylight long before human eyes can. Like some people, they tend to sit in bed having their version of pillow talk before they officially start their day. They can do this for hours. Snuggled up to Kahuna in my warm bed, I'd listen to these tiny birds discussing who knows what. "They're probably talking about us," I'd whisper to Kahuna.

One particularly chilly morning there was silence—always

suspicious when you have animals, especially toddler animals. I crept down the hallway, not sure what I would find.

As I approached their brooder—the warm nursery baby birds are kept in—I realized I had neglected to close its lid the night before. All but two babies were precariously perched on top of the brooder, as if this was perfectly acceptable behavior. They hadn't noticed me yet, so I silently watched them for a minute. They were talking to one another, quietly. I didn't even know chickens could whisper, but that's exactly what they were doing.

Finally, in a low voice, I asked: "What do y'all think you're doing?" I found myself asking my animals this question a lot. Five little chicken heads snapped to look at me. *Busted.* They immediately got quiet and froze, wide-eyed. So, they *did* know this was unacceptable behavior. And to make matters worse, all their bums were facing *out* of the brooder. It was obvious from the droppings on my floor that they had been perched there all night.

They protested loudly as I placed them back inside, one by one, and closed the lid. Of course, I made sure to express my displeasure by cuddling each one of them first. Punishments were tough on my farm.

I was still missing two chicks, but they couldn't have gone far, I told myself. The first baby I found quickly. If she was trying to play hide-and-seek, she was apparently unaware of the rule of silence. She was so excited to see me that she made trilling sounds from under the kitchen table when my feet approached. Then, she nestled into my hair as I carried her back to her nursery. Back in the brooder she went without protest.

The second baby was far more crafty. She didn't make a peep. I started to panic because she was one of my fancy, more expensive girls. I made my way through the kitchen, dining room, foyer, and living room. Then something caught the corner of my eye: my black Prada tote bag. I did a double take. There was my baby girl, hunkered down, perched quietly on top of the tote.

My emotions quickly went from relief to *please God tell me you didn't poop on my Prada!* She refused to make eye contact and stared straight ahead. It was as if the little chick thought, *Maybe if I don't move she won't notice me.* I scooped up my bad baby bird and checked. By some miracle, there was no poop. To be honest, I was proud of my fancy girl for Prada perching. I mean, Prada and peepers were two of my favorite things . . . well, along with Gucci and goats.

Needless to say, crisis averted. Paul's text had put me in a merry, distracted mood but I promised myself I would never leave the lid off the brooder again.

A Christmas Miracle

In the country, it's common practice for people to abandon unwanted animals, leaving them to fend for themselves. For over two years in Mississippi, I'd seen so many emaciated animals who had grown fearful of humans, dwelling in the woods along country roads. It never stopped upsetting me.

Luca's job was to protect and keep intruders away, so we didn't get many strays on my property, but my neighbors often had animals showing up hungry or seeking help. Tricia had cautioned me to be careful of random boxes on the side of the road. Often, they contained discarded puppies or kittens. There always seemed to be more abandoned animals during winter months. 'Tis the season, apparently, for people to leave their pets to fend for themselves just when natural food is scarce.

Two days before Christmas, I was heading home from running errands when I saw what appeared to be a little black Chihuahua running down the middle of the highway. As I got closer, I realized it was a tiny puppy. The baby was running as fast as it could ahead of an eighteen-wheeler truck. The puppy's little legs were getting tired, and it was too afraid to run off the road. As the giant semi approached, I screamed and veered into the grass, stopped, and covered my eyes. I couldn't watch what was about to happen. But, somehow, the truck driver had seen the puppy and was able to swerve. The trucker's eyes were as wide as mine as he blew past me.

I wasn't the only one who had witnessed the near miss. Several men had also pulled over and were looking toward the puppy. I leapt from my car in hot pursuit. The baby scampered off the highway. It fell on its chin several times, picked itself up, and slowed to a walk. I had almost caught up to it when it turned and saw me and went into a full-speed run again.

I chased it into thick brush and through a gully. My ballet flats filled with muddy ice water, and my nice outfit was getting ruined, but I didn't care. Then finally, the puppy's legs gave out for good, and it fell over onto its back. It was a very young baby boy. How such a young puppy was able to run like that was astonishing. Still on his back, he was a tiny, snarling ball of fleas. He showed his teeth, which made me hesitate for a second, but I grabbed him anyway, and he let out a surprised yip. I held him close while he shivered and made a tiny but vicious attempt at barking. "How are you out here all alone without your momma?" I said, assuming he must belong to someone nearby.

I went to the only house I could find in the vicinity and asked if the puppy was theirs—he wasn't. The baby was scared, wet, and skinny. I had no idea how long he'd been alone in the elements, but there was no way I was going to leave him to that fate.

The vet thought that he wasn't even six weeks old and that he was a large breed dog, probably a Labrador mixed with a Great Dane. I brought him home and, once he calmed down and was flea-free, he became friendly toward me. With a full belly, he started to play and cuddle and sleep *a lot*. Kahuna was used to being an only child in the house (Luca always slept in the barn, with his animals) and was NOT happy with the new addition. I knew we couldn't keep the puppy forever. Kahuna's life was so vastly different from when we lived in Tampa Bay, and I didn't think it was fair to force another new addition on him. He deserved to be the only inside animal (save for occasional chicks). Even so, I couldn't help but shower the lost little baby with affection. It was Christmas, after all, and my past Christmases had been tainted with sadness for so long. This was a welcome distraction.

It only took a few days to find a home for the puppy. Wonderful neighbors adopted him, and with two young girls to love him, I don't think he missed me for a second. One night they sent me a picture of "Archie" in front of his giant new dog bed, next to their Christmas tree. The dog bed was ten times too big for him. In the picture, he was surveying his toys and all the items he'd stolen from around their house. It was like he couldn't believe it was his real life. My neighbors originally said they wanted him to be an outside dog. Clearly the little guy, and their daughters, had other ideas.

I liked seeing Archie playing with his girls. If they rode their four-wheeler around, he rode right along with them. It made me smile to know I wasn't the only one with a kleptomaniac, trash-loving puppy. This life was blessing me with unexpected miracles. There were fewer distractions in the country, and that meant I could slow down enough to take note of the little things like this. Because so often it was the little things, the little moments, when life truly transformed. That puppy was proof that one interaction can change a life in an instant. It reminded me of my life-giving interaction with Paul, who was, apparently, still in the process of planning his final escape from his girlfriend.

Let It Snow

As usual, the northern Mississippi climate was unpredictable. At least in the summer, I could gauge the weather by the flying insects—if there were none, rain was coming. In winter, without bugs as forecasters, I had to rely on human meteorologists and their computer projections. Farm life had made me a constant weather watcher. There was nothing worse than having my goats get caught in a rainstorm. You'd think the goats were the Wicked Witches of the West, the way they screamed when water droplets hit their backs.

It was late afternoon on a winter day when I heard Luca howling from the back porch. "Well, that's a new behavior!" I said to Kahuna. I'd never heard Luca howl before. He sounded like he was in a full-blown panic. I threw on my boots and went out to see what was going on.

I opened the door to snow flurries. Luca had never seen snow, and he clearly had no idea how to respond. The flurries quickly turned into big snowflakes. I stepped out into the snowfall, encouraging him to follow. "Luca, baby! This is going to be your

favorite thing ever!" I said. Great Pyrenees were literally built for
this weather.

He hesitated and then, seeing me dancing around, ventured
out toward me. His eyes squinted as he looked up in the sky, fully
intimidated. He ran and sat down in front of me. He needed
comfort. "Silly boy, give it a chance. This is your kind of weather!"
The snow was coming down hard now. I took off running, knowing it would trigger him into playing. Soon, he was running and
snorting and throwing himself into the snow that dusted the
ground. I took picture after picture to share the antics with Paul.

We played in the snow for about thirty minutes, until it
stopped. The snow on the ground dissipated quickly. I was
bummed that it didn't stick, since snow was so rare in the South.

Before bed, I turned on the local weather to see what to expect
the next day. The weatherman talked of a "rain event" coming to
the area. Farther to the north, they could expect flurries and
maybe a little snow. I turned off the TV and went to bed.

The next morning, I woke up to more silence than usual. Winters
in the country were always quiet, but this was a whole new level.
It felt like waking up to a ghost world. Then, I heard what
sounded like gunshots off in the distance. Gunshots were common during this time of year when it was hunting season, so I
didn't think much of it. When I opened the curtains of my bedroom, I was surprised to see a thick blanket of snow covering
everything. The animals were nowhere in sight.

Luca greeted me on the back porch. His eyes were frisky and
full of life. Stepping outside, I saw that there were several inches
of snow. "Slight rain event, my ass, huh, big boy?!" We both took
off running to the barn. With the exception of a couple ski trips,
I had never seen this much snow in my life. The turkeys were still

roosting in the trees, their backs covered with a thick layer of flakes. Another gunshot sounded from the woods beyond my barn.

When I opened the barn door, it was evident that Luca and I were the only ones who were happy about the snow. The goats were standing at the perimeter of the barn. They wanted nothing to do with getting their hooves wet. I fed them and opened the coop door to let the chickens out. They didn't budge. I threw treats out, hoping to entice them. Still, no movement. "Okay. Stay in the coop if you like," I told them.

The turkeys, spotting the treats, flew down from their high perches. The thick skin on their legs wasn't as delicate as that on the chickens' legs. The chickens watched as the turkeys gobbled up their treats. Bria and a few other older chickens couldn't let this happen—they wanted goodies, too—and tentatively, they made their way out of the coop. The ducks and geese, meanwhile, seemed oblivious and busily stuffed their faces into the white powder in search of sunken treats.

The cold weather was giving Luca manic energy and he began dragging large, fallen branches around the yard. I heard two more shots. I looked around and noticed a lot of tree debris. Then, suddenly I realized it wasn't gunshots I was hearing; it was the sound of trees losing their branches, the cracking echoing through the woods. Like southerners who weren't acclimated to snow and ice, the trees weren't used to this either. With the new weight they were bearing, their branches were popping off with loud, eerie booms.

After farm chores, I went back inside to build a fire and sip hot cocoa made from goat milk and raw cocoa. As I helped myself to seconds, I decided to sweeten it with some of my goat milk caramel sauce. *Why not?* I plopped a heaping spoonful in and stirred it until it melted. The scent alone was decadent. "*Ohhh,*

I need to make this scent into a candle!" I said to Kahuna. I kept checking on the animals from the window. Still no sign of the goats and most of the chickens. The turkeys had flown back up to roost and sit on their feet for warmth.

At the front of the house, I looked out toward the pond. The waterfowl were actually walking on top of the water. The pond had frozen and the birds appeared to be confused, marching around aimlessly. I heated up the teakettle to unfreeze their baby pool for them.

My phone dinged. A neighbor sent a picture of the snowman they had built with their kids. The snowman was a bit disheveled. It was missing its edible facial features and buttons they had made from Oreos. It wore a scarf and appeared to once have had a nose made from a strawberry, which had now fallen to the ground. It took me a minute to realize why they sent the photo.

I zoomed in and noticed my neighbor had circled an area of the snowman stained in bright yellow. "OH MY GOD! LUCA!" He had eaten everything but the fruit, then peed on their magnificent snowman. We'd just gotten eight inches of snow, more than any time in recent history, so this was the kids' first snowman, and my dog had just had his way with it. Who knew when they would get to build a snowman again? My neighbors were great sports about it, but I was mortified.

An hour later, I opened the door to find Luca had finished off the neighbor's snowman and stolen the scarf . . . which was now a wet mess on my porch. "Luca, I really need you to grow out of stealing things." My comment didn't wipe the proud look off his face.

Within a few short hours, the eight inches of snow melted rapidly. It came down from the trees and roof like a heavy rainfall. Then my winter wonderland became a beautiful, Narnia-like memory.

After weeks of waiting for Paul to reach out with the news that he'd finally ended things with his ex-girlfriend, on New Year's Eve, he called. He was at a party and wanted to tell me I was still front and center in his mind. Although he sounded upbeat and happy to hear my voice, he couldn't tell me everything I wanted to hear. "I've missed talking to you and can't wait for all of this to be over. It's just taking longer than I expected."

"Originally you said you were looking forward to starting the new year single and completely free of any remnants of her in your house." I was finding it difficult to be understanding, not wanting to be his doormat. "Well, here we are. It's a new year."

"You're right, the holidays were difficult but this is almost over now, I promise. I'll have her get her things out this week."

It wasn't my job to nag, nor did I want to, but I had gotten my point across. I decided to adopt a wait-and-see attitude. This time, I wouldn't have to wait long.

Within the week, Paul called to tell me the good news. He was finally free.

The Ugly Duckling

I knew from experience how powerful the motherhood instinct can be. No matter how hard I tried to bat it away, it wouldn't let me go. Anything could trigger it, from simply seeing a pregnant woman to holding a baby animal.

The same can be said for animals. One of my ducks, Delia, had been devoted to her fifteen eggs for almost a month, barely moving from her well-hidden nest. Typically, the birds nested when cold weather wasn't a threat, but in Mississippi, fall through spring was very unpredictable. It had been too cold to hatch eggs, but Delia stuck to her nest anyway. The eggs were almost due to hatch when a particularly strong cold front came through and killed her unhatched babies. One by one, I candled the eggs by holding a flashlight under each one, hoping to find signs of life inside, but tragically, all the babies had died.

Delia was devastated. She moped and stayed away from the flock as she mourned. She lost weight and rarely visited the pond with the other ducks. Her pain hit me deeply; I knew exactly how she felt. My feeling of helplessness made it worse. I could fix a lot of things for Delia, but bringing her babies back wasn't one of them.

It was a hard, strange, vulnerable time for me. In my time on the farm, I'd done my best to ignore the old sorrow that darkened the edges of my mind. It had just become a part of life, avoiding these deep, complex naggings. Even so, the feelings were becoming more persistent. I stayed busy with farmwork and suppressed the memory of my own losses. But seeing Delia's sadness compounded my own.

I was talking with Paul again on a regular basis. Now that he had extricated himself yet again from his suffocating relationship, we seemed to be on the fast track to rekindling things. There was still uncertainty between us, and Gunnar was still in the periphery of my life, but the renewed relationship with Paul had brought back hope in my heart. There was still a chance, I thought. Maybe he was the person I was meant to be with, and maybe that dream of motherhood would still be available to me. During several conversations we had discussed the possibility of having children. Even though he claimed it was no longer a deal breaker for him, I booked an appointment with a doctor to have a fertility check. I was elated to find that, yes, it was still a very real possibility, even with my history.

More and more, my mind strayed away from the present, both into the future and the past. Hope is a powerful drug; it couldn't help but ignite those old memories and spark a renewed desire for a family.

I was getting ready to leave for Tampa to visit Paul when he sent an alarming text: "Sorry for getting you involved in this messy breakup but she somehow broke into my online phone account and viewed my call logs. She knows I have been talking with you. Attached is her number. If I were you, I would block it. I am changing the locks today and granting her access Sunday to pick up the remainder of her things or they're being tossed."

My phone rang. It was Paul calling to further explain his text. Unhappy and confused about the drama, I stayed quiet and listened. Then he asked for a favor. "I hate to ask this, but would you log into my phone account and change the password for me?" Given the nature of his business, he was unable to log into his account from his work computer, otherwise he would do it himself. Half understanding and half irritated, but wanting to give him the benefit of the doubt, I agreed. I'd have been pissed about the invasion of privacy, just like he was, but at the same time, it was his concern over her finding out that he was "talking to me" that struck me as odd. If they were broken up, why would Paul care if his ex-girlfriend knew he was talking to me? I reasoned that maybe he was just trying to save her feelings.

I needed a minute to process things. Was I walking into yet another muddy situation with him and his ex? I looked out the window at the animals, trying to calm my suspicions. Luca was passed out next to the barn in a deep sleep. Most of the other animals had joined him for their afternoon naps. There was only one bantam chicken who was wide awake, scratching around next to Luca. Suddenly, Luca woke up and leapt straight up into the air. A hawk was diving down to take my little hen, but Luca scared the bird away, and only missed grabbing the hawk by *inches*. I hadn't even seen the hawk coming, but somehow Luca knew. More and more, he continued to amaze me.

How did he even *know* that hawks are dangerous to the flock? His behavior varied depending on the species of wild bird. Ravens merely aggravated him, but somehow, he instinctively knew that hawks were deadly. Now, he was on high alert. He scanned the sky looking for danger. I've always believed dogs are rock stars, but after having a livestock guardian, I don't think there's a harder-working animal in the world. Luca put his life in danger every day. He was now worth his weight in gold, just as Danielle had promised.

As I logged into Paul's phone account to change his password, I remembered a night from long ago, back when I was still in Tampa. At the time, Paul had been with his current girl for almost a year, so I was surprised he wanted to see me. I assumed it was to clear the air and get closure. Instead, we talked for hours about what we wanted for our futures, about how he had never stopped thinking of me, how he knew he needed to break things off with her. During that happy hour, his phone lit up repeatedly from her calls. Each time he ignored it. As usual, we talked seriously about our desire to start a family, and how we envisioned our lives with each other. It was important to him to raise his kids as Catholic. Even though I was no longer attached to a specific religion, I had no issues with those who were and was willing to go along.

This, maybe, was part of why I couldn't let him go. I'd never talked about such serious, detailed life plans with anyone before, not even my husband. It felt kind of like planning my farm life via Excel. The passion I felt for him wasn't sexual, it was incredibly emotional. It was the opposite of what I'd had with my other relationships. Paul and I were able to map out our desires with so much specificity and vulnerability . . . and it came so *easily*. Despite the drama, despite the dysfunction, despite how dragged-out his breakups always were, somehow Paul and I just *got* each other. It was, regardless of the circumstances, an easy relationship in ways I hadn't experienced before.

My last visit to Tampa to see Paul was eye-opening for me. We stayed up late, talking. Time disappeared, as it always did.

"Did I ever tell you I bought an old convertible Mercedes, probably a year ago? It was in perfect condition," he said.

"I've always loved those!" I exclaimed.

"I know you do. I bought it with you in mind. I went all the way to Miami to pick it up and drove it back. When I got it back home, my ex immediately started hating on it. She complained so much I decided to turn around and sell it, so I actually no longer have it."

His face showed visible signs of stress. The thought crossed my mind that I had been watching both of us age for years now. He was graying, but he still had all his hair.

"Do you still love your ex-girlfriend?" I asked, wanting an honest answer.

"No," he said flatly. "I've never been in love before."

I was genuinely shocked and my anger surprised me. This was a man who had been in countless relationships, had even been married. "You've *never* been in love before? You've been *married* and you haven't been in love? You were just in a long-term relationship you've been trying to leave for *years* and you didn't feel love for her? Why on earth would you stay in that!?"

He just said, "I'm not going to do that again. I know I'll fall in love with you."

It scared the shit out of me that he'd never been in love. For as genuine as our connection felt, as wonderful as our long conversations about ideas and the future were, I knew I couldn't live without love or passion. I knew living without it would make me feel trapped. Maybe his inability to feel love explained why I didn't feel sexual passion for him. Several of his exes had openly talked of his oddly passionless sex life. I rationalized their words away by telling myself that it would be different with us. And yet, here we were. His words settled like ice in my veins. I could feel my body stiffen as I processed his truth. My gut told me that if he didn't have a heart to follow and only honored his feelings of guilt, he might never have the strength to set boundaries with his ex or with his mother, who, he said, was still pressuring him to go back to his ex.

My mind grappled with the idea that he'd never been in love before. Are people who don't feel romantic love even capable of romantic passion? I decided to press him further. "But . . . I don't understand how in every social media picture she tags you in, you look like the epitome of the happy smiling couple . . . I just don't get it."

He looked me in the eyes. "None of that was real."

His words hit me like a punch to the stomach. I'd never been one to believe people should smile through misery. I cringed at the thought of someone I cared for being that inauthentic to me. I'd hit my threshold. Finally tired of talking about his past, I decided to drop it and hope for the best.

Paul still had his green thumb. I especially loved his plumeria tree, and he had saved a piece for me to plant when I returned home. He gave me instructions on how to help it grow and flourish. It was a sweet, simple gift.

On the long drive back to Mississippi from Tampa, I received a call from Hayden, who had become my regular farm sitter. I'd cautioned her about not collecting the green eggs a hen was sitting on. All the other eggs should be collected daily. She updated me: "Hey, Jake! I collected the eggs and put them in the refrigerator egg basket. Also, I was able to milk that goat but she was really mad, so I couldn't get much but at least the pressure is off her udder for now."

When I got home, I heard a goat screaming. Hayden had milked the wrong goat. The goat she milked was nursing babies and didn't need milking. No wonder she was angry. Later, my niece Krissy informed me that she had taken eggs out of my refrigerator. When she went to crack one into a pan for breakfast a fully formed, dead chick fell out. There were so many variables to animal care and farm life. Even with the help of temporary caregivers, it was getting harder and harder to leave.

A couple weeks passed after my Tampa visit and the weather had been oddly warm. The Noonans invited me to a cookout. I had my friend Kathryn and my niece Krissy with me, and they tagged along.

It was still daylight when we arrived, and as always, the tortoise sex was in full, slow-motion display. We also noticed that one of the Noonans' ducks had a large number of ducklings, walking freely around the farm. The mother duck was solid black and all her ducklings were black copies of her, except one, which was completely white and followed far behind his mother and siblings.

When I got closer, I could see that the white baby was missing down and had sores all over his body. Periodically, the mother and her other ducklings would turn and attack the little white duckling. He would run for cover, squealing into the woods, only to come back out and attempt to join his family again.

The Noonans said they felt awful for the little duckling; its mother and siblings had been hateful toward him since the day he hatched. They wanted to help him, but the little guy was too scared and fast for them to catch. It was heartbreaking, and I wanted to do something. They said that if I could catch him, I could have him.

Eventually, with the help of others at the cookout, we caught the duckling. The poor baby was dirty, scared, and covered in sores from his own mother's attacks. I had no idea what I was going to do with him, or if my ducks would accept him. I was worried he might experience more of the same attacks and stress.

Back at my farm, Delia was alone in the pen while the other ducks frolicked on the pond. Her depression over her lost babies had been a lasting one. We brought the crated duckling into her pen. She was so withdrawn that she didn't even look up to acknowledge us. When we reached into the carrier to retrieve the duckling, he loudly protested the contact. His squeaks immediately caught Delia's attention. We placed the duckling on the ground with her and stepped back to watch, hopeful but concerned.

The baby ran toward a corner in the pen, and Delia ran after him. We held our breath as she cornered him, bracing for the possibility of an impending attack, preparing to rescue the baby again. But instead of attacking him, Delia, without making a sound, somehow calmed him down. Within *minutes* she had him sitting quietly next to her, snuggled up, her wing draped over him lovingly. She began making soft sounds and gently sifted through his matted down. It appeared as if they were quietly talking to each other. None of us could believe our eyes.

With Delia's love and watchful care, the baby would heal quickly. In less than a week, Delia had her adopted baby swimming on the pond with the other ducks. The entire flock had welcomed him. He looked nothing like the others, but this ugly duckling finally found a family of his own, and a mother who loved him fiercely.

When Delia lost her babies, I had grieved along with her. But now I found myself thinking, *If Delia could have a happy ending, maybe I can, too.*

It was early on a dark evening when Krissy, who was staying with me at the time, came running into the house. "There's a possum in one of the baby chicken pens!" she yelled. I jumped up and called back to her, "Open the gate and let Luca in!" Luca was barking like mad. He had already seen the predator.

As I ran out the door, Krissy opened the gate. Luca went straight for the possum. As far as I knew, this was his first face-to-face meeting with a possum. I'd seen him kill snakes and other smaller, faster animals, but never one with teeth like this.

By the time I made it to the pen, Krissy was inside checking on the adolescent chickens. "It already killed a couple," she said, upset and deflated. Before Luca could get to the possum, it escaped into the next pen through a hole in the back. Luca didn't skip a beat and headed it off in the next pen. He grabbed the possum by the neck and shook it violently. He then walked over to a metal pole and slung the possum against it. I'd never seen a dog make a brutal kill like this before. Usually, Luca's kills were accidental, so I had no idea if his behavior was normal or not.

My mind raced, considering what to do. Should I get a gun to finish off the possum? But instinctively I knew Luca needed to have this experience and handle it himself. The possum was limp and appeared to be dead. Luca kept looking at us, almost as if for encouragement, so we gave it to him with a round of high-pitched "Good boy!"s. He dropped the body and nosed it around. Then he picked it up by the back and, while making eye contact with me, bit down on the possum, bones cracking under the pressure of his jaws. Chills ran up my arms, it was disturbing. I wanted to break his eye contact, but I knew he needed it. If I was asking him to do this, to take another life to defend the animals, I had to be there with him. Considering what the possum had just done to my expensive adolescent chickens, who I'd been nurturing and loving for months, I wasn't in the mood for mercy. Plus, I didn't want to alarm my neighbors with a gunshot so close to the house.

Luca dropped the limp predator and lay down next to it. We tended to the chicken carnage and checked for injuries. Krissy went to bed and I followed soon after. I was glad Luca had the experience, but I wished I hadn't had to witness it.

Fifteen minutes later, he was barking hysterically again. Through a long process that lost me a lot of sleep, I was starting to learn the meaning of his different barks. If we were going to be a team, I had to know when he needed assistance. I went onto the back porch off my bedroom, jumped over the railing, and hit the ground running.

The possum, it turned out, had been playing dead. I'd heard about this before but didn't know it was a real thing they could do. Luca seemed astonished that the animal had sprung back to life. It couldn't really get away with its cracked bones, but it was dragging itself, trying to escape. I can't stand to see anything in pain and struggling, but Luca needed to see this all the way through if he was going to learn properly.

"Finish it, Luca," I said, calmly but firmly. This time, he did. It was a tough lesson for both of us, but at least it was one he would never have to learn again.

Darwin Award Nominee

It was a beautiful day on the farm. Every window was open to the breezes. Adding a screen door to the front of the house was one of the best investments I'd made. I loved how it creaked when it was opened or shut. I loved the little bit of character it gave my drab house, but mostly I loved that it ushered the fresh air inside. The new door also allowed me to easily hear the animals going about their day . . . *usually*.

I was minding my own business, enjoying an unseasonably warm breeze and making lunch, when suddenly I had the feeling that I was being watched. This wasn't unusual; often, I *was* being watched by various animals. I looked up and glanced around at the windows, expecting to see a cat, chicken, or even a turkey being a voyeur. But the windows were clear of the usual suspects. Kahuna was headfirst in his lunch bowl. It wasn't him. "*Hmmm. Weird,*" I said, starting to feel creeped out.

I went back to cooking when, a minute later, I looked up from the stove to see my buck, Valentino, standing in the living room—all one hundred and twenty pounds of pure muscle. He was perfectly relaxed, there on my white carpet, chewing his cud, staring at me. His beard still held the braid I'd added that morning. I had no idea how long he had been in the house. *Shiiiitt. This could be bad,* I realized.

I couldn't alert Kahuna to the fact that there was a goat in the house. The feud between my little city dog and the goats was like my own farm version of the Hatfields and McCoys. I only had a few seconds to escort my wayward buck outside before all hell would break loose. Bucks are 100 percent muscle and 100 percent stubborn and so they can cause a tremendous amount of damage. Add a small dog and my china cabinet into the mix and I'd need to call my insurance agent immediately. *Would a goat break-in be considered an "act of God"?* I wondered.

I did my best to quietly lure Valentino back through the screen door that he had somehow opened. Trying to be nonchalant, I casually walked over and grabbed his collar. Just as I was about to open the door, Kahuna came around the corner to find that his nemesis was in *his* house, with *his* mom. Kahuna's expression quickly changed from shock to determination.

Picture, if you will, an old Hollywood western in which someone gets thrown through a door or window.

At the sight of seven-pound Kahuna barreling toward him, the dog's legs moving so fast he slipped all over the tile foyer floor, Valentino reared up and launched himself through the screen door with the power of the space shuttle. My fingers still wrapped around his collar, I went with him. Before I knew it, my feet left the ground with the force of jet propulsion and my life flashed before my eyes.

As I soared through the air on my goat rocket ship, the first thought that entered my mind was, *So this is how it all ends.* Then it was, *How will anyone know I didn't throw myself through my own front door?* and, *I'll be one of those people who wins a Darwin award for dumbest death,* and finally, *And this bastard will be far from the scene, munching on my shrubs as if nothing happened.*

I've seen those funny videos where someone could easily just LET GO of the object of their torture. I can even recall yelling at the screen, "JUST LET GO!" There are so many scenarios where someone can simply let go and yet, we stay latched on defiantly, linking ourselves to our doom. We all do this, metaphorically and literally. This time, for me, it involved a goat. I blame my hand. It had a mind of its own. I don't know why it didn't let go of his collar. Maybe it was purely for my animals' entertainment, maybe it was a metaphor for everything that was to come, who knows.

After crashing through my door and being airborne for what felt like an eternity, I landed hard on the back of my head and back. My legs were sprawled across the steps high above my head. Every limb hurt and my ribs were bruised from hitting the sharp corner of the brick stairs. If this has never happened to you, let me tell you, rocketing through a door of wood and wire is . . . unpleasant. I looked up at Valentino, my hand still grasping his collar. Blood was running down my pinkie finger.

Valentino was wide-eyed and breathing heavily but, thankfully, he had stopped moving. He could have easily kept dragging me behind him for some distance. I lifted my head to look back into the house. Kahuna was standing in the doorway, in all his bowlegged glory, with a satisfied expression, not at all concerned by my awkward position and destroyed door. He won that round against the buck, and that's all that mattered.

As the shock wore off, I slowly assessed the damage. Even with all my scrapes and bruises, I made it through the ordeal much better than my now barely hanging screen door. The wood frame was splintered in several places, dangling from the hinges, and the screen itself was toast. Later, when I told Kathryn, she was laughing hysterically even before I finished the story. "I'm sorry but the visual of this is hilarious. It's the perfect metaphor for what happens when we stay too long in a bad relationship. Life comes along and throws us out of our comfort zone, onto our asses. The fact that you got thrown out by a goat named Valentino is priceless!"

The Flower of Lies

After weeks of warmth, the weather had turned frigid again for Valentine's Day, my all-time favorite holiday. A lot of people consider it a boring obligation manufactured by greeting card companies. And most single people seem to despise it. But I always loved it because it's the only holiday that doesn't revolve around religion, nationality, race, age, or anything other than the noblest of sentiments: love.

When I was growing up, my mother never made Valentine's Day about romance; it was always about *any* kind of love. I would make colorful shoeboxes covered with construction paper, paper hearts, and lace, with a slit in the top for sweet Valentine's messages. My mother always encouraged me to give Valentine's cards to everyone. It wasn't about sexual attraction or obligation. It was about inclusion and appreciation. I wasn't going to let commercialism limit my dedication to the holiday for all kinds of love.

My visit to Tampa had been only weeks ago, and since I'd returned home, I'd felt uncertain about things with Paul. He had grown distant in the days before the holiday, and I could feel his confused energy; I knew his mother and ex-girlfriend were chewing away at his sanity and it was entirely possible for him to backslide. He had already stayed with this girlfriend, according to him, year after year because of external pressure and guilt. But do you remember what I said about clinging to the things that cause us doom? In my mind, clinging to something out of guilt is not only dishonest, it *always* leads to misery.

I tried to maintain my holiday bliss with treat-making and a bit of decorating. The urge to do anything at all was how I knew I had hope for the future; it had been years since I felt inspired to decorate for any holiday. My phone dinged with a text from Paul. "Do you like roses?" he asked. For some reason, something about the message felt forced and gave me a slightly sick feeling. I never wanted anyone to do anything for me out of obligation. But I wanted to give him the benefit of the doubt—maybe he was just trying to get to know more of my likes and dislikes. I responded, "I love roses, just not red ones."

In my early twenties, I had worked at a flower shop, where I made far too many red rose bouquets for men in the doghouse. A couple men in particular were there often. They would come in and have me make two or three red rose bouquets. One for their wife, which they always carried out themselves. The others for girlfriends, which I had to deliver. Usually I loved delivering flowers and seeing people light up when they answered the door, but I hated handing these poor, clueless women their roses. Ever since then, to me, red roses have been the flower of lies.

That Valentine's Day, I was startled out of my decorating bliss by the sound of a doorbell. No one had ever rung my doorbell before. There was a delivery guy holding a long box. "That was fast!" I said out loud. I inhaled the scent of the boxed roses deeply. In the kitchen, I opened it. There, lying on their side, were a dozen individually wrapped red roses. *Well, crap.* I thought of my text to Paul and felt like an awful person. I carefully unwrapped and arranged them in the accompanying clear glass vase. I should have felt happy, but there was a knot in the pit of my stomach.

At that moment Paul called, and I summoned the cheeriest voice I could muster and gushed over his thoughtfulness. He apologized and said he had already ordered the roses prior to asking me. His energy was miserable and weak. I knew what was coming next.

He asked for more time. He wasn't ready to do this, but said if I lived there things would be different. It was a cop-out. He said he needed to be alone and away from the women in his life to get his head straight—and that included me.

Paul dumped me on Valentine's Day. My favorite holiday. It hurt, but at the same time, it was the first honest thing he had done for himself. He'd spent years filling my head with fantasy and hope, but there was no substance to any of it. There never had been. He was a coward, but I had been a fool. *When would I learn that my instincts never lie?* All that talk about the future we would share, the family we would create—without action behind those honeyed words, it was meaningless. I think I knew all along that he was an emotional lightweight, but if I were brutally honest with myself . . . there had been no other viable options around, so out of fear, I had been willing to settle. Some people want to fall in love just to change their life and leave their past behind. I had always tended to judge those people but, I realized now, I was that "some people." Somewhere inside, I wanted to be saved from the part of myself that felt empty, sad, and not good enough for something great. I'd already experienced being in the middle of a less than good marriage when my parents were together; now here I was about to do the same thing to any potential future children. I had repeatedly ignored the red flags, stubbornly holding on to my own dream of a family. Granted, it was a dream he was also trying to sell me. But yet again, it had no real substance and, like a rainbow, it evaporated.

This was the final lesson I needed to trust my own intuition, to sift through fear versus instincts. It had taken me until my early forties to learn this, but so be it. I would stay single forever before I would settle again.

Quietly weeping, I repacked the holiday decorations. Heart-shaped decor and flowers couldn't pull me out of my funk. I tossed his lying roses in the trash.

The next morning, I was in a terrible mood. I was hurt and angry that I let things with Paul go on for so long despite knowing better. I was embarrassed that I had wanted it so badly I had even had a fertility checkup. Now, I felt stupid for having hope at all. Stupid for not putting the quality of the relationship ahead of my stubborn dreams.

Overnight, the warmer weather was replaced by a severe cold front, which was fitting for my now frosty heart. I bundled up and trudged out to feed and water the animals. The cold air stung my skin and made my nose run. It felt like even nature was conspiring against me and I was unable to stop my rage spiral. The waterline in the barn had burst yet again, and water was turning to ice on the barn's concrete floor. "Oh my god! Can't you guys leave the insulation alone for once?!" I snapped at my chickens. The birds had a thing for eating the insulation on pipes, or anything else I was trying to protect. To stop the fountain of water I had to climb into the sketchy crawl space under my house to shut off the barn valve.

Back inside the house, I filled the buckets from the kitchen faucet. *This blows,* I thought, growing increasingly agitated. On my way back to the barn, lugging two heavy buckets, I tripped and spilled half the water on myself. The water was shockingly cold as it saturated my clothes and went down my boots into my socks. When I looked back, I realized I'd tripped on a giant frozen turkey turd. *Fitting metaphor,* I thought, even more pissed off.

Now I was fuming, in full fight mode. I reared my leg back and kicked the frozen shit with full force. It seemed to be cemented to the ground and didn't budge. I stubbed my toe and the force of my own kick threw me onto my butt, dumping the rest of the water onto me. Now my toe hurt, my butt hurt, my ego hurt, and I was soaking wet. Blood boiling, feeling like my life was a total nightmare, I silently finished my chores and went back to bed.

I thought I had gotten pretty good at outrunning my misery. For years I used clothes, events, parties, and other distractions to keep it at bay. And then, when I felt the chill returning, I left Tampa to buy a farm in the middle of nowhere. The farm had been a complete change from my previous routine, but it had taken awhile for me to understand what I had actually done: Moving here had been the *ultimate* distraction, just like shopping or clothes. It staved off the depression and loneliness that had followed me throughout my adult life—but it didn't make it vanish.

All the anguish, all the hurt and trauma was finally catching up to me. I felt trapped by my own choices, with nowhere left to run. I couldn't go back to Tampa; I wouldn't be any happier there. There was no distraction powerful enough to cover this up. The truth was like a bottomless hole. I would always let people cross my boundaries despite my own instincts screaming at me. I would never be a mother. I would never have a family of my own. What I'd had with Paul had felt like my last thread of hope, and now it was gone. I was hurt. I was enraged at myself and at the world.

As I put the box of Valentine's Day decorations back in the garage, I saw Kahuna sniffing around a small black Chanel box. I hadn't noticed that box before. "Why would I have left that box in the garage?" I wondered aloud.

Opening the lid was like a hard slap across the face. There, carefully placed inside the box, were mementos of my previous relationship and last pregnancy. I had thrown all this in the trash after my last miscarriage, which I'd had while I was with Chad. The box was full of little things, some I remembered and some I hadn't seen previously. Old movie ticket stubs, dried flowers, little love notes.

At the very bottom of the box was my last sonogram picture. My breath caught. I had told Chad that I didn't want the memories and had thrown the images and video away. But Chad must have fished them out of the garbage when I wasn't around. Just months ago, my mother and stepfather had picked up the rest of my things from the storage unit in Tampa that I had once shared with Chad. Chad, knowing they were bringing me my things, must have slipped the box of mementos in with my belongings. Of course I wouldn't ignore a Chanel box, he must have known. At some point, I would see it and open it. Maybe Chad was being thoughtful, but it felt, in this moment, like his way of sticking it to me one last time.

I remembered when Chad had bragged to me about being good at manipulating people. That was the first crack in our foundation. Horrified, over time I started noticing the truth in his statement. In conversations with clients, for example, he lied about small things. On one hand, I knew this was easy to do with clients who had no boundaries and high expectations. On the other, it made me wonder how easily and often he was lying to me. By my last miscarriage, the basis of our once loving relationship was all but gone. During that pregnancy, I felt the stress of not knowing how I would parent our baby alone, because I knew I couldn't count on him. As it turned out, it wouldn't be a challenge I'd have to face, but the memory of that stress sealed our fate. It would take several more months before I had the courage to walk away.

Now, impossible to ignore, here were the pieces of my last and most painful loss. It's funny, the negative things your mind will fixate on when you're falling apart. In that moment, I looked down at my chipped, tattered nails that had once been mission critical. I grabbed a piece of my hair and saw the split ends. It was all too much. I felt old. Ugly. Ruined.

At that moment, four little words entered my mind . . . *ruin is a gift.*

"FUCK YOU, ELIZABETH GILBERT!" The words exploded from me.

Waves of emotions bombarded me. They were heavy and confusing, and I didn't know which one to follow. My skin pricked as if crawling with ants. I could feel someone new inside me rising as the compliant soldier I had always been was struck down. The misery that had ruled me was replaced by fury and a desperate desire for freedom. *And it felt good.*

The sudden anger that erupted was so massive it was too big for my body to hold all at once. It was primal. It was dangerous. And it was *overdue*. I had nothing left to lose. It felt like the rage of a thousand warriors over a thousand lifetimes who returned home from battle to find nothing left of everything they had fought for. And like them, I had nothing to show for my staying power . . . had I not been a good soldier? Had I not kept going through every one of life's blows? I was livid. Red filled my eyes. I wanted retribution. I wanted to fight God. No. I wanted God to *pay*. To pay for every lost life, every torturous event, every bit of lost innocence.

Years of pent-up powerlessness and grief funneled into rage that permeated from every part of my body. I was electrified. Furious. I could sense the familiar feeling of death I'd now experienced so many times. Like the predators I'd battled, I wasn't going down without a fight. But unlike them, I was looking for it.

Kahuna, sensing I wasn't okay, pawed at me to be picked up, but I wanted to be alone. On autopilot, I threw the Chanel box in the trash. Its contents scattered over Paul's obligatory red roses.

Ignoring Kahuna, I made my way to the front door. The air was cold and raw, and I was relieved when I didn't see Luca or any of the animals. Alone, I marched to the pond and stared in defiance at its frozen banks. For so much of the year, this pond was overflowing with life. Right now, it appeared dead and still.

In the silence of the winter air my anger burst forth; I screamed, "If this is all there is, then I'm DONE!"

I waited, as if expecting a response to my challenge. There was nothing but the mocking silence.

With no resistance to meet my outrage I felt unheard, ignored. Exhausted and defeated, I crumpled to the ground and lay staring at the icy water. The cold earth felt good on the side of my face, still hot from emotion. Large tears welled up uncontrollably and rapidly rolled down my face. I was so damn tired. Tired of feeling like I wasn't good enough. Tired of feeling like I was barely staying above the sadness and fear that wouldn't let me go.

My gloveless hands turned pink from the freezing air and started to shake. These feelings were repetitive and paralyzing, like an awful, unsolvable riddle. *This couldn't be the rest of my life.* I didn't want to spend my days slowly dying inside, mourning what I'd lost, hating other people for living the life I didn't have. It was like a prison in my head, the weight of my past and the anxiety of my uncertain future. Even surrounded by fresh country air, I felt I was suffocating. Making money and having babies were what people seemed to be valued for and I had ultimately failed at both. There was nothing left and there was no more point to all this. I had a physical desire to open my chest, rip out my heart, and leave it there on the icy banks for God to see what he'd done.

Just then, a giant white paw landed silently in front of me. Luca sniffed at my face with his cold nose. His winter coat and size made him look like a white lion. When I didn't respond, he whined and laid his big body next to mine, blocking me from the water. I didn't make any effort to comfort him. I didn't acknowledge him or move. I just lay there, expressionless, staring into his fur until I could no longer see at all.

I was in my early forties, and it felt like time had run out. I'd never see my mother holding my child or reading bedtime stories. I'd never watch my kids playing on the pond catching tadpoles or cupping chicks in their hands. There would be no ballet classes, no school pictures, no holidays. My life had grown quiet since moving to the farm, and while that quiet was needed, my lack of busyness gave the dark thoughts strength. What ran through my mind were a million memories I'd never have, and frightening ones I'd tried to keep away for decades. Every day. Every night. Every weekend. Every holiday. I could see it in vivid detail. Now, more than anything, I felt forgotten, without a legacy to leave my mark on the world.

I had to accept what was lost. I had to redefine the rest of my life and try to meet a future I dreaded. But how the fuck was I supposed to do that?

While each pregnancy varied, with different cravings and different symptoms, each miscarriage was the same. They started with the feeling of abruptly being alone, followed, hours or days later, by an intense pressure inside my uterus.

I had my last one while I was with Chad. I was self-employed and without maternity insurance. When I felt the time come, I had lain in the shower and relived every feeling and symptom of the previous losses. Yet again, I fought my body. Yet again, it fought back. This time, with the rush of pain and fluid, I looked down to find my little baby resting on the drain. The water from the shower rained down and made him appear alive.

I held my baby in one hand and stared through swollen eyes. I was holding a tiny miracle and even in my despair, I still marveled at the perfect little hands and feet. His mouth was open. I gently tried to close it but it fell open again. It was so delicate the skin sloughed off with my touch.

I've heard over and over again from the medical community that miscarriages are like heavy periods. I've had enough experience to know this to be complete bullshit. The physical and emotional pain, not to mention the blood and fluid loss, the elevated hormones and the tiny body of your child—this is nothing like a "heavy period." It's a horrible trauma, and trying to minimize it didn't change or help anything.

People like me have nothing to show for our past, for our never-ending heartbreak, for the internal scars. Words like *orphan* and *widow* exist to communicate a specific kind of loss, but there's no word for someone who has lost a baby or child. It's an unspeakable kind of grief, and despite the fact that a part of you lives in that moment forever, it goes unrecognized by the world.

If I wasn't going to be a mother, then who was I? What role did I have in society, if any at all? Was my life considered valuable as a childless, single woman? Did *I* even value it? The chill in the air by the pond was no match for the freeze that had developed in my heart.

People talk about hope as if it's a good thing. Yet there are some types of hope that only set you up for brutal heartache. I could now see that I had never even loved Paul, but for a chance at motherhood and stability, I had been willing to settle for a passionless and loveless man. This time, when the self-hatred welled up inside, instead of pushing it away, I allowed it.

Even with over forty years of life under my belt, I still needed to learn some simple things.

I'd always had an inner guidance, a quiet whisper that reminded me of my personal truths. The problem was, I usually didn't listen. Life had a way of seemingly offering me something *almost* good enough—a relationship that was *almost* good enough, a home that was *almost* good enough—and yet it was, deep down, unfulfilling. It was as if I were being tested repeatedly. Would I agree to that? Would I settle for something less than what I was giving? Would I stick up for myself when I should? Or would I finally learn my lessons and value *myself*, despite the uncertainty that sometimes came with it?

Choosing your truth isn't always the easy choice. Other options promise escape and they're often just golden handcuffs cleverly disguised. Merely temporary rainbows and instant ego gratification. There were so many mediocre relationships that promised exactly that. But when I chose those, when I took a step down the path of fear avoidance, life had its own way of course-correcting. It pulled the rug from under me, and rightfully so, because living through fear with a false foundation isn't living at all. Now, I knew that the love I'd always wanted could only be found through respecting myself and honoring my instincts.

Like a zombie army breaking through the ground, more memories started pouring in. But I wasn't afraid anymore. They could take me. I was ready to go. And into the darkness they pulled me.

I was a little girl. It was the last time my molester approached me wearing his disgusting grin. I knew all too well what he wanted. But for some reason, this time was different. I was different.

I had been playing with an airplane-shaped clock radio. As he came up to me, my hand gripped the radio tightly. I was fully prepared to bash his head with it if he touched me again. My heart beat fast, like a rabbit's. Then, as if someone else took control of me, I heard myself say, "If you ever come near me again, I WILL TELL MY MOM!" He looked shocked and slunk away, never to try that shit again. I wondered what got into me that day and, more important, why, as an adult, I had solely focused on the trauma and never pondered how the abuse stopped. What was different about that day, versus all the ones before? What changed? I had finally set a powerful boundary, and for some reason I had never given myself credit for that or even allowed myself to remember what I had done, the courage I had summoned, until now. There on the icy banks of my pond, this realization took my breath away.

My mother once told me about my great-grandmother, Sarah. She, too, had a farm in Mississippi. She had eight sons. She lost her husband to the Spanish flu shortly after her last child was born. Sarah was highly educated, a violinist and poet. After my great-grandfather died, she became so distraught that she would frequently leave her boys, go into the woods, and scream. The parallel to my life and Sarah's didn't escape me. I wondered about Sarah's sadness and if it all stemmed from losing her husband, or if it went even deeper. Sarah died almost a year before the day I was born, but I had always wished I had known her. As I lay by the pond on that bleak and frozen February day, thoughts of her kept entering my mind.

Luca was still by my side, keeping me warm. I slung my arm around him and felt his heat radiating into my body. Grabbing a handful of his thick, white fur, I sank my fingers down into his undercoat. My hand slowly stopped hurting from the cold. The thought of leaving my animals to an uncertain future gave me a pang of guilt.

I looked toward the sky, closed my eyes, and whispered, "*Help me.*" I didn't know who I was talking to, but I felt compelled to say it out loud. I opened my eyes and watched as my breath spread out into the winter chill. Luca, still guarding me from the water, let out a sigh and laid his big head between his paws. Yet again, there was no response. The cold air stung my eyes, so I closed them again. Then, behind the darkness of my eyelids came a burst of light. The light broke apart into what seemed like millions of stars. The stars started spinning rapidly together and formed the shape of a butterfly for a couple seconds, then disappeared.

In that moment, something shifted inside me. It was the simplest realization of the tiniest desire. I wanted to be released from these emotional swords. I wanted to be *truly* released. I didn't want to live this way anymore, missing or fearing something that was gone for good. I could only put a bandage over my wounds for so long. Bandages weren't enough. I wanted to be *free* of them.

Within that desire shone the smallest light. It was a little breath of hope, but this was a different kind of hope than I'd ever experienced. It was hope I had from within, hope I could actually count on. Hope that was *mine*. That desire had been there all along, obscured by my resistance and desperation. But acknowledging it suddenly gave it power and I could feel it spreading warmly through my chest.

For so long, I had avoided the feelings and memories that were slowly choking the life from me. But avoiding wasn't the solution; I had to see, and accept it. I was ready to allow myself to evolve, to see my value. I thought of my birds, how they go through the annual process of losing their feathers, growing new, shiny, protective ones to replace the old, tattered, sun-bleached ones. This isn't something they force to happen; it's a natural process. This was how I wanted to shed my old life—not by running away, but by letting go naturally. It was dawning on me that this was a choice I could actually make for myself.

Destruction is often part of creation. This is what Elizabeth Gilbert meant and why those words stuck with me for so long. Life had gifted me with immense freedom, and I was only beginning to see it for its possibilities. Now a new dream could emerge. And I would meet it with an open heart.

Like the seed that destroys itself to make way for something larger, I had to transform. Now, I could clearly see this metaphor across all life. Birds and butterflies have to extricate themselves from their eggs and cocoons. It's the struggle inside that gives them the strength needed to survive. It's pressure that makes gemstones. It's agitation that makes pearls. The beauty of being human is that we can choose what we become. Everything transforms. The choice is to transform through growth or rot, through expansion or contraction. We may not have control over many things in life, but we can decide our truth and how we will live it. My spirit had been contracting long enough. It was time to allow the force inside me to break my outer shell.

When I was back inside, I found a message on my phone from one of my Tampa friends. Her IVF transfer had failed. Her dream of pregnancy, for now, was not to be. I was heartbroken for her, because I knew how badly she had wanted this, for so many years.

As the news sank in, I had a strange realization: With so many women who had never even had the chance to carry life, for any length of time, *I* was one of the lucky ones. Even if my experiences were incomplete, they were something that not everyone was fortunate enough to have had.

The next morning I was startled awake by a loud voice saying: "*There's always a light. Look to Aurora.*" I jolted upright, full of adrenaline. The voice didn't sound masculine or feminine but it was very real. I looked around but there was no one there. Kahuna was still asleep at the end of the bed.

"Look to Aurora?? What does that even mean?" I said out loud. But the only response was the roosters crowing. The sun was coming up. I pondered what the voice had said, then I remembered . . . Aurora was my grandmother on my father's side. Like the quintessential flapper girl of the 1920s, she was brazen and had a quick, naughty wit that both delighted and embarrassed me as a kid. Like me, she had a masculine-sounding nickname, Billie. *Look to Aurora:* I had no idea what that specific message meant, but I knew I was being told to have faith.

After all that emotional release, of course I got sick. Within days, I was so ill that if I moved too much, I'd vomit. My body was hot with fever and my mind was delirious. Each purging session was followed by a twenty-minute window in which I was slightly mobile. I took these windows to attempt to eat, drink, and feed the animals. Putting on normal clothes wasn't an option, it only wasted precious energy and induced more vomiting. At least the nip in the air through my flimsy nightgown was a welcome sensation to my fevered body.

On the last day of my sickness, I tried to trudge to the goat pen. But I was too exhausted. I lost all sense of vanity and concern for cleanliness and collapsed to the ground. I lay there as the animals surrounded me. They'd never seen me like this. When I opened my eyes, I saw my goats, chickens, geese, and turkeys in front of me. I tried to tell them that I was okay, but all that came out was projectile vomit. I actually threw up on my animals.

After their initial two seconds of shock, the goats, turkeys, geese, and chickens dove in like I'd provided a gourmet buffet. I tried to kick and swat them away, but I was too weak. *Screw it.* I lay there quietly and watched as they cleaned up my mess.

Eventually, after lying mostly bare-skinned in the winter air, my body grew cold enough to motivate me to move again. I mustered enough strength to make it to the chicken coop, but that was all I could manage. I collapsed into the straw on the floor of the coop and passed out. When I woke up, who knows how long later, some of the hens were perched on top of me. I could feel their warm softness dispersed around my body. I was too tired to care and fell back asleep.

The brunt of the illness only lasted a couple of days, but it felt like a forced rest, a final cleansing. When the sickness lifted, somehow, everything was new.

The Confession

In those late winter weeks, after the brutal breakup with Paul and the discovery of the box of lost dreams, then being laid up by illness, I saw Gunnar occasionally, but I never told him what I'd been through. Somehow, he instinctively gave me the affection and support I needed, without asking any questions.

Gradually, I began to find the unquestionable good in what had happened. Being with Paul would have meant leaving this life I was building for myself, trading my farm and my beloved animals for what surely would have been a subpar relationship and predictable future. Deep down, I knew that what I had here was better than anything he could have given me.

It was around this time my friend Kathryn called me out. "You're always talking about living authentically but you don't post *any* pictures of yourself on the farm. And worse, most people *still* don't know you're not in Tampa!" She was right. For years now, I'd been a closet farm girl, afraid of my own damn truth. I still felt somewhat fragile, and occasionally still wanted to stay in my safe little cocoon. But in the name of truth, and change,

I decided it was time to out myself. Besides, I reasoned, hidden things can't inspire. They are connections lost. It's why we get so excited when old things are found or new things are discovered. They have a story to tell. I decided I wouldn't hide any longer.

Social media made it easy to tell the whole world at once. I made a simple declaration that I had been secretly living a farm life for quite some time. With my heart beating in my ears from nervousness, I took a deep breath, pressed the post button, and braced myself.

Later, when I finally got the guts to check my dinging phone, I was amazed by the outpouring of support. I received several private messages from people who were contemplating making a major life change as well. Many wanted advice and asked how I came to make such a big choice.

Late that night, my head was still buzzing from the excitement of hearing from so many people who also wanted to change their lives. Their support felt like virtual hugs and high fives. I was too amped up to sleep. I left Kahuna snug in bed and made my way out into the dark to visit the animals in the barn. Trying not to alarm my sleeping birds, I quietly sat next to Luca and the goats, amid the smell of straw and animal warmth. Luca wagged his fluffy tail and it thumped loudly against the ground. I petted his big muffin head and kissed his velvet nose. Maybelle came to sit on the other side of me. Luca put his big head on one leg and looked up at me. Maybelle stretched her neck across my lap and sniffed at her big, beloved dog, then she, too, laid her head on my other knee. I leaned my head back and cried. This was my family, my home; this was the life I had built for myself. This time my tears welled up from an overwhelming sense of love, gratitude, and a new perspective.

The next night, one of my Tampa friends called. She had been at the salon earlier in the day and overheard one of our friends talking about me to their stylist. She recalled what this other woman had said: "Did you hear Jake moved to a farm in Mississippi? I think she's lost her mind."

That judgment was exactly why I'd kept quiet for so long. It stung, especially since I'd thought the other woman was a friend. But the truth was, she was right. In a way, I did lose my mind. But I was also finding my heart and discovering a powerful new person emerging.

I was on my own journey. And I was finally okay knowing that not everyone would be coming with me. I knew that to open other people's eyes, I had to keep opening mine.

Witnessing Miracles

Every once in a while, if you really stay present, you can witness small miracles. For me, one such miracle was found in my rooster Marcel.

Marcel was a Black Copper Marans rooster, a French breed that lays a prized, dark-chocolate-colored egg. He was sickly from the moment I brought him home from the breeder. I tried desperately to help him, but he was near death for well over a year. He didn't crow, his comb and wattles were under-developed, and physically, he was small, barely the size of a young female.

At least four different times I found him lying on his side, close to death, too weak to move. He had a clear will to survive, and yet nothing helped him. He wouldn't gain weight, barely ate, and showed zero interest in girls. It was as if he had extreme depression. None of the usual remedies or medicines helped. I resigned myself to the fact that I just had to wait for him to die.

I was out of town on a rare business trip when my new farm sitter sent a picture of Marcel looking very dead, lying on his side in the pen. My heart sank. I asked her to put him in the barn and told her I'd take care of him when I returned the following day.

The next day, however, when I walked into the barn, to my surprise, Marcel was standing in the barn looking at me. "Hi, sweet boy!" I cooed. He cocked his head and replied with a low *churr*. I got him to eat and drink but still, nothing brought the glow of life into his eyes. Some animals want to live; others give up easily. Over time, I had learned to see it in their eyes. Marcel was stubbornly clinging to life, and now I had a renewed inspiration to do the same. I would continue to help him as long as he allowed it.

A few days later, out of the blue, a social media farm friend gifted me my dream chickens. I called them Lemon Chiffon Brahmas, otherwise known in Europe as Lemon Pyle Brahmas. The variety was extremely rare in the United States.

I kept the new birds separated for a while to make sure they were healthy. When I finally allowed the flocks to mix, I watched Marcel amble over to a particularly lovely Brahma girl, Sophie. They locked eyes for at least two long minutes. I realized what was happening was unusual and stopped my chores to pay attention.

Right before my eyes, Marcel's puny pink comb and wattles turned bright red as he stared face-to-face with Sophie. She returned his stare. They didn't move or make a sound for several more minutes—just stood beak-to-beak, zero personal space between them. I sat down, mesmerized. I was witnessing love at first sight, chicken style. To them, I didn't exist. Nothing did. A miracle was happening two feet in front of me.

Almost overnight, Marcel was a new man. He started eating with a hearty appetite and did everything Sophie did. He stood taller and his eyes brightened. After over a year of silence, he started crowing within two days. The lovebirds were inseparable.

They were two peas in a pod. Within a couple weeks, Marcel transformed into a real rooster. He grew an enormously large comb and wattles and filled out nicely with a proud, broad chest. He strutted and danced for Sophie, and *only* for Sophie. The once-bullied boy now defended his girl ferociously. For the first time, he freely explored the property with his new love. It was utterly romantic.

I'll never know what was wrong with him, or how he could hover so close to death for well over a year, living for so long by sheer willpower. Love is powerful, poetic medicine. Everyone should be so lucky to have a Sophie or Marcel. They showed me that real love was healing, and worth the wait.

The business trip had thrown me back into city life for a few days and I hated to leave the farm. One evening, one conversation in particular stuck with me. A man who knew about my farm life asked in an arrogant tone, "What's it like being back in the *real* world?" I thought about his question for a moment before replying, "City life isn't the real world."

I saw it differently now: City living was perfectly orchestrated and man-made. It was a bubble that required a level of disconnection and self-importance that I hadn't experienced in rural living. I still liked visiting my old friends, and I loved the excitement and opportunities of the city. But having experienced both lifestyles, I saw the clear advantage of living closer to nature: There was no pretending. No living by a clock or strict schedule. No pesticides or dirty air. No drinking water that smelled like a public pool. No *fake it 'til you make it*. No people blindly walking past a homeless person in need. None of the things that disturbed me about urban living, where I had to constantly distract myself and disconnect from realities directly in front of my face. My life on the farm was raw, often unexpected, and required my purest presence and attention. There was nothing about it that wasn't as real as it gets.

A New Role

After almost two years of lovely casual dating, the time came for Gunnar to graduate and leave Mississippi for a new life. For our last evening together, he invited me over for dinner at his new apartment. Before I made it to his building, I could hear mood-setting music streaming from his door. He had candles lit, wine poured, and dinner on the grill. *If only he were twenty years older,* I thought to myself for the hundredth time. We watched the sun set from his patio while we ate and talked about what was next in his life. His sweet hospitality helped me overlook the terrible food: the rock-hard chicken cutlet, the mushy asparagus that dis-integrated when I tried to eat it. One day he would be a great cook, but today wasn't that day. He was only twenty-two, after all.

Gunnar had another confession for me. He pulled out his acoustic guitar. "I wrote a song for you," he said, smiling.

"*Wait,* what kind of song?" I blushed.

"Don't get mad . . . but I do refer to you as my Mrs. Robinson."

"Oh god. *That's* not embarrassing at all!"

"Just let me play it before you start getting all judgmental."

I braced myself. He started to play, and from the first few

notes alone, I loved it. The song, he said, was called, "Jake." He started to sing:

"She was my version of the graduate, she was my Mrs. Robinson . . . she taught me how to fly . . . she taught me how to survive . . . she said walk that walk, talk that talk . . . I was fire, she was wind . . . together we were like a storm blowing in . . ."

Other than the Mrs. Robinson reference, I loved the song and was surprised by his lyrics and what he had taken from our relationship. And he played it beautifully.

The night was bittersweet. We had been in each other's lives for over two years, and he had made me feel important. But there was no future for us other than friendship. The life mileage between us would have been enough to break us. But I will be forever grateful to this sweet guy who was there to unknowingly pick up the pieces that other, lesser men had left behind.

Becoming a Badass

I was out doing the P.M. feeding and putting the animals to bed when I realized one of my new turkey poults was missing. The poults were still in that awkward, gangly teenage stage. Once they got to this point, they could usually take care of themselves, but the missing poult was a special little girl. She was paralyzed from the neck up when I got her from the flea market. The paralysis greatly limited her mobility and created a hump in her back. It was amazing that she was alive at all since she was such easy prey, but I felt it was important that she get as much exercise as she could.

I was searching for her when I noticed a large hawk sitting at the top of a very tall tree at the side of the property. Luca was silent but he had seen it, too, and he kept his gaze on it. The hawk had a perfect view of the barnyard. My heart sank. This was bad.

I walked around the property looking for feathers or other signs of my poult. I stared the hawk down with as evil a look as I could muster. The bird seemed to be eyeballing me back. And then, all of a sudden, it took a nosedive off the top of the tree. Birds of prey have been known to attack people, especially when they came between the predator and their intended food source. This damn bird was coming for me. For a second, I froze. Then, adrenaline kicked in.

I thought of turning to run, screaming like a little kid, but there was no time for that. This bird was about to deliver an ass-kicking directly to my head. How to defend myself? I positioned myself in a fighting stance and decided that I would swing and try to punch the raptor out of the sky. Yes, that's right. I was planning to *punch* a large bird with huge talons out of the sky. I balled my hands into tight fists and put them up to protect my face. I was about to Muhammad Ali this bitch.

I looked down to check my footing and saw a bundle of dried cornstalks someone had donated to the farm for the animals to pick on. Luca loved to drag them around the property. I reached down to pick up the six-foot-long stalks, some of which still had corncobs attached to them. *Good, there's some weight to my weapon,* I thought. I decided to use the bundle like a baseball bat and knock the big bird away from me. Feeling bold, I yelled to the hawk, "BRING IT!" It needed to know that I was a crazy person and ready to rumble. I grasped my weapon and planted my feet like a batter on a baseball field.

As the bird swooped toward me, I couldn't believe its audacity. I braced myself, but just as I was starting to take my swing, I recognized the bird. It wasn't a hawk. It was my sweet, formerly paralyzed turkey poult!

I abandoned my makeshift bat midswing, the stalks flying all over the place and barely missing my girl. I ducked and she landed just behind me, safe and sound.

At this point, several things occurred to me. One: I'd never seen a turkey that high in a tree, perched at the very top like a raptor or buzzard. Two: Considering the fact that I didn't expect this bird to live past the first night, she now had mad flight skills.

Three: Had I paid attention to Luca, I would have noticed that he was completely unconcerned for my safety or the safety of the animals. He always barked or growled when danger was present. His lack of concern should have clued me in to the fact that I had nothing to worry about from the faux hawk. That dog wouldn't let a crow land on the property, much less a hawk.

Then it dawned on me. Did I really think I was going to *punch* a large bird of prey? As ridiculous as that was, I realized that, for the first time, I had done something without a trace of fear, intimidation, or hesitation to act. In my early forties, I was finally becoming a badass.

That day, I thought about how I wasn't meant to have a traditional life—and so what? At this point, I realized that my willingness to accept my unknown future was the key. With that acceptance, I could redefine who I was going to be from here on out. Life was open-ended, and defining myself was no longer a burden; it could now be freeing and fun. I could live exactly as I wanted and on my own terms.

I felt like a survivor. I stood there on my land, surrounded by animals—animals who gave me inspiration every single day. If my turkey hen could miraculously overcome paralysis to fly higher than any turkey I'd ever seen, who knew what I could do?

That night I woke up to loud gobbling from Rupert. When the toms gobbled at night, it was a response to either thunderstorms or a predator. When I heard Luca's barking far from the house, I jumped out of bed and opened the glass door of my bedroom porch to listen for thunder. Rupert and the boys gobbled again from their high perches in the trees. There was no thunderstorm, which meant Luca needed help.

Then I heard the yipping, howling, and barking . . . coyotes.

They had surrounded the property and Luca was trying to fend them off. I immediately screamed in the direction of the pack, "GET OUT OF HERE!" I grabbed my gun, which I now kept next to the bedstead, and leapt over the deck railing, calling for Luca, who appeared within seconds. He was in a panic. He barked at me, turned, and took off running toward the woods. I ran after him but found nothing. The coyotes had gone silent. My determined voice had scared them off. Luca stood at the edge of the woods, barking in their direction. For good measure, I yelled into the forest, "AND DON'T COME BACK!"

I thought of my first night in the moving truck after my initial encounter with the coyotes. Had I only known then that my voice could be a powerful, lifesaving weapon.

No longer afraid of the night's hidden creatures, I followed Luca to the driveway and lay down. I gazed intently at the vastness of the night sky, hoping my relaxed state would ease Luca's stress. The pavement still held the warmth of the day's sun and felt good against my skin. Fireflies, despite the cooling night air, were out. As they accentuated their starry backdrop I was struck by how beautiful it is that they shine as brightly as they can to attract a mate in the darkness. I lay there watching their showy signals until the tension left Luca's body.

After Luca calmed down, I checked on the animals. Rupert and Luca were increasingly working in tandem to keep our little farm safe. My guardians were brave creatures, and on this night, I was finally brave enough to help them.

Look Back to Move Forward

Now, after several years on the farm, I was determined to consolidate all my old boxes. For hours, I dug through decades' worth of my worldly possessions. When I came upon a small notebook I'd kept during my childhood living in Guam and the Philippines, the years when my stepfather was stationed abroad at Naval Air Stations, I started to read.

The world looked very different to my eighth-grade self. In pages full of large, loopy Catholic school cursive, I described the joy of waking up each morning to the loud screeches of wild parrots flying by our house. I recounted the lyrical awesomeness of the monsoon rains, and how they brought forth a thick white fog from the ground. I wrote of sneaking out of my room at night to watch the tropical wind push the palm fronds around, making them look like they were hula dancing against the backdrop of the sparkling bay. I illustrated how the people were beautiful and soulful. How they truly *lived* and respected nature.

The parallels between then and now were stark. My neighbors in rural Mississippi were equally as kind and resourceful as the people I'd known in the Philippines. Nature and faith were front and center in their lives. And, much like the Philippines, Mississippi had a brain drain of monumental proportions. Often the best and brightest left to find opportunities elsewhere due to the lack of financial prospects and limitations from the corruption of those in power.

Closing the notebook, I looked across the room at my computer. The screen glowed with my Facebook newsfeed and a crawling string of posts. Photographs of friends from another lifetime; self-affirming messages; pictures of trendy restaurants that weren't Cracker Barrel; words of advice people wished they could give their younger selves.

I clicked on my personal profile page, which I rarely posted to anymore. As I made my way through years of posts, it was hard to recognize my former self. Worse, I didn't really like what I saw. It was full of friends, events, and smiling faces, but it was also full of restaurant check-ins, random daily thoughts, selfies, and my trivial, biased opinions. I realized how bored I had been, and how much I had needed validation from others to prop up an unfulfilling life.

Mississippi had stripped me down completely, but it was giving me my soul back. Like the Philippines, Mississippi was madness and magic. It was the full circle of my life—reconnecting to what lit me up as a kid turned out to be exactly what I needed as an adult. I had to return to the child I had been to rediscover life with more freedom, free of trauma.

I shut down my computer. I took a cup of tea and a jar of fresh caramel sauce to the front porch. Rupert took his usual position, standing silently in front of me. He was still losing his feathers from molting, but the new ones coming in were shiny and perfect. I spoke to him in a low voice, telling him how much I loved him, how gorgeous he was. His head turned turquoise with content.

Soon Hazel, a young chicken I'd kept inside over the previous winter, showed up as well. She had never really acclimated to being a chicken. She preferred being inside the house with her diaper on.

As I sipped my hot tea and spooned goat milk caramel sauce into my mouth, I looked over the property I loved so much. But, like every picture-perfect moment on the farm, there was an interruption: A fly arrived and kept coming at my face. I swatted at it repeatedly and noticed Hazel watching intently. Finally, the fly gave up on me and flew down to buzz around Hazel. On its third flyby, Hazel was ready for it. My little chicken promptly plucked it from the air and ate it. Have I told you how much I love chickens?

As I was praising Hazel in my baby-talk voice, I heard an unfamiliar sound. I looked up to see a neighbor's herd of brown-and-white pinto horses running through my property at a thunderous gallop. *I have to be hallucinating,* I thought. I wasn't. The large group of horses ran past, galloping into the woods, whinnying and calling to the rest of their herd. It was astonishingly beautiful.

Now I Get It

I feared that after Gunnar moved away and there was no one to replace him (or Paul), I would slip back into my previous trauma state. After all, it had ruled over me for most of my life. But months had passed, and I still felt a sense of freedom that I appreciated more each day.

That Halloween, my friend Brooke and her husband included me in their family holiday plans. Usually, family holidays like this were searingly painful, but this time felt different. I was excited. I couldn't wait to help their little boys get in their costumes. Everyone was in good spirits, and I was thoroughly immersed in the kids' perspectives and the variety of costumes. I was delighted by the creativity and happiness around me. I was actually *enjoying* myself, and for once, I wasn't thinking about what I'd never have.

That night, I went to bed happy. I didn't cry a single tear. For the first time in years, I didn't feel sorry for myself, didn't fantasize about the costumes my own babies would wear, or dream of taking pictures of them for their grandparents.

But I wasn't ready to let down my guard entirely. In the following weeks, I still braced myself for the heartache to return. Christmas was the big test—but it came and went with the same new perspective I had at Halloween. The death grip on my heart was gone. Just like that: *gone.* The grief, regret, and anger I thought I'd carry to my grave were somehow replaced by strength and excitement for my unknown future. I knew that my little ones might not be visible, but they were with me, and they always would be.

As the sun started to set on Christmas Day, I stoked the fire and cuddled with Kahuna on the couch. The last rays beamed into the windows and caught my attention. There, reflecting on a windowpane, was the distinct shape of a butterfly, about fourteen inches in diameter. I must have looked out that window hundreds of times. Over the years, my fingerprints against the glass had created the perfect shape of a butterfly. There were no fingerprints anywhere else on the window.

A feeling welled up inside me. I have no way to describe it other than . . . spiritual effervescence. It bubbled up and took over my body for less than a minute, as if every cell in my body was on a natural high. It didn't make me want to weep. Instead, I felt full of happiness and love. I felt the need to speak. I smiled and whispered, *"I'm really happy."* And I was.

The holy water of solitude had washed over me. No one else had the power to define what my life would be anymore. My faith was renewed, redefined, and I no longer had a fear of being alone. In fact, I'd rarely met anyone who had been more physically alone than me—and not only was I fine, I was starting to truly love and appreciate it.

Every once in a while we have to redefine our relationships, even our most essential relationships; even our relationships with ourselves. That's not only okay, it's healthy. I had learned that I had choices. That I had a certain power over my own life. My filter had become much thicker; I was careful about what and who I let into my life, and I was learning the power of no.

That evening, I fell asleep thinking of family and friends who had passed on. I had a vivid dream. In the dream, I was walking through my woods alone. None of my animals were with me. As I walked, I came to a giant oak tree. I noticed it had stairs that led up to a beautiful carved wooden door in the tree. I made my way up the stairs, put my hand on the ornate handle, and pushed it open.

I found myself inside a bright white room. There was a man, sitting in a modern-looking white chair, one leg crossed over the other. His face was hidden by a newspaper. "Where am I?" I asked. The man put his newspaper down and looked at me. It was a young version of my grandfather, who had passed years ago.

"Grandpa!? What are you doing here? You look amazing!"

Getting right down to business, he said, "It's time to share your life with others."

I protested, "But I don't want to. I don't want to teach anyone anything!"

He nodded and calmly responded, "Sharing isn't always about teaching, sometimes it's just about *showing*."

I wasn't following. "But how am I supposed to do that?"

He produced pictures of my future farm life. He held them up for me to see. One was an image of me with my white Sebastopol geese I had recently procured. The picture showed me mesmerized by their impossibly soft feathers that hung like loosely curled ribbons draped down their sides. Each time I ran my fingers through them, it felt like I was putting my hands into tendrils of warm gentle air, or maybe even heaven. Another photo showed me interacting with their newly hatched goslings. The joy on my face was obvious. He continued, "Show your life with pictures. Restart your blog and show with words."

But even in the dream, the thought of putting myself "out there" made me feel anxious and exposed.

"I've been so quiet for so long. I don't know if I can do this."

Again he nodded and said, "There are different ways to be a lantern. Everyone who speaks has a voice and yet not everyone is heard. The key to being heard is to speak in a way that others can understand. You don't need to be a teacher to shine a light for others. The ones who need to hear it will find you. This is how it is. Wake up and start your blog, *now*."

Startled awake from my dream, I grabbed my bedside notebook and scribbled down my grandfather's words.

Years earlier, back in Tampa, I had started a blog, only to abandon it completely when I moved to the country. The ironic thing was that the more interesting my life had become in Mississippi, the more quiet I became. I was still unsure about this, but I felt determined. I threw my hair into a ponytail and grabbed my laptop.

In an echo of my dream, it was around this time that my new Sebastopol geese started laying eggs. I decided to let Poppy, my sole Sebastopol female, hatch her eggs and raise the babies herself. Each day she laid an egg I would try to collect it before Luca could find it, and I'd bring it inside for safekeeping. She laid eleven eggs, two of which Luca found before I did.

When I suspected that Poppy was ready to settle in and sit on her eggs, I made a big nest of fresh straw inside an old doghouse. The doghouse only had a roof, no sides, so Poppy could see 360 degrees around her. I placed the nine remaining eggs in the nest, closed up her pen, and watched from afar. An hour later, she was fussing over the nest. She was in the zone, meticulously placing each piece of straw, woven along with soft, white down feathers she plucked from her belly. She continued making a circle around the eggs, building it as high as she could. When she finished her masterpiece, she gently rotated each egg and gingerly stepped into the nest. Then she dipped her webbed foot into the pile of eggs and shimmied them around before finally settling in.

For a month, Poppy rarely left the nest. Every day or two she would get up, take a bath, and have dinner for a few minutes. During cold snaps, she wouldn't budge.

After the first week of sitting, she rolled two eggs out of the nest. By the time I found them, they were already cold. Usually this means the eggs aren't viable or the embryos are early quitters. With only seven eggs remaining and a cold front coming, I was afraid it would be another failed season with no goslings. Waterfowl hatchlings seem to be difficult to hatch.

After a couple weeks of sitting, I noticed her legs becoming paler, drier, and weaker. I doted over her constantly, giving her greens and deep bowls of warm water to dip her face in.

About a week before the goslings were due to hatch, Lucian, my Sebastopol gander and Poppy's mate, went into extreme protective mode. He wouldn't leave Poppy's side. At first, I made him leave the pen each day, to keep him from disturbing Poppy. Then I noticed that he was chasing all the other animals away and seemed to be standing guard around the pen. He and Poppy were chatting quietly to each other from their respective places in and outside the pen. I finally saw his overprotective behavior for what it was and opened the door to allow him access to his mate. He immediately went to her side and stayed with her or paced the perimeter, chasing away random chickens and attacking any goat who had the nerve to come too close. He was a nervous expectant father waiting on the delivery of his child.

Two days after the official, expected hatch date, nothing seemed to be happening. Then I saw Lucian walk over to check on Poppy. She lifted her wing and he stuffed his face under her into the nest. That's when I heard the sweetest peeping. I went into the pen and sat next to her. "Can I see your baby?" I asked, and to my surprise and delight, she lifted her wing. There, tucked inside her soft down, was a newly hatched, drying gosling. It squeaked, objecting to the rush of cool air, so I retracted my hand and Poppy put her wing back over the baby.

A day later, Poppy held fast to her unhatched eggs. Her first gosling, a bouncing baby girl, was already out of the nest exploring her new world with her daddy. Lucian could barely keep up with his naughty little offspring. This one-day-old baby was far too independent for both our comforts. I put her back under her mom about thirty times before I finally gave up. Lucian followed her everywhere and doted on his tiny daughter while still constantly checking on Poppy. The poor guy was being run ragged.

After the second gosling hatched, Poppy was coaxed off the nest by her mate. Their two kids were a workout for all of us. Herding goslings is a lot like herding cats. They kept their parents very busy and kept me on the constant verge of a heart attack. It turned out that my goose pen wasn't built for holding rubber-ducky-sized babies; they went in and out through the wire fence at their pleasure. I had no choice but to open the gate so their parents could follow them. At least the goslings would have some measure of protection as they explored.

After a couple more days, the babies started to communicate and listen to their parents (for the most part). I let them out on supervised excursions around the property for short periods of time. At one point, I walked to the pond and the geese followed me with their littles in tow. Luca and I watched as the parents tentatively allowed the babies to walk into the water and float around the shoreline. I said, "This is seriously the cutest thing I've ever seen. No offense, Luca."

To Luca, they were like bossy squeaky toys. Fortunately, Danielle's assurance that Luca would grow out of his accidental killing spree had proven correct. As he aged, he simply stopped that behavior. Now I could trust him with even tiny goslings. He had become the cornerstone and protector of my farm.

Luca and I watched as Poppy stayed on the shore and Lucian waded out to shield the babies from the deeper water. He let them paddle around the shallows for a couple minutes, then nudged each little bum back to their mom onshore. After that, they kept the babies away from the pond, which was probably for the best.

Still thinking about the dream of my grandfather, I documented everything I could through pictures. I learned what amazing fathers and partners ganders could be. I posted about my experiences and started sharing my photos via social media and my blog. Now that I was no longer afraid of the darkness returning, a new chapter of my life was beginning, and it was one that I'd share with the rest of the world.

A farm is a complete sensory experience. Hearing the wind blow through the leaves from miles away, or through the chimes on my porch. Feeling breezes brush across my face and playing with my hair. Touching impossibly soft feathers or assisting babies being born. Feeling the searing pain of losing a beloved animal or the exquisite comfort of having one fall asleep in my lap, knowing that it trusts me completely. Deeply inhaling air untainted by exhaust and drinking cool water pulled from deep in the ground. Tasting fresh cream, those first sweet pecans in fall, the wild mulberries in spring. Finding something long buried and forgotten. Learning, unlearning, and relearning. These were the things that made me feel alive and connected. Life itself, in all its facets. Love, in its purest forms. It all changed me.

How did I overcome the sexual trauma, past losses, and fear of the future? I gutted through it. I stopped ignoring the dark feelings of fear, and I no longer punished myself for having them. It was okay to finally get mad, but I didn't hold on to it; that would have been just trading one prison for another. Ultimately, I didn't drink or drug or sleep or shop or cope the feelings away. I let them wash over me with their icy waves and I accepted them, not knowing where they would lead me, not knowing if I'd ever find my way out of the darkness.

I processed my emotions lightly with my friends, Kathryn and Brooke, who had the lives I'd always thought I wanted, filled with partners and children. Both gave me new perspectives on freedom, motherhood, and appreciating what I had. I stopped fearing my depths. Then on that one day by my icy pond, the fog lifted, without warning. Just like that. Gone. I waited for the other shoe to drop—waited for the feelings of sadness to come back. They didn't. What has shown up in their place is a new perspective and fierce sense of freedom.

It's not that I know exactly where or how I fit into society, or what my future holds, or if I'll even stay on the farm forever . . . it's that I'm no longer concerned about it. From spiders to loss and loneliness, life has given me everything I've ever feared. Not only am I still standing, I'm now free from that fear, and appreciative. My biggest realization was that I didn't have to fight my demons. Ignoring them for years *was* the fight. My demons weren't trying to drown me, they were trying to *free* me. By finally acknowledging and accepting them, they not only loosened their grip on me, their power was *transferred* to me. Through the seclusion, accepting my past and overcoming the fear of an unknown future, I found my life's passion: self-empowerment through self-reliance. I finally had the purpose I'd always heard about.

I had lost much of my former identity and no longer wanted anything small. My past would always be a part of me. I didn't beat it, or overcome it—I integrated it and now I no longer had to *live* there. It turns out that within Edward Bernays's methods of manipulation lies the antidote: By questioning my own preferences, habits, behavior, and propaganda I began to find myself and discover what truly resonated with *me*.

My life before had been busy, filled with distraction. But what was the point of all that busyness? On the farm, I stopped feeling guilty about having free time, alone time, naps, and uncommon preferences—now, I revel in them and wear them happily. I know I'm not perfect, but I'm good the way I am. I'm not only *enough*, I have value. I actually really, truly like myself, the people in my circle, and the future I'm building. I've finally given birth to life. My *own*, unshackled life. And now, I'll be the one who decides how I live it.

Acknowledgments

I'd like to lovingly acknowledge my family, friends, and community for unknowingly being my rock. It's a daunting task to try to thank everyone who has played an important role for this book, but it also shows me I have incredible and interesting people around me.

Wesley Webb: Thank you for being annoying and constantly nagging me to write a book. You believed in me even when I didn't.

My mother, Patsy Reilly: Thank you for showing me the art of finding hidden treasures, for all your love, sacrifices, and giving me wings. I'm finally learning to fly.

My father, Dr. Edmund Keiser: You've always demonstrated the importance of laughter and following my passion, and I will forever be grateful. Also, I promise not to use more than a nickel's worth of dish soap.

My stepmother, Sue Keiser: You've always been a true dream maker for others. Now I hope you make your own. Thank you for all you've done for me.

My stepfather, Edward Reilly: Thank you for giving me a high bar in relationships, for giving Mom and me the world and loving me as if I were your own.

Tommy Tucker: Thank you for making all this possible, for your big heart and honesty.

Mark Keiser: Your unwavering support has meant the world to me and I'll always be grateful.

Titi: The beauty and creativity you express have always inspired me. Thank you for helping me start this crazy journey and for not giving up on me.

Mary Beth Reilly: You are my sister, my confidante, and champion, and I can't thank you enough.

Skip King: Your kindness and generosity touch so many lives. I'm grateful to have it touch mine.

Kristina Keiser: Thank you for all your help and loving the farm and animals as much as I have.

Kelly Smith: Thank you for years of fun, laughter, craziness, and your undying support.

Brice and Danielle Noonan: I'll never be able to express how much your friendship and all the laughs have meant to me. Thank you for getting me started on this satisfying and healing path.

Kathryn Dilworth and Brooke Bridge: Meeting you was destined by the stars. Thank you for sharing your families, wisdom, and incredible mind- and soul-expanding friendships with me.

Kelly Yario: You're one of the most solid, bighearted people I know. Thank you for being there when I felt small.

Cindy Sturdivant: You coming into my life was a blessing. Thank you for the helping hand as I emerged from dark days. You are a badass.

Gunnar: I truly appreciate the music, moonlight, and mostly, your beautiful presence.

Della and Todd Grzech: Thank you for your generosity, kindness, and friendship.

My neighbors: I can't tell you how much I appreciate all your help and being my safety net while I evolved out of my rural ignorance.

Adria Rhoads, Nicole Uihtoven, and Angi Taveekanjana: My Tampa girls, thank you for your friendship and great memories—the good times are far from over.

John Howard: Your friendship and life insights have enriched my life. One day I'll write about you . . . and the proper way to make cornbread.

My agents, Michelle Brower and Becky Sweren: Thank you for finding me and forcing me out of my comfort zone.

My editors, Anna Pitoniak and Annie Chagnot: I know it can be tough to wrestle a writer into relevance, but thank you for believing in me.

Luca: You've devoted your life to our farm. You are my real-life hero.

ABOUT THE AUTHOR

JAKE KEISER is a former city girl currently creating a fabulous farm life in Oxford, Mississippi. Her farm is where children and families come to learn about raising animals and empowering oneself through self-reliance.

ABOUT THE TYPE

This book was set in Caslon, a typeface first designed in 1722 by William Caslon (1692–1766). Its widespread use by most English printers in the early eighteenth century soon supplanted the Dutch typefaces that had formerly prevailed. The roman is considered a "workhorse" typeface due to its pleasant, open appearance, while the italic is exceedingly decorative.